Affect Ethnography

Also available from Bloomsbury

Symbiotic Autoethnography, Liana Beattie
Affective Performance and Cognitive Science, edited by Nicola Shaughnessy,
Bruce McConachie, Rhonda Blair, Amy Cook, Anna Furse and Erin Hood
Post-Qualitative Research and Innovative Methodologies, edited by
Matthew K E Thomas and Robin Bellingham

Affect Ethnography

Exploring Performance and Narrative in the Creation of Unstories

Cristiana Giordano and Greg Pierotti

BLOOMSBURY ACADEMIC

LONDON • NEW YORK • OXFORD • NEW DELHI • SYDNEY

BLOOMSBURY ACADEMIC
Bloomsbury Publishing Plc, 50 Bedford Square, London, WC1B 3DP, UK
Bloomsbury Publishing Inc, 1359 Broadway, New York, NY 10018, USA
Bloomsbury Publishing Ireland, 29 Earlsfort Terrace, Dublin 2, D02 AY28, Ireland

BLOOMSBURY, BLOOMSBURY ACADEMIC and the Diana logo are trademarks
of Bloomsbury Publishing Plc

First published in Great Britain 2024
Paperback edition published 2026

Cover design: Grace Ridge
Cover image © YBCA and Tommy Lau

A catalogue record for this book is available from the British Library.

Library of Congress Cataloging-in-Publication Data

Names: Giordano, Cristiana, 1971- author. | Pierotti, Greg, author.
Title: Affect ethnography : exploring performance and narrative in the creation of unstories /
Cristiana Giordano and Greg Pierotti.
Description: London ; New York : Bloomsbury Academic, 2024. | Includes bibliographical references
and index. | Summary: "Playing with the relation between truth and representation in the stories we
tell as ethnographers, this book contributes to the current debates around experimental research
methodologies and ethnographically grounded theatrical forms. It departs from other studies in the
field by proposing a unique and easily followed methodology that brings together theatrical devising
practices and anthropology. The practice described in the book, Affect Theater, also emphasizes
embodied and affective approaches to empirical research and defines a process for rendering this
type of material into imaginative academic writing, collaborative performance, and other inventive
forms, applicable across a range of academic disciplines"–Provided by publisher.
Identifiers: LCCN 2023048295 (print) | LCCN 2023048296 (ebook) | ISBN 9781350374812 (hardback) |
ISBN 9781350374850 (paperback) | ISBN 9781350374829 (epub) | ISBN 9781350374836 (ebook)
Subjects: LCSH: Theater–Anthropological aspects. | Experimental theater.
Classification: LCC PN2041.A57 G56 2024 (print) | LCC PN2041.A57 (ebook) | DDC 792–dc23/
eng/20231218
LC record available at https://lccn.loc.gov/2023048295
LC ebook record available at https://lccn.loc.gov/2023048296

ISBN: HB: 978-1-3503-7481-2
PB: 978-1-3503-7485-0
ePDF: 978-1-3503-7483-6
eBook: 978-1-3503-7482-9

Typeset by Deanta Global Publishing Services, Chennai, India

For product safety related questions contact productsafety@bloomsbury.com

To find out more about our authors and books visit www.bloomsbury.com
and sign up for our newsletters.

A mia madre ed amica, Rosanna Colonna
To my father, Rob Pierotti, and to Bug

Contents

Figures

Acknowledgments

This book is the result of a rich and generative collaboration not only between us the authors but between us and many collaborators with whom we engaged along the way. We are deeply grateful to Tristyn Caneso, the designer and illustrator who helped us translate our performance score of *Unstories* into Chapter 2. Her creativity and skill were an invaluable contribution to the book. We would also like to thank the three other artists who contributed their work to Chapter 2: Ramzi Harrabi, Homiex, and Naichè Luzzana.

This book would not exist without the collaboration and energy of those who participated in our two year-long workshops that resulted in the performances of *Unstories* (2017) and *Unstories II (roaming)* (2018). Each with their unique perspective and background enriched not only these performance events but also the theoretical and practical underpinnings of our work: Sarah Hart, Ante Ursic, John Zibell, Regina Gutiérrez, Álvaro Rodríguez, Ugo Edu, Maria Massolo, Bettina Ng'weno, Rima Praspaliauskiene, Morganne Blais-McPherson, Adam Kersch, Julian Gatto, Mercedes Villalba, Arielle Estrada Solomianski, Camilla Hawthorne, Carolina Novella Centellas, Maria McCavish, Keith Williams, Matthew Nesvet.

Throughout the devising of *Unstories* we could not have shared the ethnographic material from Italy with our collaborators in California if it wasn't for the three amazing translators who patiently and rigorously rendered each transcript, field note, news article, legal document, and medical record into English. Thank you, Daisy Ament, Greta Anders, and Elisa Massenzio who, at the time, were majors in Italian studies at the University of California, Davis. Margherita Besuschio was instrumental in transcribing interviews conducted in Italian. For documentation of the performances and workshops we are indebted to Jorge Nunez, Matthew Nesvet, Lisa Stevenson, and A.S. Krause.

In these workshops, our focus was on the empirical material that Cristiana drew from her fieldwork in Italy. We are particularly grateful to Ramzi Harrabi for his generosity, inventiveness, and warmth. His guidance and welcome in Siracura inspired many summers of research and play. We owe special gratitude to Homiex for sharing his original artwork and unique experience, to Antonino Audino for our long conversations about his background as a coast guard in the

Sicilian channel and his insightful writings, to Carolina Cardillo for her guidance in working with the youth. Special thanks go to the young men who participated in the theater workshops in Siracusa during the summers of 2015–18: Ibrahima Sliou (Stoneboy), Amadou, Mohammed Mesoud, Dudu, Saliou, Abdullah, Alex, Lamine, Said, Ahmed, Austin. It meant a lot to Cristiana to have two colleagues and friends accompany her in parts of fieldwork in Sicily: Kelly McKinney and Anne Lovell, thank you for your company and engagement.

Part of this book emerges out of research Cristiana conducted at mobile clinics and ports of entry with the Italian humanitarian organization _Emergency_. Andrea Bellardinelli opened the doors to _Progetto Italia_ (Project Italia), the Italian branch of _Emergency_ which serves different underserved and marginal parts of the country. With her wit and brightness, Maria Izzo was an extraordinary collaborator and traveling companion. We also thank Daniela Porcu, Loredana Carpentieri, Giulia Chiarenza, Luca Corso, Maria Perri, Sergio Serraino, Marie Kolie, Jean De Dieu Bihizi, and all the doctors, cultural brokers, and nurses who passed through the mobile clinics during Cristiana's field research. Maria Romana Giordano introduced us to several of her colleagues who work as social workers in migrant shelters and with foreign minors. We especially thank Viviana Martinoli for sharing her experience engaging with the "refugee emergency" and "crisis" of these last ten years. From the _Associazione per gli Studi Giuridici sull'Immigrazione_ (Association for Juridical Studies on Immigration), we are grateful to Donatella Bava for her time, knowledge, and insight into the intricacies of the legal system. Dr. Franco Zulian, legal doctor, took time to explain the medical exams required to establish a foreigner's age in order to grant access to services and rights. His words shed light on medical procedures and legal processes that inspired one of the central episodes of _Unstories_ (2017). Rosanna Colonna, Paola Giordano, and Guido Besuschio were delightful interlocutors who helped us clarify Italian terminology and colloquial expressions.

Many friends and colleagues have read parts of the manuscript and offered generous and helpful feedback. In particular, we thank Rima Praspaliauskiene, Anne Lovell, Eric Taggart, Dominique Behague, Luca D'Isanto, Bettina Ng'weno, Kevin Byrne, Ana Martinez, Laura Meek, Kelly McKinney, Fiamma Montezemolo, Tarek Elhaik, John Zibell, Gino Forlin, Aurora Donzelli, Antonella Giordano, Rhiannon N. Welch, Debarati Sanyal, Gabriel Dattatreyan, Andrea Muehlebach, Stavroula Pupyrou, Claudia Mattalucci, and Alessandra Brivio. We presented early drafts of some chapters in seminars and workshops. We would like to extend our gratitude to Dominique Behague, Kenneth MacLeish, and Jonathan

Metzl for inviting Cristiana to the workshop "The Global Psyche: Experiments in Ethics, Politics and Technoscience" at Vanderbilt University in spring 2017. The collegial and supportive group they brought together offered helpful feedback. In February 2018, Heike Drotbohm and Hannah Brown invited Cristiana to their workshop on "Care in Crisis—Ethnographic Perspectives on Humanitarian" at Johannes Gutenberg University Mainz, Germany. This workshop provided generative feedback for several parts of this book and created a space for thinking inside and outside of crisis. In Italy, the graduate students in the Ph.D program in anthropology at the University of Milano-Bicocca were attentive and insightful readers of drafts of Chapter 4. Special thanks to Richard Schechner and Sarah Ellen Brady for their insightful notes, support, and inclusion of our work in *The Drama Review*.

This book is also deeply informed by many of Greg's previous collaborators and co-investigators within the discipline of theater of the real. We want to thank members of Tectonic Theater Project Leigh Fondakowski, Moisés Kaufman, Stephen Belber, Steve Wangh, Andy Paris, John McAdams, Barbara Pitts-McAdams, Kelli Simkins, Amanda Gronich, Mercedes Herrero, Jeffrey LaHoste, Sarah Lambert, Betsy Adams, Matt Joslyn, Greg Steinbruner, and Michael Emerson, as well as Tony Taccone, former Artistic Director of Berkeley Repertory Theater.

Anitra Grisales copyedited an earlier version of the manuscript and provided her usual nuanced feedback which always makes books better than what they originally were. Jamie Davidson was our star in putting together this manuscript. She assisted us with careful editing, astute comments, and with much care and kindness. Melissa Wilfley was an effective and generous research assistant, Edoardo Andrea Assandri was instrumental in the final push of reference checking, and Federico Belcredi for image editing.

What also shaped this book are the many informal and cross-disciplinary conversations we have had over the years with Eugenio Barba, Eduardo Kohn, Suzana Sawyer, Joe Dumit, Marisol de la Cadena, Fatima Mojaddedi, Lisa Oxley, Li Zhang, Janet Roitman, Giovanna Parmigiani, Mauro Ivo Van Aken, Jessica Maerz, Dara Culhane, Lochlann Jain, Sophie Sarcinelli, Ivano Gamelli, Margaret Kemp, Michael d'Arcy, Taylor Bell, Muneeza Rizvi, Wendell Beavers, Jiwon Chung, Steve Wangh, Peter Lichtenfels, Josh Moses, Krista DeNio, Valentina Napolitano, Lynette Hunter, Charles Briggs, Clara Mantini-Brigg, Tomás Sánchez Criado, Monika Weissensteiner, Gabriel Dattatreyan, Setrag Manoukian, and Carol Martin.

Each time we do an Affect Theater workshop outside our institutional affiliations we encounter groups of vibrant and curious students and colleagues who contribute to the unfolding of our practice and enrich our engagement across disciplines. Over the years, we have had the pleasure to share our work at Goldsmith College, London (UK); McGill University, Montreal (Canada); the University of Pennsylvania; the University of Milano-Bicocca (Italy); Texas State University; the UC Collaboratory for Ethnographic Design (CoLED); and the Cittadellarte Fondazione Pistoletto, Biella (Italy).

We are fortunate to be part of a community of friends who have kept us company in different ways throughout the birth and life of this project, by providing delicious meals, offering emotional support, coming to our performances, taking us on walks, and encouraging us to delve deeper in the exploration: Deborah Gordon, Jil Geller, John Hill, Ari Langer, Giedrius Praspaliauskas, Catherine Fitzmaurice, Laurie Kappe, Isaac Cohen, Maddalena Ughi, Laima Kreivyte, Tamar Rapoport, Julia Morales Fontanilla, Adrian Yen, Tanzeen Doha, Diana Pardo Pedraza, Dale Griner, Bob Koherr, Simon Donavan, Vida Cechaviciene, Kastis Cechavicius, and Samuele Collu. The presence of those who have passed while working on this book accompanies us in invisible ways: thank you, Rami Geller, for your loyal, warm, and playful energy; Sibyl Pierotti, David Anderson, Lorna Kelly, and John McAdams. You are all deeply missed. Ugo Fabietti, thank you for your mentorship and kindness: you passed the day of our first performance which we silently dedicated to you.

In fall 2021, we held a residency at the Center for Experimental Ethnography, at the University of Pennsylvania, where we taught a seminar and a workshop. This time away from our respective universities allowed us time to write and further explore our shared practice. It also broadened our cross-disciplinary conversations with students and colleagues. We are deeply grateful to Deborah Thomas for welcoming us into the Center's vibrant community and supporting our scholarship; to Alissa Jordan for her endless support; and to the graduate students who engaged our practice and helped us see it through their perspectives.

Different funding institutions supported our research and performance events: the Davis Humanities Institute, the Mellon Initiative in Comparative Border Studies, the Yerba Buena Center for the Arts; the University of California Summer Grants; and the University of Arizona's School of Theater Film and Television and College of Fine Arts. For rehearsal and performance spaces, we are grateful to the Department of Theater and Dance at the University of California, Davis, and to Yerba Buena Center for the Arts in San Francisco, CA.

At Bloomsbury, we would like to thank Maria Giovanna Brauzzi for believing in this project; Laura Gallon, Sarah McDonald, and Susan Furber for guiding us through the process of production; and the anonymous reviewers who provided encouraging and useful comments that helped us shape the manuscript.

We are so grateful for each other and the playful and nourishing collaboration we have. Finally, we are especially indebted to Franz Ferdinand and Sparks for creating our theme song, "Collaborations Don't Work." https://www.youtube .com/watch?v=tGAwp5syXyE

Preface

Cristiana Giordano and Greg Pierotti

Cristiana: In your own words, what does "*bighellonare*" mean?

Guido: *Bighellonare* means to wander around without any purpose. Milling around without any real reason.

Paola: Exactly, without a goal.

Rosanna: Really to waste time.

P: To waste time, or even to relax.

R: Without knowing where to go.

G: To spend time with friends.

R: . . . I mean *bighellonare* . . . you really don't know where you want to go. You go out just to go, without any goal at all.

G: With your friends, you go for a walk, you chat, it is just to be together, and you'd hang around Corso Cavour and the porticos.

P: Another example, someone who skips school and just wanders around town *bighellonando*.

C: Can you describe how someone walks when they're *bighellonando*?

P: Hands in their pockets. . .

G: Looking at the road ahead. . .

P: Looking at shop windows. . .

G: But for the hands in the pockets it depends, nowadays everyone puts their hands in their pockets.

P: No, but "hands in the pockets" is also a metaphor, it's the ethic of the *bighellonatore*. [laughs]

C: Do you walk quickly or slowly?

Everyone: Slowly!

P: Because you don't have a goal. A fast pace is for someone who knows where to go. You need to pass the time. . .

R: You look to the right, to the left, you stop to look at things.

In the fall of 2015, we started a collaboration between theater and anthropology by designing workshops: thinking and rehearsal spaces where a dialogue between disciplines takes shape. We create non-narrative performative dramaturgies through theatrical-devising practices to slow down thinking and to create new relations with our empirical material.[1] Instead of thinking at our desks and computers, we practice thinking with what we call the elements of the stage. Throughout this book, when we refer to the elements of the stage, we mean anything that is used in theatrical composition. The list of these elements emerges in response to the research material and can be quite extensive. They might include light, sound, props, costumes, architecture, spatial relationships, texts, acting choices, gesture, music, emotion, and so on. We engage with our research material by mixing these compositional languages with texts. Their interaction creates multiple layers of collaboration: between theater makers and anthropologists, between theory and practice, and between theatrical forms and empirical material.

The opening conversation is drawn from one of those workshops. This is how Cristiana Giordano describes its genesis in her fieldnotes.

One night, in late December 2016, I was sitting at the dinner table with my family in the mountains in Northern Italy, and as we were sipping grappa and coffee after the meal, we had this conversation. The occasion was the research I was conducting on the "refugee crisis" in the Mediterranean, and the collaborative theater project Greg Pierotti and I were leading with a group at UC Davis to turn the empirical material into a performance. We were working on some field notes and transcripts from earlier that year, when I visited the Prefecture of my hometown in Piedmont to meet with Viviana, a social worker in charge of the program for the reception and housing of "unaccompanied foreign minors." We sat in her cluttered office, surrounded by piles of folders and unfiled, dusty paper. We were discussing how, despite the insistent media coverage and political debates on the "refugee crisis," the Italian state had not declared a state of emergency, which would grant regions and municipalities the power to take quick and incisive decisions on important matters such as granting asylum, finding housing, providing medical care, and deciding on deportation. She faced millions of emergencies daily, mostly regarding accommodation and medical care for all the foreigners who were arriving by the hundreds every week. Right in the middle of our conversation, the Prefect himself walked in, unannounced, to fill Viviana in on the latest about the migrant shelters in town. A tall man in his late sixties with an important long mustache, he hurried to inform her that the problem was not where to host them, but that the soup kitchen was in a separate building, a few blocks away from the shelter: "People in the community are annoyed because they see the refugees walking back and forth on the street, not because they live in the neighborhood. They just bighellonano *in the streets, and that is the problem!"*

The Prefect's interruption intrigued me as something that might direct our research focus away from questions of crisis and emergency to seemingly minor, marginal concerns with a strong affective charge. The "public security" issue, as he made clear in his appearance in Viviana's office, was not the crisis of housing, or the emergency posed by the high numbers of foreigners applying for asylum in a country already overwhelmed by a slow judicial system and scarce resources, but the way young African men walked in the streets! I had heard the term bighellonare *related to migrants walking around Italian towns and villages before but hearing it in that context had a different impact. It seemed like a needless distraction from Viviana's emergencies, an irrelevant detail amid more important concerns.*

When I brought my field notes from this encounter to the group of theater collaborators at UC Davis, bighellonare *became an embodied occasion to practice and relate to a way of being in space that none of us quite grasped. Greg and the other members of the workshop asked me what* bighellonare *really meant. I tried to mimic it, then attempted to guide their walking in our dance studio in a way that resembled a casual and relaxed pace. Also, my somewhat literal translation of the Italian term into "wandering around," "walking around," "hanging out," left us unsatisfied. Greg suggested we do more research around it, to have more empirical material to play with and devise performance material around the concept. And so, I found myself at the dinner table conversing about* bighellonare *with my mother Rosanna, my sister Paola, and her husband Guido.*

Working with our empirical material in this way allows us to relate to field research and writing in more affective and embodied ways. French anthropologist Jeanne Favret-Saada has reflected on anthropological "participant observation" as a moment when rather than observing and participating from a purely scientific position, the researcher needs to "be caught" in the webs of relations, emotions, and affects that make up any given world in order to experience it rather than understand it (Favret-Saada 1980). Similarly, she argues, when we set out to write about the empirical material collected in the field, writing should not be a distancing moment to reflect *upon* research, but a process of "getting caught again" in the same intensities and webs of relations that caught us in the first place when we started our empirical work. Our collaboration takes up this challenge to experience the affective dimension of research. This opens new experiments in our disciplines and ways of relating to worlds.

Looping back to our exploration of *bighellonare*, we immersed ourselves in a practice of walking that the official press and discourse use in Italy to describe African refugees' aimless wandering around towns. We followed our hunch that *bighellonare* was not just a way of representing the "other," but also an affective (minor) element taken from our research material that reflected not only a nonlinear way of walking observed in the field, but also something we could use to do research and create narratives. Noticing the Prefect's interruption and his concern for refugees' ways of walking created a shift in our encounter with the field. We noticed something that escaped the logic of crisis and emergency, but that was nonetheless pregnant with analytical and conceptual potential for our affective knowledge of the contemporary moment. It also allowed us to connect with the performative power of the empirical material that emerged through an interruption in a conversation, which led to other conversations and experiments. The practice of *bighellonare* in the workshop became a form through which we could interact and present stories and other material drawn from the fieldwork.

These oscillations between empirical material and theatrical vocabularies are the purpose of our practice. As we describe in Part I of this book, we collaboratively produce an affective context in which the tactile, sonic, and visual are woven together with modes of thinking. This work need not culminate in a performance. This type of dramaturgical process can be used to create nonlinear structures, not only for playwrights working with the real, but also for social scientists and humanities scholars who can learn a more playful approach to research and curating texts, which can also translate into other forms such as essays, plays, short stories, etc. It allows writers to form structures for chapters, essays, traditional plays, and books in nonlinear ways. In Part II, the workshop experience informs other ethnographic and essayistic writings, beyond the production of performances. In Part III, we further explore the question of narrative in theater and propose pedagogical exercises that can be used in different educational settings.

In our methodological experiments we practice with and reflect on these questions of participation, observation, and affective resonance. We simultaneously engage theatrical-devising practices, anthropological modes of attending to forms of life, and affect and postdramatic theories to create a practice we call Affect Theater. This approach also provides an analytical lens through which we may attend to transcripts, archival documents, visual material, and field notes. Our practice/performance as research (Riley and Hunter 2009) resonates with the human geographer Derek McCormack's idea of "radical empiricism" where, as he describes it, "concepts participate in the felt process of being drawn into, and drawing out, the affective qualities of worldly experience rather than distancing thinking from that experience" (2013: xi).

In Affect Theater, we immerse ourselves in the empirical material through the senses and, in choreographer Mary Overlie's language, different Viewpoints (2016).[2] For her, *The Six Viewpoints* (Space/Blocking, Shape/Design, Time, Emotion, Movement, and Story/Logic) is a composition technique and "practice of not knowing, as opposed to knowing" (2016: 189), which prepares artists for making art through experiential practices that explore the relation between themselves and the various performance elements.[3] In line with this, ours is a creative process and a type of listening that allows for multiple and simultaneous modes of attention and analysis, which results in more affective re-presentations of research in the here and now.

When we reflect on affect as a research and writing modality, we add another layer of complexity to the task of representation. Affect has often been invoked and engaged (as an experience and an analytic) as alternative to representation, as a mode of presence and of experiencing the worlds around us that challenges the distinction between subjects and objects. Deleuze understood it as force and intensity, as the capacity to affect and be affected, and as the experience of what emerges in-between the potential and the actual (1988). As intensity, affect emerges in what passes between bodies, the elements of the stage, and worlds at large. As Melissa Gregg and Gregory Seigworth put it, "Affect is found . . . in those resonances that circulate about, between, and sometimes stick to bodies and worlds. . . . Affect is in many ways synonymous with force or forces of encounter" (2010: 4). Our practice is an attempt to engage in and be engaged by these very forces. These attempts occur in the workshops, which we consider to be spaces for thinking and practicing.

Hans-Thies Lehman's theory of the postdramatic as a theater that decenters narrative as its primary organizing element is a helpful frame. In describing the shared experience between audience and performers, he writes:

> In postdramatic theatre, breath, rhythm, and the present actuality of the body's visceral presence take precedence over the logos. An opening and dispersal of the logos develop in such a way that it is no longer necessarily the case that a meaning is communicated from A (stage) to B (spectator), but instead a specifically theatrical, "magical" transmission and connection happen by means of language. (2004: 145)

Similarly to Lehman's reflections on theater, Stuart McLean (2017) has argued in anthropology for a form of fidelity to the real that does not strive for representational accuracy, but rather for questioning what is assumed to be real within the social sciences:

> The real that anthropology engages is often a source less of certitude than of doubt and disorientation. Rather than a restraint or limit, might not such a fictionalizing real (in Deleuze's and Nietzsche's sense) serve as an incitement to experiment, . . . by lingering in those spaces and moments when realities and representation, and with them anthropology and literature . . . are rendered truly indiscernible? (McLean 2017: 48)

Lehman's magic in between performance and audience, and McLean's experimentation in between the real and fiction, resonate with our devising practice in Affect Theater.

Performance, Ethnography, and Theater

Interdisciplinary experiments between anthropology and theater go back to the work of Zora Neal Hurston (Hurston and Hughes 1931) and Katherine Dunham (Chin 2014) and their experiments with ethnographically grounded plays and dance performances. Other experiments, such as those developed by Edith and Victor Turner (1982) and Richard Schechner (1985) have focused on performing ethnographies or have used performance as a metaphor for understanding the social (Goffman 1959, Conquergood 2013). In the 1970s, Eugenio Barba (2005) started the tradition of "Theater Anthropology," which investigates different theatrical traditions and how they inform and impact performance and presence.[4] While inspired by these explorations, our workshops make yet another turn. We do not make performances that recreate or represent our research, nor do we draw from a broad array of theatrical history and traditions.

Our work is part of an exciting conversation on multimodality and experimental collaboration that has animated anthropology and the social sciences at large in the last twenty years (Collins, Durington, and Gill 2017, Estalella and Sánchez Criado 2018, Biddle and Lea 2018, Kazubowski-Houston and Auslander 2021). This body of research explores ways to create spaces of invention and collaboration that enable generative engagements in the field and ways of producing knowledge collaboratively (Marcus 2008, 2010, Myers and Dumit 2011, Ossman 2021, Elhaik and Marcus 2019). Many of these scholars share a general critique of the academic text as the main product of anthropological knowledge (Conquergood 2013, Madison 2018) and an interest in challenging common forms of representation to allow new relations, forms, and worlds to emerge from anthropological encounters (Elliott and Culhane 2016, Dattatreyan and Marrero-Guillamo 2019, Vidali 2020).[5]

More specific to our work, over the past few decades, experiments with performance and performativity as a form of representation, analysis, and ethnographic process have gained currency. We acknowledge the inspiration provided by scholars such as Conquergood (2013), Madison (2018), Denzin (2003), and Fabian (1990), and their contributions to performance ethnography as a research methodology that cross-pollinates ethnography, arts, and performance to find novel ways to share empirical research material in embodied and emphatic ways that reach beyond conventional written texts and academic audiences. These scholars are concerned with different registers of performance and performativity: the dramaturgy of social interactions and the performativity of social life broadly conceived, the performativity of fieldwork where in order for the ethnographer to do research she has to weave her life-worlds with the ones of her collaborators in the field; and, last but not least, performance as a method to translate the experience of fieldwork into a performable play. In this kind of work, theater has often figured as both an ethnographic research methodology and a form of representation that emerged from intense collaborations with research participants to translate fieldwork material for the stage, something D. Soyini Madison calls "a performance of possibilities" aimed at creation and social change (2005: 172). Johannes Fabian, for instance, conceives the ethnographer as a "co-performer" (1990: 7) doing research *with* and not *of* others, and of the anthropological encounter as performative more than informative; for him, theater taps into those aspects of knowledge that can only be embodied in performance, and not in conversations or texts. Dwight Conquergood, in his vision of a committed performance ethnography that challenges the hegemony of academic writing and elitism, argues that "performance as a complementary or alternative form of 'publishing' research" is "the most deeply subversive and threatening to the text-bound structure of the academy. [. . .] It is quite another thing, politically, to move performance from hermeneutics to a form of scholarly representation. That move strikes at the heart of academic politics and issues of scholarly authority" (2013: 96–7).

It is maybe, in part, to take on this challenge, that more recently anthropologists have actively incorporated in their monographs their direct work with theater as a participatory ethnographic practice and a form of being implicated with others in the fieldwork experience (Kondo 2018, Vidali 2020), using performance of the material itself as a way of rendering, giving back, sharing, and producing knowledge otherwise. This has allowed the visual dimension of performance to counter and complement the often highly verbal anthropological account (Kazubowski-Houston 2010), offering a nuanced analysis of ethnography as cultural performance and an occasion to produce a stage play with a community (Hartblay 2020), opening anthropological practice to embodied collaborative performances (Vidali 2020), and blurring the line between the real and fiction (Kondo 2018). Our work is embedded in this conversation but also diverges from it with its emphasis on method and attention to affect as a mode of relating to the empirical in every step of the process: fieldwork, analysis, representation, and creation.

Affect Theater is also in conversation with and emerges out of a prodigious tradition of western documentary theater or Theater of the Real (Martin 2013). Moreover, our practice, while different, resonates with performances that originate from fieldwork and empirical research. The plays of Zora Neale Hurston are an example of more observational and ethnographic approaches to performance making where fictionalized characters play out plots of local legend and engage in real behavior, language, and cultural practices observed in the field.[6] The choreography and teaching of Katherine Dunham infused contemporary dance with a new movement vocabulary drawn directly from her field research.[7] We are also inspired by postmodern theater artists—such as Ron Vawter, Leeny Saks, Spalding Gray, Karen Finley, Holly Hughes, Elevator Repair Service, and The Wooster Group—who explore performance as an analytical frame and engage in the deconstruction and reconstruction of meaning through the use of the elements of the stage in nontraditional dramaturgies in research- or interview-based work. Finally, like many others working in the Theater of the Real, we are indebted to the groundbreaking interview-based works of Anna Deveare Smith[8] and her explorations of the ways in which language, speech, and behavior can construct meaning, culture, and character.[9]

Interrupting Crisis

Returning to our workshops, the scenes that unfolded for us from *bighellonare* are examples of how the process of Affect Theater and ethnographic devising allowed us to investigate the tensions between typical crisis narratives around migration and borders, and the affective material and minor stories that those types of narratives leave out. To work around—rather than about—the issue of "crisis," our group's collaboration rendered empirical material about movement and borders into performances that not only inform about events but also elicit affects and blur the line between the cultural tendency toward crisis narratives and the bias against the uneventful.

Since 2015, an unprecedented number of people from Middle Eastern and African countries have been crossing borders into and within Europe. The deaths resulting from such crossings have also multiplied, often turning the images of borders and seas into cemeteries of people on the move. This time has been described by the media, the nation states, and various political actors as an "emergency" and a "crisis" that challenges the core of European values and human rights principles. The statistics that result from such movements have turned migration into a metric of crisis, positing Europe as a "civilization" currently in a "state of crisis" (Davis 2015).[10] If migration has become a metric of crisis, crisis has become a narrative device (Koselleck 2002; Roitman 2014) that allows for certain questions to be posed and others to be foreclosed. Framing this time as such implies approaching the present moment as a state of emergency that activates the different functions and modalities of sovereign power. European nation states and supranational organizations are mobilized to simultaneously save and care for lives in need of rescue, on the one hand, and to enforce stricter border control, on the other. Both postures of sovereign power are framed within a grammar of life that identifies certain events as worth accounting for and as crisis producing, and others as ordinary, thus uneventful and unaccountable (Povinelli 2011). This is the departure point for *Unstories*, our first collaboratively devised performance out of which this entire book emerges.

Affect Theater is a process that allows us to wander and err through minor sites of attention and pose questions outside of master narratives, and to be surprised by the answers. For example, in *Unstories*, our question was: How can we narrate outside of the "crisis" paradigm and sensationalist representations of violence? Our social imaginary has been colonized by a narrative binary where migration is either represented as a linear process, with one (state-determined) temporality of people leaving, arriving, integrating, and becoming a new citizen-subject, or never arriving and dying during the crossing. Our task, then, was to devise theater and performance that acknowledged the reality of borders, tuned in to the elusiveness of lived experience, and cut through the numbing resulting from the public's saturation with violent images and terrifying statistics about migration. Our embodied dramaturgy becomes both a heuristic method and a tool of representation to explore how affective performances can produce new political reflections on experience. In the same way, it can also function as a pedagogical tool for students involved in the process as either devisers or spectators. For instance, one of our students, after watching *Unstories* (2017), described the value of this work: "Taking the stories off the page and bringing them into a visual and aural dimension made them much more impactful. It increased my knowledge of the human behind the ethnographies." In the third section of the book, our collaborators (students and colleagues) offer depictions of the ways that the work affected their research.

In the case of *Unstories*, our exploration centered on the experience of migration and borders. As a result, our book devotes many pages to themes and stories on this topic. These are offered as examples to demonstrate the ways that Affect Theater helps artists and social scientists in their research and writing around any subject. Our book should be understood to be as much about the *method* of Affect Theater as about the *content* which revolves around questions of borders and migration. Our practice includes an engagement with the full spectrum of narrative values. At one end of this spectrum lies traditional types of theatrical and cultural storytelling with solid dramatic action that rises toward a crisis. In the middle lie minor stories and association and, at the other end of the spectrum, the direct experience of affect and non-narrative performance. The subject matter of *Unstories* certainly profits from an engagement with and juxtaposition of these various narrative and non-narrative dramaturgies, but this is a book about a process/method that may be applied to any empirical research.

The Dramaturgy of this Book

Unstories is a performance and a book that, rather than informing about current events, attempts to play with the ways in which we think we know, and to work differently with empirical material, giving precedence to affect over analysis, intuition over interpretation, slowness over fastness, nonlinearity over linear plots. Our intention is to transport the listener/reader/spectator into the affective field of experiences, rather than simply write about them. It is an experiment at listening around the stories we are told about migration, or any area of research, to recuperate other rhythms of narration that remain uncaptured by official discourses.

This book is divided into three parts. In Part I, we present Affect Theater as our process of working and writing with empirical material (Chapter 1), and experiment with a performative text of the piece we produced for the stage in 2017, *Unstories* (Chapter 2). Part II is composed of three chapters and two essays (*Associations*). Here Giordano continues writing from the empirical material, not in the same performative form of Chapter 2, but letting the process of the workshops affect her more ethnographic and essayistic writing. In Part III, Pierotti addresses some of the perils that come with being positioned as a representer of the "real," and he examines the challenges and benefits of working with affect and narrative when engaging the empirical. In Part III, we also detail our experimental pedagogies between theater and anthropology by sharing practical exercises, workshop prompts, and additional resources that can be brought to the classroom or used in a workshop exploration of one's own research. Four essays by our collaborators in *Unstories* (Carol Garcia, Morganne Blais-McPherson, Rima Praspaliauskiene, and Lisa Stevenson) are included to share with the reader different ways in which Affect Theater has impacted the work of others in the field and in the practice of writing, beyond theater and performance making.

The reader will notice that parts of the research engaged in the script of *Unstories* (Chapter 2) reappear in different forms in the chapters of Part II. These reverberations and the enactment of our thinking about them in space help us access the power of association and allow collaborative thinking. This book's experiment is not only to un-story discourses on movement and borders, and to decenter narrative more broadly, but also to share methods for *making strange*, as Bertolt Brecht would say, anthropological ways of relating to and knowing the real. The *Associations* interspersed throughout the book think through unexamined aspects of the surrounding chapters, making further estrangements and associations.

The practice and direct experience of un-storying empirical material in Part I enables the perspective of the minor (Deleuze and Guattari 1983) through which the chapters of Part II are written. There, Giordano thinks with this question of the minor in its various valences and, in line with the process of Affect Theater, decenters dominant discourses around migration and borders, and unstories anthropological ways of writing them. Unlike in the performative text (Chapter 2), Affect Theater provides her a way into minor sites of attention and practice where different accounts of movement form, and allows her to approach ethnographic sites through details, unofficial documents, objects, debris, and the ways in which they open (minor) ways of narrativizing the world (Stewart 1996: 29).

In Chapter 3, Giordano explores the expression "the funnel effect of immigration." Since 2015, this phrase has been used to describe the drastic increase in numbers of people arriving in Italy, turning the peninsula into the main gateway to Europe. This also points to the contradictions at the heart of the European Union's management of the "refugee crisis" and the frontline role the Italian government and civil society have played over the years. Through the disembarkation procedures that people rescued at sea go through when they arrive at Italian ports, she approaches the *sbarco* (disembarkation) as an assemblage of techniques that mirror sovereign power's modalities, to then trace the emergence of worlds beyond the scrutiny of the port.

In Chapter 4, Giordano explores this emergence by attending to a Tunisian artist's installation entitled "Museo dei sogni frantumati" (Museum of fractured dreams). Ramzi Harrabi created this work with the debris left over from the shipwrecks of those who attempted to cross the Mediterranean into Sicily (Italy). Giordano pays attention to minor details such as the shoes, ripped documents, a torn Koran, unopened cans of food, and worn-out life jackets that Harrabi recuperates at boat cemeteries and dumps throughout Sicily and transforms into artwork. The whole installation was meant to perform the traces of the crossing that exceeds the *sbarco*. By displaying it in an unconsecrated Church in Sicily, first, and later at the Strasbourg European Parliament, Harrabi performs a different account of movement and experience in a minor register and provides a political critique of the crisis narrative from within official institutions. In this way, he re-stories the crisis from within, and gives space to sites, objects, and their uncanny relations to the humans—foreigners and Italians alike—that are interwoven with them.

Chapter 5 continues to work around the grammar of crisis and the forms of care that it simultaneously enables and disables. Inspired by the relationship between two painters—from Tunisia and Nigeria—and their forms of therapeutic and ethical explorations through art, Giordano attends to practices that unfold through other grammars, or the lack thereof. These practices are the expression of a denial, or, better, of an interruption in the language of the crisis and pathology. She focuses on the paintings of Homiex, a young Nigerian man who arrived in Italy as a minor, entered the system of humanitarian protection, and spent his first several months at reception centers drawing and learning how to paint. Although he was invited to draw and paint his "refugee experience," he refused to do so. In this chapter, Giordano experiments with forms of experiencing and representing that belong to the performativity of creation and the potential that is exemplified by the gesture of Melville's character, Bartleby, when he says: "I would prefer not to."

Part III examines narratives from the theatrical perspective, as well as providing some pedagogical applications of Affect Theater for the classroom or studio. It opens with Chapter 6, where Pierotti unpacks Bertolt Brecht's theory and dramaturgy of *Verfremdungseffekt* (making the familiar strange), as he reflects on the ethical complication of narrativizing the real in both traditional and unconventional documentary forms. He discusses his collaborative process as a member of Tectonic Theater Project when they co-created *The Laramie Project*, the play about the homophobic attack and murder of Matthew Shepard, the trials of the perpetrators, and the impact of these incidents on the town of Laramie, Wyoming. He explores how devising the play revealed to him both the power and the dangers of engaging strong narrative practices when working with the "real." Developing the question of estrangement in theater narratives, he explores the kind of experimental dramaturgies and logics that can emerge in contemporary forms of performance based on different conceptions of what counts as the "real," and the ways in which theater can "perceive reality without collapsing it to fit particular agendas," so that old assumptions cannot be taken for granted and new understanding is possible (Barnett 2014: 77–8).

In Chapter 7, Pierotti and Giordano develop a pedagogical journey that can be extended to various classroom formats and disciplines, with exercises and workshop prompts that originated in their Affect Theater experiments.

Also included in Part III are *Reverberations*, short reflections written by four of our collaborators. They each have participated in our seminars and or the making of *Unstories* (2017), and *Unstories II (roaming)* (2018) as anthropologists, writers, and/or performers. We invited them to reflect upon their own experiences and how the engagement with our process of Affect Theater may have influenced their own practices of writing, performing, acting, doing research, or simply observing and working with images.

The sections entitled *Associations*, interspersed throughout, are written in the mode of the *post scriptum*, taking on a question, a thought, or an image that remained unexplored in the preceding chapter. They are conceived in the spirit of yet another association that keeps expanding the affective qualities of the material at hand, but also inviting the reader to keep on imaging connections and possible associations on their own. Part of our process of making empirically based performances is to create a list of theatrical episodes that we later compose in sequences with more or less narrative logic that form a performance event. Similarly, the reader can treat each section and chapter of this book as an episode in and of itself that can be put in alternative sequences with the rest of the material contained here.

Part I

Affect Theater

A Collaboration between Theater and Anthropology

Cristiana Giordano and Greg Pierotti

In the early 1980s, French anthropologist and psychoanalyst Jeanne Favret-Saada outlined a research method and a practice of writing that challenged the common idea of "participant observation" in the social sciences, and that resonates with our experiments between theater and anthropology. She emphasized the paradoxical nature of this common anthropological research method, an oxymoron, "to observe while participating, or to participate while observing, is about as obvious as savoring a burning hot ice cream" (1990: 190). Instead, in her work on witchcraft in the Bocage, France, she proposed a different kind of presence during fieldwork, something that she called "getting caught." She argued that this is a way of letting oneself be affected and positioned by the language, grammar, and network of relations that make up specific worlds. She further elaborated: "To accept to 'participate' and be affected has nothing to do with understanding." Research, then, implies being affected by the intensities of relations in the field that exceed the possibility of being understood and represented through participant observation. Like in a dream, a lot of what happens during our research processes can only be grasped through the affects that are produced in us and the kind of oblique associations we make while immersed in the experience of it. Her reflections may help any research that engages empirical material. For anthropologists, one might include the experience of the intensities that go with research rather than taking a distant observer position. For theater makers working with the empirical, or some kind of "real" (Martin 2013), one might choose to avoid the pressure to reduce their experience into simple and legible narrative arcs that exclude these intensities in their representations.

When social scientists (or theater makers) start writing from empirical material, Favret-Saada warns against moving from being "caught" to "catching" things in an analytical or representational frame, creating accounts from an unaffected and comprehending posture. She suggests instead that we need to be "caught again." For her, writing is not a distancing process that allows for objectification, but rather a way to tap back into the intensities we experienced while doing research. It is also a way to create new relations with the empirical so that our sense of separateness from our objects of inquiry continues to be challenged and blurred. Informed by the psychoanalytic understanding of transference, Favret-Saada sees in writing the need for "a second 'catching' and not a 'getting uncaught'" (1980: 14).[1]

Mary Overlie's theorizing of postmodern choreographers and theater makers helps us respond to Favret-Saada's challenge. Inspired by Overlie's Viewpoints, workshop participants in our groups respond to the empirical sources not with the posture of a creator of art, but rather by becoming "absorbed in a dialogue with the material," where listening to all the materials available (including the empirical) allows them to become at once participants and observers and thus avoid working from "the prejudice of the creator" (Overlie 2016: 189). In this way, Overlie provides a reframing, through theater practice, of the anthropological understanding of participant observation, which is at the heart of Favret-Saada's conundrum.

The primary devising technique that influences us is the practice of Moment Work (Brown 2005, Kaufman et al. 2018), which was developed by Tectonic Theater Project, where Greg worked from 1996 to 2015. Moment Work is a practice for the construction of performance from what the company calls "non-theatrical source material"; it was used to collaboratively develop plays like *Gross Indecency* (1996), *The Laramie Project* (2000), *Laramie: 10 Years Later* (2008), and *The People's Temple* (2004). Like most devising practices, it differs from traditional theater in which a text precedes the staging of the play. In Moment Work, the finalized text is unearthed, or written, by the devising company in collaboration using all the elements of the stage, including text-based research materials, simultaneously. This practice emerged in the context of postmodern theatrical experiments (1960s-1980s), specifically Overlie's teaching and Viewpoints theory.[2] In Moment Work, text (any written or spoken language) and narrative are just two of many theatrical elements that, while not dismissed, are temporarily decentered.

However, Moment Work differs from Affect Theater, as well as from other devising practices, in that at a certain point text and narrative reassert themselves in their traditional position at the center of the theater-making process. The objective of Moment Work is similar to the work of more conventional theatrical models: the creation of a textual artifact, a play-script with a traditional dramaturgy, that can be published and reproduced independently by other interpretive artists. With Affect Theater, on the other hand, we are developing a new practice for engaging the empirical, creating knowledge, and sharing our research findings in less linear presentations. Our experiment utilizes aspects of Moment Work but might be better characterized by Hans-Thies Lehman's concept of the postdramatic. Lehman writes, "When the progression of a story with its internal logic no longer forms the center, when composition is no longer experienced as an organizing principle, but as an artificially imposed 'manufacture' . . . then theatre is confronted with the question of possibilities beyond drama" (2004: 26).

For example, in the course of our collaboration we have worked with two bodies of empirical material: one relating to police violence in the United States, and one to migration in Europe, which is the research we engage primarily in this book. In the productions of *Unstories I and II*, the 2016–18 theatrical events around issues of migration in the Mediterranean, we drew from our research at ports of entry in Sicily where boats of "refugees" arrive from Northern Africa.[3] We observed that upon disembarkation, as people were received by humanitarian organizations, they were immediately given a pair of fake crocs and their old shoes were thrown away.[4] During our devising explorations, the crocs emerged as a form that could provide non-narrative structure. They allowed the company to move in and out of character; they also formally enabled representations of the care and control of the state, gesturing toward specific translations of the foreign body into legal categories ("refugee," "victim of human trafficking," "economic migrant," "unaccompanied minor"). Dramaturgically, they created structures within which the empirical material could be presented. Here, rather than a story, it was a pair of crocs that enabled the recitation of text from interviews, archival documents, observations from field notes, and so on. Stepping into crocs allowed the conveyance of bureaucratic and legal voices of policymakers and humanitarian agents. Stepping out of crocs allowed for language to be spoken that exceeds the rhetoric of the state. This is a non-narrative, affective dramaturgy. Audiences responded to the use of the crocs in less conceptual ways. For example, at our University of California, Davis, performance (May 2017), some audience members *felt* the constraint of the theatrical form of the crocs rather than understanding it; others had a bodily experience of the crocs as a physicalization of being categorized.

In Affect Theater, the language of our empirical research is transformed from a currency invested in the creation of meaning or logos into, as Lehman puts it, a "dance of language gestures" (2004: 145). For us, the "'magical' transmission and connection" (Lehman 2004: 145) happens not exclusively through language but through the fluid and affective relations that occur between language, space, elements of the stage, performer, and audience.

Affect Theater also challenges the prevalent practice in much contemporary theater and anthropology of single authoring our pieces of writing (articles, books, plays, and essays). The most traditional model of play making utilizes a singularly authored text created prior to the collaboration in the rehearsal room. When anthropologists analyze and write, they often stop co-laboring with those we have worked with in the field. In our joint work, we ask how theater makers can learn new relationships to their narratives from anthropological questioning, and how anthropologists can learn from theater devising to write in more collaborative and visceral ways.

The Workshops

For our first workshop, in the fall of 2015, we used a shared body of research, primarily interview transcripts collected for a play Greg was writing about police violence in Baltimore. In the spring of the same year, he was inspired to tell the story of twenty-five-year-old Freddie Gray, a Black man who was illegally arrested by the Baltimore police and died as a result of injuries incurred during the violent encounter. The play explores the often-contradictory understandings and negotiations of race and the practices of institutional violence in American society.[5] In 2016–18, our second and third series of workshops focused on material that Cristiana collected concerning borders, and what the mainstream media and academic discourses have described as "the refugee crisis" in the Mediterranean and Europe. This material investigates the narratives, spaces, and experiences that discussions of this "crisis" erase or marginalize.[6]

For both projects, we experimented with staging what we call theatrical episodes using theoretical and historical texts, to weave them into the empirical and blur the lines between the two. In the Baltimore project, *b more* (Figure 1), for example, one of Frank B. Wilderson III's scholarly writings on anti-blackness features as a voice in the play's conversation around police violence, race, and Freddie Gray's death in custody. Greg placed Wilderson III's words (2014) in conversation with journalist Antero Pietila's (2010) account of Baltimore's complex urban and social landscape (including the history of redlining).[7] In a further complication throughout the play, there are episodes where white actors draw a map of Baltimore's streets across the stage space with painter's

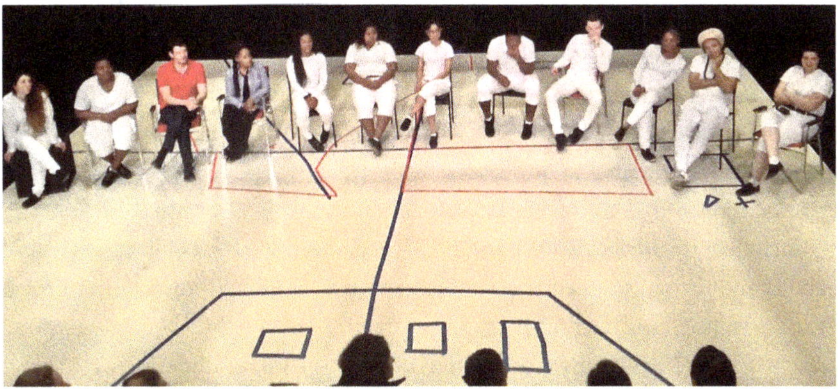

Figure 1 From left: Adriana Pinkerton, Jasmine Washington, Greg Pierotti, Margaret Laurena Kemp (talk back moderator), Natsumi McGee, Tyler Crawford, Rufayda Dhamani, Gabriel Lee Johnson, Taylor Church, Ugo Edu, Sergio Bitencourt Ferreira, and Caitlin Sales. Audience Talk back for b more, written and directed by Greg Pierotti, University of California, Davis, March 2016. Photo by John Zibell. Reproduced by permission of John Zibell (first published in TDR 2020).

tape. This action interrupts the play and prescribes the physical territory where actors representing people in the city would be allowed to move or perform. These scenes introduce questions about who controls the representations we see. Additionally, whenever the dramaturgy of the play becomes too narrative, an episode centering this map-drawing disrupts the performance, interrupts the flow of theatrical time, and breaks up the performance space.

For *Unstories*, we put anthropologist Janet Roitman's reflections on "crisis" and "anti-crisis" on stage (Roitman 2014) and draw from Favret-Saada's work on different modes of research (1980, 1990) to think through our positions as theater makers and social scientists. Throughout both series of workshops, we were guided by Favret-Saada's provocation of "getting caught."

In order, however, to better convey the ways in which our workshop enables this process, we want to describe in more detail how the practice originated, and how we are using it now in our collaboration. Workshops usually comprise three phases that, while deeply interconnected, are also discrete practices: (1) Research, (2) Episode Composition, and (3) Dramaturgy.

1) Research

During the research period, the group investigates an initial area of inquiry; for example, Freddie Gray and anti-blackness, or the Italian refugee "crisis" and theories of "anti-crisis." Having chosen a topic, narrative, or theme, each member then conducts scholarly research or field work to generate a body of primary and secondary sources encountered within the sites of inquiry. In the cases of our two projects, because we lacked sufficient funding and time, this model of research was modified.[8] We conducted our research individually and only briefly overlapped in our research sites; later, we shared the content of our investigation with the company that collaboratively devised with it.

Included in the research period is the gathering of specific visual, aural, tactile, and textual source material. For example, while Tectonic Theater Project was devising *Gross Indecency: The Three Trials of Oscar Wilde* (1996), costume designer Kitty Leech pinned renderings of men's Victorian underwear that could have been worn by the prostitutes Oscar Wilde hired to the wall of the rehearsal studio. We also draw from secondary research, as when in *b more* Greg staged excerpts from Pietila's *Not In My Neighborhood* (2010) to evoke Baltimore's history of redlining. Researchers also gather material from their direct experience in the field. For instance, during the creation of *Unstories,* Cristiana introduced artwork that Homiex, a young Nigerian artist she met in Siracusa, Italy, shared with her. This material was used to create a character in the performance who emerged through images rather than text; another example of an approach we found to represent narratives that exceed state categories. Finally, this material may include seemingly unrelated design elements pulled directly from transcribed interviews because they strike us. During one interview for *b more*, Greg was struck when community activist Mama Ama described a cabaret show she was doing with her band following Freddie Gray's funeral.[9] Greg used the song *I Like it* by DeBarge, which she referenced in the interview, to create atmosphere and point to differences in cultural contexts between Black and white characters as well as in audiences. We always mine the collected interviews for references to any design element that might add to the theatrical world we create.

However, as Favret-Saada observed, research is not just about gathering material but about being affected by an atmosphere and the subject positions assigned to us while in the field. In her work on witchcraft, she references the ways in which her interlocutors positioned her as a potential un-witcher who could undo the consequences of a spell (1980). In other words, she was caught in the force field of witchcraft by simply being placed in a set of relations organized through the discourse of magic.[10] Similarly, because he is white, when Greg arrived in Baltimore, his interlocutors positioned him in the field of race relations in ways he had little control over. This is a sort of affective space that Greg could not evade and in which he also found himself actively participating through his own projections and anxieties about race relations. This aspect of his research becomes an important part of what is represented in *b more*. When Cristiana entered an Italian ethno-psychiatric clinic exclusively for foreign patients as part of her research (2002–4), she was often positioned as a therapist simply because she was a white Italian and a researcher. This allowed certain experiences and narratives to emerge in her relationships with patients that she could not imagine nor control before entering that specific therapeutic setting. All these positions are forms of "getting caught," of stepping into different sites and their discursive practices. This creates a set of obligations we don't master, but that guide us through our fieldwork and inform our creative productions in unexpected ways. Affect Theater engages with and attempts to share these complexities.

Before getting into the second phase, Episode Composition, it is important to point out the dialectical nature of all three phases of our devising process. For example, research is shared with other collaborators when composing episodes. This sharing of our empirical material through theatrical compositions redirects group members' ongoing research agendas. Similarly, research impacts episode composition and dramaturgy phases. There are points in the process where research is paused to focus exclusively on making episodes, phase two, which is our way to resist "catching" our empirical material in a merely descriptive or narrative frame.

2) Episode composition

Whether writing ethnographies or plays, text and narrative tend to crowd out other forms of communication between creators and audiences. In Affect Theater, we begin our work by leaving text and storytelling aside. We start by constructing short theatrical events, what we call "episodes." An episode is framed by the words, "We Begin" and "We End." This deceptively simple framing device allows us to think in a structural way about the discrete units of theatrical time that make up an entire performance progression. We are signaling to the group that the theatrical material being presented for analysis is only what exists within this frame. Successful episodes will later constitute the building blocks for the creation of an entire performance score (or play) and are analyzed by the viewers at the time of their presentation, as we will describe shortly.

To do this compositional work, it is helpful to distill the theatrical languages discovered in the research phase into their basic parts. We generate a list of the elements of the stage besides text that are available to us, and we explore each element by creating individual episodes that investigate their actual sensorial qualities. Initially, we explore them from a phenomenological rather than a semiotic point of view. We look for their theatrical rather than their narrative potential. For example, if we want to make an episode with a banana, we don't represent eating the banana (the sign representing itself), nor do we "answer" the banana, pretending that it is a telephone receiver (the sign representing something else). Instead, we construct an episode that explores its softness or its yellowness; its scent and sound as we open it; what the pulp within the skin can do; how it smashes and looks on various surfaces.

At many of her research sites in Italy, Cristiana had noticed a variety of garbage, litter, and other detritus. In the workshops for *Unstories*, collaborators brought in an array of junk: crumpled newspaper and paper towels, cans and bottles, plastic bags, dirty clothes and blankets, bicycle wheels, broken toys, destroyed books, plastic cutlery, and so on. Rather than simply scattering them around as set dressing, as one might do in response to a play's stage direction, we spent time exploring the sensorial qualities of our stuff. A cloud of white shopping bags speaks a different language than a neat shimmering stack of black trash can liners, which again emits a different affect than a pile of crumpled dirty blankets. When we needed a heap of garbage as set dressing (the sign representing itself) we had this material at hand, but we were also able to utilize the specific poetry of each kind of garbage after our phenomenological explorations. Black bin liners can become comic when worn as a dress or can create a claustrophobic oily enclosure (the sign representing something else), but they also evoke a feeling of freedom and spontaneity when thrown high in the air and allowed to float gently back to earth (phenomenological exploration).

In Affect Theater, we explore our research material by experimenting with the elements of our theatrical world to find out what they can tell us rather than to make it function in the way we have decided it must, or in ways that we are used to. For Favret-Saada, it wasn't until she let herself be caught again through the power that words carried in witchcraft that she could start experiencing, rather than understanding, their performativity, and to be surprised by the unpredictability of relations, both human and nonhuman, that made up her field of inquiry (1980). Similarly, for us the practice of composition takes our experience of "being caught" in our research phase and extends that into the phase of analytical engagement with our research so that writing or devising can be a way of "getting caught again." Based on our associations and intuitive hunches, we create episodes using the elements of the stage and engage them through different types of analysis, which allow the material to speak back to our initial impulse. This dialectic creates something unexpected and unintentional, giving the material a liveliness that must then be encountered and grappled with in the present episode.[11]

For both theater makers and social scientists, letting go of the urge for signification, even temporarily, can be challenging. Rarely do students or professionals come easily to the notion that the theater and the elements of the stage could be agents not just in the making but also in the unmaking of meaning. Even for those of us who are very interested in working with and through narrative, these early explorations can free us and create instead an affective space where we can play with phenomena and spectacle for their own sakes. This allows us to be drawn anew into the world where field research has taken place. Echoing Helen Vendler, in our workshops we "pull the energy of the performing arts into the social sciences in order to make it easier to 'crawl out to the edge of the cliff of the conceptual'" (Vendler 1995 quoted in Thrift 2007: 79).

Because affect is "found in those intensities that pass from body to body" (Gregg and Siegworth 2010: 4) to get caught again or *anew* while writing, one allows the human and nonhuman bodies that inhabit the stage to interact with the empirical material. We think and engage with the material in ways that may blur the distinction between subject and object, between subjects, and between objects. For example, during an *Unstories* workshop our collaborators Sarah Hart and Regina Gutiérrez made a few versions of an episode that we titled "GPS Head Inside/Outside" (Figure 2). Their impulse was to investigate problems of translation and movement. Each time one of them made a version based on her hunch, the other would revise based on her intuitive response to the last version shared, until finally they had collaboratively developed an episode that they documented as follows.[12]

Episode—GPS Head Inside/Outside

We begin.

Regina calls Sarah on her cell phone, which is on loudspeaker.

Next, Regina addresses the audience. Speaking in Spanish, her words reverberate through the phone as she welcomes them and tells them they are going to go on a tour of the UC Davis campus. She asks seven audience members to put on pairs of crocs (but she only has five pairs, so some people are left out).

She asks all the people with crocs to follow her outside. She is very animated in her instructions in case they don't understand Spanish.

The group with crocs exits the theater space with Regina, leaving the others still sitting in the audience but able to hear the tour through Sarah's phone.

The tour group disappears outside but eventually becomes visible again through the windows.

Sarah enters from backstage with her cell phone on her head. Slides of google map images of the UC Davis campus are projected on the back wall. Over the course of the episode, these slides expand out to include the city of Davis, the state of California, etc., until finally the entire globe is presented in the slide show. Then the slides progress back down in scale focusing on Italy and finally on Siracusa.

Regina's instructions are always audible from Sarah's phone.

Regina tells the group outside (in Spanish) to walk straight, then turn right, etc. Clear directions. (If they do not appear to understand, she clarifies with a word or two in English, like "walk please"). Sarah, inside, follows Regina's instructions physically on the stage.

The group outside returns after a few minutes, entering the theatre and taking their seats, as instructed by Regina. By this time, the slide projections have completed their full trajectory panning out from Davis and then focusing in on Siracusa.

Regina says these words from Cristiana's field notes:

"Welcome to Siracusa. You will need to find your way to processing. Please be careful as you walk down the ramp from the boat."

One person hands bottles of water to the tour members as they head back to their seats.

The phone call ends.

We end.

In the group's analysis, we found that no one knew or agreed on what the episode "meant," but there was a strong positive response to the ways it seemed to blur the discreet distinctions between a number of bodies and concepts: the real bodies of performers in spatial relationship to each other; the represented bodies of migrants in movement; the complications of borders, migration, and translation; the distinctions between outside and inside and between spectators and performers; the complexities and pervasiveness of cell phone technology and the implications of their use in state and corporate surveillance, along with the opposing implications of being guided and assisted by those same technologies and institutions; the mapping of the performance venue as a place for constructing meanings and narratives, and the mapping of the earth by satellite showing where larger dramas of bodies in movement play out.

Figure 2 From left: Ugo Edu, Maria Massolo (foreground), and John Zibell, in *Unstories*, written by Cristiana Giordano and Greg Pierotti, directed by Greg Pierotti. Yerba Buena Center for the Arts, San Francisco, September 23, 2017. Photo by Tommy Lau. Reproduced by permission of Yerba Buena Center for the Arts. San Francisco, CA.

In Affect Theater, the body is one of many elements that moves through and connects with other elements, including our texts. It may become a tool of expression rather than being a signifier in a story (Thrift 2007). In this context, the body is not a place where experience is merely embodied, absorbed, and conveyed, but it is an element in the same way light and sound can be. Just as in our practice when the text is at first decentered and put in relation to other elements of the stage, similarly the body may not take center stage but can function as one element among many creating relations, disruptions, and producing affects and effects.

In anthropology, the debate around embodiment has challenged the long-standing western philosophical tradition that posits the mind/body divide, by positioning the body as the primary site of experience and authenticity (Csordas 1994, Kirmayer 1993, Desjarlais and Troop 2011, Farquhar and Lock 2007). We draw from these debates on embodiment, but we don't consider the body a privileged site of performance and knowledge. Rather, we approach and use it as an element of the stage that creates and is created by relations with other elements in the production of theatrical episodes. This allows us to see the set of relations, the affective "in betweenness," that makes up a theatrical episode (or sequences of episodes) as the locus of experience where connections and constellations of knowledge between research and the stage take shape.

As our collaborator Regina Gutiérrez, who is trained as a dancer, put it: "I have always thought through my body. I am becoming more analytical, and the anthropologists [in our group] are becoming more bodily in their thinking." She referred to the body as a place of and for thinking, as a site that can create relations with other bodies, objects, and words: the human and nonhuman presences in the workshop.

Looping back to the actual process of composition, after an episode is presented within the frame "We begin"—"We end," viewers—not the episode makers—engage in a structured critique that unfolds in three parts. The first step is noticing what we particularly loved within the episode, for any reason (Lerman and Borstel 2003). If a lot of interest has been generated, we move to the second part, which is *structural analysis*: a precise description, without interpretation, of only what we saw and heard, similar to the "GPS Head Inside/Outside" documentation above. Another example: in analyzing an episode of gesture we might comment, "You said 'we begin' standing upstage left and looking downstage right. After about ten seconds, you took five steps on the diagonal towards center stage. You pointed your face towards the floor and slowly lifted your hand with splayed fingers and covered your entire face. You said, 'We end.'"

This is followed by part three, the *interpretive analysis*, which describes any meaning attributed to the episode. In the interpretive analysis, we are always careful to link the narrative we "made up" to the material elements of the episode that were discussed in the structural analysis. An interpretive analysis of the same episode might be: "Because of the slow pace of your cross and the lowering of your head, I made up that you were in deep grief. Because of the tension in your fingers and the way you grabbed your whole face, you seemed to be expressing some rage and violence. The pace and the size of the emotions that I was imagining you having felt like Greek tragedy."

As they listen to the group's structural and interpretive analyses, the presenters of the episode do not respond or explain (Kaufman et al. 2018: 50–3). This is important because to correct the viewers and describe our intention in making the episode—what it "really meant" to the makers—short-circuits the generative analysis that arises in our misunderstanding and the varieties of interpretations among the viewers. Putting an episode in the space without being able to defend or describe it to the viewers allows for a continuation of this sort of affective theorizing. This is a different kind of analysis from what we are accustomed to in either the social sciences or in the narrative practices of theater. It's important to note that unlike analysis in many product-oriented devising practices, our analytical process is as much an end product as the performance itself. The generative thinking that arises in between our various interpretations and that allows for new insight into the empirical material is one of the principal goals of Affect Theater: the process of "getting caught" *anew*.

It is in the gaps between what we mean and what is received and fed-back that a dialectic arises between the collaborators, and between the group and the shared empirical material. It is a way of thinking collaboratively, in and out of meaning. Instead of interpreting our material and using it to frame our theoretical arguments, this approach allows us to respond more affectively to what we see and hear, and to experience the material in tactile and sensuous new ways.

While we place a lot of emphasis on trying to leave text and storytelling out of our process for a while, the phenomenological does not have a privileged position in our work either. If an episode is powerful because it creates a surprising and shared interpretation or even narrative among some of the viewers, that is useful. If we find an episode compelling or theatrical for any reason—because it tells a great story, or because it teaches us something fascinating about an object, light, costume, or another element of the stage—we title and document it. We create a list of episode titles, which becomes a catalogue of possible material for the larger piece.[13]

Over time, as we begin to add more elements to our episodes, and the episodes become more complex, they can create more associations in the minds of the spectators, and therefore more narrative and metaphor tend to arise for them. Finally, we introduce language. We choose our texts from the body of shared research by simply tuning in with language that we love or find compelling. Some texts emerge out of the vast array of the material because they seem to capture everyone's attention. We are learning about the affective nature of our textual content by attending to the group's feeling about the words. We are guided by what we are drawn to through intuition and association. The addition of text increases the capacity of each episode to signify further. We do this by layering language into episodes that have already been made and listed, or by creating completely new episodes from and with language.

For example, when we worked on the transcript of a conversation with Dubarak, a young man from Senegal we met in a shanty town in the South of Italy where he worked as a seasonal worker, we engaged with his description of life in the fields and the "ghetto," as he called the place where he lived. Despite its hardship, the shanty town was in the open fields. Living there, and not in the city, where people like him were often stopped by the police and asked for documents, he said: "Deep down [here] I am free." A majority of us, without consulting each other, were inspired to make episodes using this line. When portions of texts are selected repeatedly in the workshop, they affect the whole group. Through repetition the text becomes other than the words uttered, and it also may start mobilizing certain narratives or associations. Through this utterance, Dubarak mobilized a critique of power and surveillance, which the group picked up and further developed, responding to it through our devising practice. In the process of episode making, who is mobilizing what narrative is blurred, and the author of the statement blends with other bodies, voices, objects, lights, and space. When we performed *Unstories II (roaming)* in June 2018, this text was used in relation to piles of trash and actors' bodies being entangled in red yarn.

Our challenge is to put words into conversation and conflict with the other elements of the stage, as opposed to having the elements simply demonstrating what the words are already describing. For example, rather than offering an episode where a performer is dressed in an evening gown seated at a piano playing Chopin accompanied by a voice-over text, "She was a concert pianist who loved Chopin" (this would be an example of the text and the other elements of the stage doing the same work), we might present the same theatrical image accompanied by the text, "The most widely prescribed medications for depression are SSRIs, selective serotonin reuptake inhibitors." In this second iteration, text and the other elements are not in a completely coherent relationship to one another; nor are they so distanced from each other that no connections can be drawn. The tensions between them require that the audience participate in meaning construction; it raises questions that the spectators must answer for themselves. Who is this woman and what has she got to do with depression? Is she depressed? Is she depression itself? Is she on these drugs? Again, the practice of making episodes, like many postmodern theatrical techniques, decenters the text. Eugenio Barba calls this working *with* the text rather than *for* the text. To work *with* the text implies that the text is one of the many materials of a performance rather than the blueprint that dictates how the various other materials will be used in the construction of a representation (Barba 2010: 123).

3) Dramaturgy

Dramaturgy is the third phase of our workshop. At its heart, dramaturgy is an organizational process. After we have generated many complex episodes and documented them, we start to narrow them down to a manageable number that we can work with and organize into a performance. For example, if we have devised for two years toward the creation of a full-length play, we might have 400 episodes that we want to narrow down to thirty or forty. To do this, we begin to look for the commonalities among particular episodes. These shared properties can be of any sort. We may notice that one specific object keeps getting included in episodes over and over, while others seem to be lying fallow, or that a certain colored light gets used repeatedly, that a certain subject or theme arises in different text-based episodes. Moreover, we may find that performers repeatedly function in certain ways (as actors in a company, as anthropologists making observations, as capoeiristas, etc.), that certain interlocutors in our research emerge as central characters in numerous episodes, or even that stories rise to prominence. All these common threads begin to interweave into possible structures for the piece—some narrative and character based, some thematic and language-based, and some entirely performative. Having narrowed the episodes down, we start to consider larger structures within which we can place them. This sequencing is in fact a form of writing. Like all writing, it is messy and difficult to articulate. The process is intuitive. We are not only creating narrative and text-based structures, but also physical ones, based in the elements (light, objects, architecture, etc.).

For example, in *Unstories* one of the collaborators, Ante Ursic, made an episode where he took a piece of paper from a pile of research and read a section of a transcript about a young Tunisian man who drowned while crossing the Mediterranean. After reading this passage, Ante folded the page into a paper boat and placed it into a fishbowl full of water (Figure 3). During the analysis, each collaborator appreciated its simplicity but also noticed its many theatrical ramifications—both representational and affective. Of course, the episode referenced the boats used to cross the Mediterranean. For some of us, it also pointed to the impossibility of representing through language—in this case, the written language of our research—the lived experience of those who cross borders. From then on, the image of the paper boat began to recur frequently in other episodes made by other collaborators.[14]

The boat brought to light the affective quality of the texts, allowed for a material form to carry what text alone could not, and so allowed the group to be

Figure 3 From left: Ante Ursic (partially obscured), Greg Pierotti, Maria Massolo, Mercedes Villalba, Ugo Edu, Sarah Hart, Cristiana Giordano, Regina Gutiérrez in the talk back of Unstories, written by Cristiana Giordano and Greg Pierotti, directed by Greg Pierotti, University of California, Davis, May 7, 2017. Photo by Jorge Nunez, reproduced with permission.

"caught again." It complicated the textual content by placing it into relationship with the felt experience produced by water, paper, fishbowls, lights, and the associations and interpretations of each spectator. Because we had all been studying the empirical material and the ideas embedded in the field research, this episode stuck with the group. It engaged us in new relations with the research, enabling an analysis of the episode that was generative and escaped predictable theoretical frames.

This process resembles the work that the unconscious does to produce dreams, which Sigmund Freud called "dream work" (Freud 1899). It also resembles the associations one finds in interpreting a dream after the fact. For Freud, awake, we think in concepts; asleep, we dream in images. Since dreams form by means of condensation and displacement of objects, words, people, and, more broadly, symbols, we can think of them as associative compositions. The images that make up a dream are the product of the unconscious dream work accomplished in sleep, which allows for the emergence and rearrangement of unconscious material. Just like in dream work, or in free association, things are brought together in a logic that is non-literal. In our workshop, it is through an affective movement from one object to a text to a shade of light, and so on, that chains of associations and overlays are formed, creating more evocative responses to our research. As our collaborator Alvaro Rodriguez put it, the theory "leaks out" in the space produced in the associations between bodies, texts, and the elements of the stage, and between the accords and disagreements among observers in their analyses afterward. Relations between interpretations of what the paper boat episodes actually "meant" gave rise to all sorts of new relations to the empirical material and allowed for the development of a dramaturgy, a performance score.[15]

Arriving at the dramaturgical phase, because many paper-boat episodes had been generated, we found that this form could serve as a non-narrative throughline. The episodes created in phase two were more concerned with the exploration of the theatrical language of the fishbowls and paper boats, and less with where the episodes took place within the stage space. In structuring the piece, we used a new fishbowl for each of the boat episodes. We lined them up at the downstage edge of the playing space. Each time a boat episode was performed, a paper boat was placed in a fishbowl starting at stage left and moving to stage right. This created a physical throughline that our audience could follow through the performance.

We also found this form could act as a dramaturgical container for other texts. For example, in the original episode we replaced the original text with a new one: field notes about the arrival of refugee boats at the port. The actor, in the role of an observing anthropologist, read the field notes, instead of the text from Ante's initial episode, and then performed the folding of the paper boat as in the original. Lastly, she walked downstage and very deliberately placed the boat in one of the fishbowls.

Three episodes later in the play, we used the making and placing of another paper boat in a fishbowl as a refrain. Each time we presented an episode that contained empirical material on paper, we ended it in the same way: an actor folding the research material into a paper boat and placing it in one of the fishbowls that lined the downstage edge of the playing space. After the second, or third of these episodes, spectators began to understand that the fishbowls would be filled with boats over the course of the piece. For the audience, this became a reliable physical throughline they could follow during the entire performance but that had nothing to do with narrative—except in an associative way. For us, it provided one of the central dramaturgical structures for the play, relieving us of the pressure of narrative.

The fishbowls example points to another shift in the way the dramaturgy of Affect Theater works. We often discover the formal container for a theatrical episode first, which then points us back to our research to look for the language that it can contain. This is in extreme opposition to traditional play-production models where a script exists prior to the production process and all the other forms are put in service of the text. In her teaching on writing and devising, Leigh Fondakowski calls this very different practice "writing into form" (2018).

In our collaboration, one of the primary goals is the discovery of theatrical forms that can contain as well as disrupt textual narratives (Giordano and Pierotti 2018). This practice is a way of creating an experience with the material that does not necessarily lead to storytelling, meaning-making, or knowledge. It produces, or re-produces, an affect. It moves away from analysis; it resists the temptation to explain things away and make everything clear to us and to the viewers.

For instance, in *b more* Greg used painter's tape to mark a map of the city on the floor while the performance unfolds. In relation to the selected texts in the play, this allowed the audience to imagine how streets and neighborhoods shape the life of inhabitants. It also performed the ways in which city planning inscribes/prescribes the spaces in which a black body may or may not move. By having a white actor create these boundaries, the mapping in the play enacted what the planners produce in the city: On the one hand, forms of discontinuity, division, and interruption; and on the other, forms of communication, community, and flow.[16] In this case, the tape mapping, like the fishbowls, functions as a recognizable throughline for the audience. Unlike the fishbowl form, however, the tape mapping also produces its dramaturgy through interruption as well as continuity. When the narrative drive of the play picked up too much force or pace, mapping undercut story.

Affect and Association

The theatrical devices mentioned in this chapter are means of making what in the Preface we refer to as affective re-presentation or our empirical research in the here and now. This is a process of decentering the literal meaning of texts so that language becomes more sensorial and imagistic in its encounters with other materials. This workshop re-presentation shares the same paradox as any other representation, that of doing something in the present that is not in fact present. The practice of composition foregrounds this way of working at the border between the real and the imaginary (McLean 2017), the actual and the potential (Deleuze 1988).

Engagement with affect generates different non-representational theories that challenge the hegemony of meaning and the divide between theory and practice by blurring the boundaries of each (Thrift 2007). It emphasizes a mode of perception that is not necessarily subject-based or narratively driven. Our devising practice proposes an associative rather than representational approach to research, creating non-narrative performances. We perform our thinking. We pay attention to elements of the stage and their relations—literal or oblique—with transcripts, legal documents, and field notes. We attend to empirical details, finding and following associations between the materials we work with and the workshop space (in all its visual, sonic, and tactile aspects); in relationship to other elements; and to other Viewpoints (Overlie 2016). This practice affects our writing in other ways, as the reader will see in the following chapters.

Episodes are the result of a series of these affective associations that arise in response to what we create with objects, sounds, lights, texts, and so on. We follow our hunches in making these associations. For example, we don't always understand why we may use red yarn in relation to the words of an African man describing working conditions in the tomato fields of southern Italy (*Unstories II* 2018). Or we are not fully aware of why we decide to print the text of field notes about the disembarkation of people rescued in the Mediterranean labeled "refugees" on a roll of wax paper. All the elements in an episode have what anthropologist Marilyn Strathern calls "partial connection" with one another (Strathern 2004).[17] A line from our field notes—"May I steal your shade?"— strikes us as curious, and so we create a movement piece where performers chase the holder of a shade-giving umbrella repeating the line over and again (Figure 4).

The red yarn may be connected to feeling trapped in an exploitative seasonal labor market, or it may relate to the color of tomatoes. Something about the ephemeral and disposable nature of wax paper may resonate with the fictional nature of the descriptions and interpretations that comprise field notes, but not only. This is not a symbolic approach, but an evocative and associative one. Coherence is not the logic/force that animates a good episode. Instead of creating a linear relation among the elements that make up an episode, we mix elements in the workshop space to evoke many associations.

Framing the episodes suspends the rush to storytelling, opening a gap in linear time, creating a space for exploration and inquiry, not necessarily into our research, but into the theatrical world that is emerging out of and in relation to that research. This could be text but could as easily be a tree branch or a shaft of light. This space is open to different times and intensities that are conjured when bodies, theatrical elements, and texts interact in-between "We begin" and

Figure 4 From left: Arielle Estrada, Maria Massolo, Sarah Hart, Rima Praspaliauskiene, John Zibell, in Unstories II (roaming) written by Cristiana Giordano and Greg Pierotti, directed by Cristiana Giordano and John Zibell, University of California, Davis, January 25, 2018. Photo by Lisa Stevenson, reproduced with permission.

"We end." The purpose of devising episodes is to set in motion their poetic and creative potential. The frame allows the materialization of our thoughts and the pursuit of our intuitions. Affect Theater is a practice of writing *in collaboration with* our research. In this partial relation, the empirical material directs us in a series of associations, and in associating we, in turn, give new shape to the empirical.

Psychoanalyst Christopher Bollas writing on free association says: "We may extend the domain of free association to the world of actual objects, where the way we use them—and how they process us—is another form of the associative. There are many different ways to think; one way we think ourselves is through our engagement with, and use of, evocative objects" (2009: 2). In our workshop, elements of the stage become evocative rather than signifying objects. We practice a form of associative thinking in space that brings to the fore aspects of the material that are not apparent if we interpret them through their literal meanings only. We create lines of relations between the various elements, and we follow different directions and tap into unspoken and unexamined aspects of the empirical, among collaborators and between performers and spectators.

Lehman writes:

> In theatre the specific time of the performance with its particular rhythm and its individual dramaturgy (tempo of action and speech, duration, pauses and silences, etc.) belongs to the "work." It's a matter of the time no longer of one (reading) subject but of the shared time of many subjects (collectively spending time). In this way, a physical, sensual reality of the experience of time is inseparably interwoven with a mental reality. (2004: 153)

For us, the physical/sensual becomes inseparable from the mental/theoretical. This particular power of real, or shared, performance time allows ethnographers and dramatists working with "the real" to re-experience the material in the creation process. It allows audiences to enter into an unfolding conversation with the empirical rather than receiving a transmission of what's known.

Our student Adam Kersch, who did fieldwork in Siracusa, Italy, and who was a spectator at the first showing of *Unstories* (2017), described his experience of it: "When I was watching [*Unstories*], I felt like I was dreaming my research notes, . . . it was in some ways like the unconscious part of dreams made explicit. . . . I felt like all my field notes were in my head and were jumbled around and spat out into a dream."[18]

The associative is a movement of affects and images, thoughts and words that access the "unthought known" of the empirical material, something that can only be experienced, not fully put into words (Bollas 2009: 19). Or, in our parlance, an affective knowing rather than a rational understanding. If writing for Favret-Saada is not a process of distancing oneself from the experience of fieldwork, but rather a re-immersion in the relations and intensities of the field, then writing becomes a process of re-presenting in the here and now the affective relations that we create anew when away from fieldwork. Between "We begin" and "We end," we get caught again in our material, and a new experience emerges. Erin Manning writes: "Direct experience takes place not in the subject or in the object, but in the relation itself" (2013: 3). This is what Affect Theater encourages.[19] Episodes, like affects, become "a contact zone for analysis" (Stewart 2007: 5). They form as a set of relations between elements of the stage, texts, and bodies, not as a mere montage of discrete entities (Strathern 2004).

Looping back to the question of dramaturgy, how does one combine an affective relation to material and worlds, and also tell a story? After all, the purpose of Affect Theater is not to move away from representation altogether, if that were even possible. It is to trouble storytelling, to explore different pathways to narrative that are slower, more inclusive of the contradictions of the "real." For example, when working on the Baltimore transcripts, we didn't have to represent narratives about issues of race and violence, nor did we have to talk about them from a purely conceptual or theoretical perspective, because, as mentioned earlier, in the process of creating and analyzing episodes our felt experience leaked into the workshop space and troubled our theoretical frames. The frictions of theorizing race are embedded in the composition and analysis of the theatrical episodes themselves, as well as in our positions as observers and makers.

Remembering Favret-Saada's invitation, we propose that Affect Theater may be "thinking enough." By bringing together different representational and affective practices that are interdisciplinary, we are developing practical methodologies that the artist/ethnographer can use to "get caught again." Favret-Saada does not describe a way to do it. We think we have added to her contribution a practice that engages with associations by colliding the empirical, stage elements, and the imagination of audiences and company members. When that happens, new worlds become available for both creator and spectator that are neither true nor fictitious, but nonetheless real.

Association #1

How to Read the Following Performative Text

Cristiana Giordano and Greg Pierotti

Dear reader,

What follows is the performance score of *Unstories*. *Unstories* was a montage of theatrical episodes that took flight from empirical research around issues of migration in the Mediterranean. It was performed by "actors," some trained in theatrical disciplines and some in anthropology. The score continued to be developed, designed, and reframed until the very day it was performed. It included descriptions of complex staging, movement sequences, and the execution of design elements: light cues, sound cues, costume changes, and so on, which performers implemented during the live event. Because the goal was to create a thinking space rather than a "show," emphasis was never placed on creating polished representations, and as such the performers worked with scripts in hand.

In translating our script into a book chapter, we marked Actors with numbers (#1–#9), instead of using performers' names. In our performance we used visible costume changes and the device of the narrating company members transforming themselves into a named character to disrupt the audience's trust in character, reminding spectators that each utterance and action was performed by an actor standing in as a person we met in the field and was not pretending to personify their experience. We also hoped that this change—along with the fact that the actor was reading directly from field-note transcripts—would serve as a reminder that company members representing "real" characters from the field also had a hand in determining which of these characters' utterances the audience would hear. Performers spoke the words of the characters they represented without portraying them. We performed the relation between performer and character.

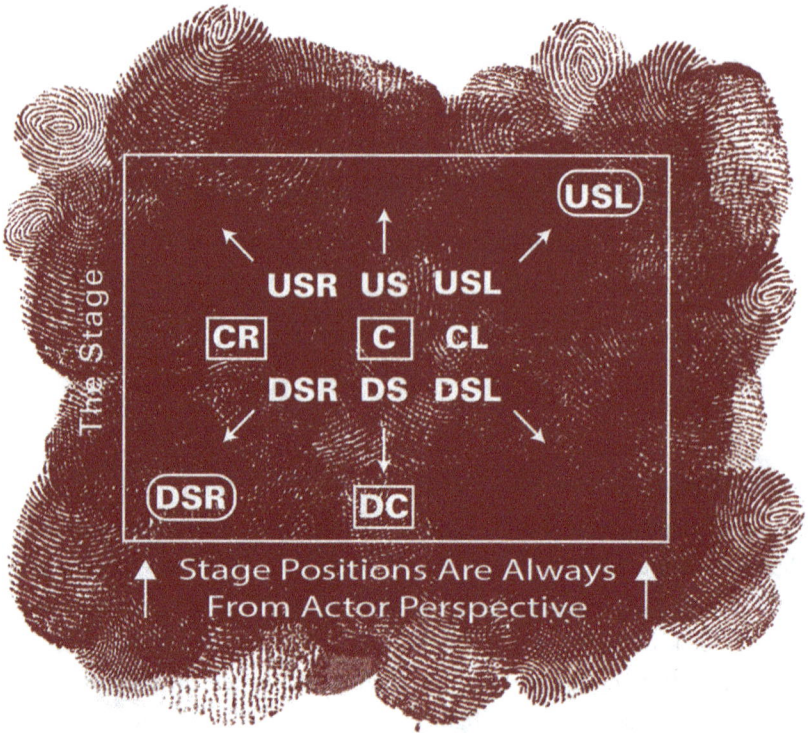

Figure 5 Stage directions. Image design by Tristyn Caneso and Greg Pierotti.

The resulting text can be read in several ways. It can be read as a play with illustrations. This will certainly convey aspects of the research that Cristiana collected in the field. It can be read as a performative text; in this case, a slower engagement with the material and some contemplation about how the text and visuals interact, disrupt, and support each other may provide a more affective experience of the content. Finally, it may be read and performed by you, the reader. You will encounter "stage directions for the reader" in light blue font. It is our hope that many of you will accept this invitation and participate in a more embodied and performative reading of the chapter.

A practical note: for those not familiar with theatrical jargon, when you see a series of capitalized letters, they stand for stage positions (Figure 5): "USR" means Up Stage Right; "DSL" means Down Stage Left. "SR" means Stage Right; "US" means Up Stage; and "USL" means Up Stage Left. "CL" means Center Left. "DC" means Down Center, and so on. These directions are from the actor's perspective.[1]

2

Unstories

A Performative Text

Cristiana Giordano and Greg Pierotti

UNSTORIES

by
Cristiana Giordano
Greg Pierotti

Illustration and Graphic Design

Tristyn Caneso

Comics and Paintings

HomieX

Additional Illustration

Naiché Luzzana

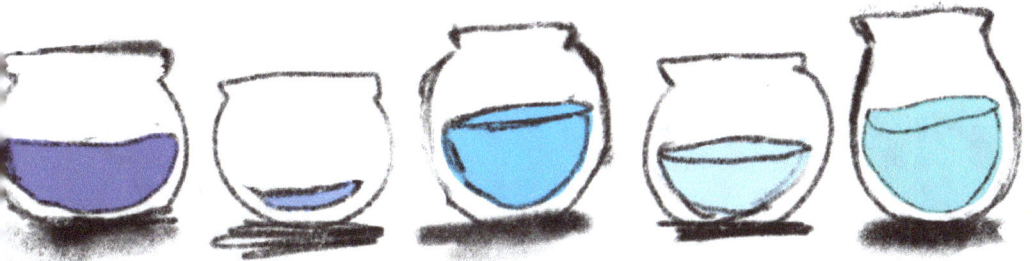

Stage direction for the reader:

TO BEGIN YOUR JOURNEY, PLEASE TEAR OUT THE FOLLOWING PAGE AND FOLLOW THE INSTRUCTIONS

1. Fold your paper in half on the vertical line and reopen the paper

2. Fold your paper again on the horizontal line

3. Fold the top corners in

4. Fold up the exposed edges on both sides

5. Grasp the center bottom edges and pull them away from each other and flatten into a square

6. Fold front and back layers up from the bottom to make a triangle

7. Grasp bottom edges from the center, pull apart and flatten

8. Pull top flaps outwards

9. You almost have a boat! Test your vessel in a bowl of water. Finesse the shape so it floats upright

10. Fill a fishbowl or another container with water. Now you are ready to sail!

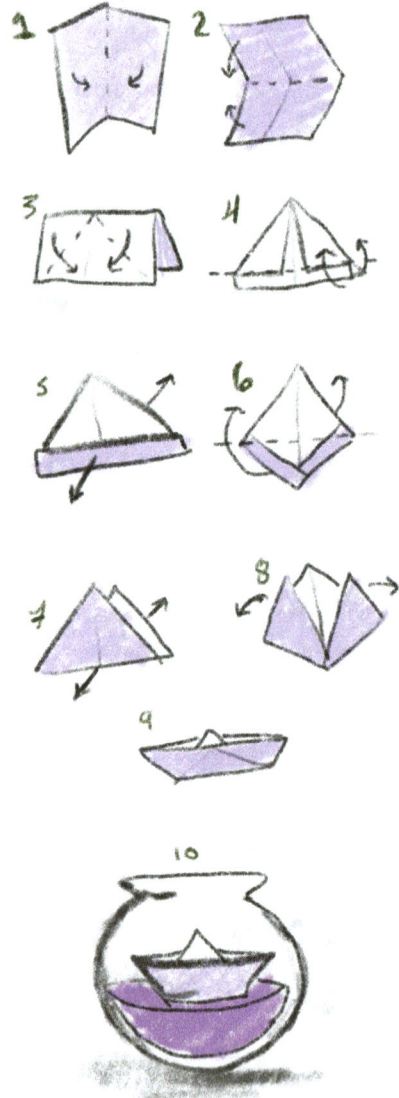

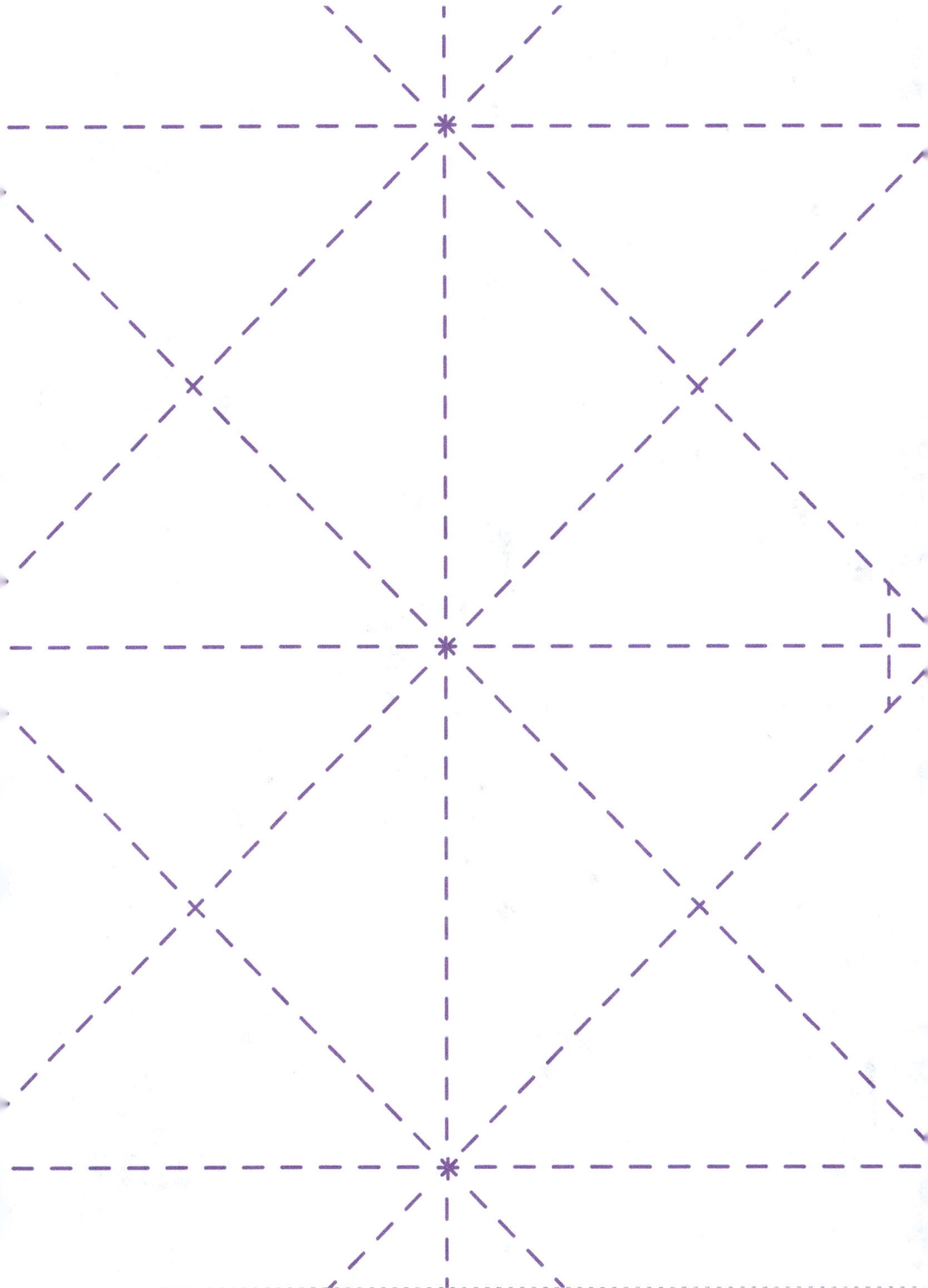

Painting by Ramzi Harrabi

Episode 🩴 GPS Head Inside Outside

tage directions for the reader: using your GPS discover the
ravel time from where you are to Syracuse, Italy. Write
hat time on your boat.

pstage (US) curtain is closed. ACTOR 1,
CTOR 2, and ACTOR 3 enter from DSR.

CTOR 1 calls ACTOR 2 on cell phone,
CTOR 2's phone is on speaker and is ampli-
ed. Audience hears ACTOR 1's lines through
eaker phone. ACTOR 1 addresses the audi-
nce in Spanish. She pulls six people from the
udience.

CTOR 1: Me gustaría que vinieras con
igo y por favor pónganse un par de
apatillas Crocs.

he only has four pairs, so two people are left
 the audience while the others follow ACTOR

CTOR 1: Todos lo que tengan las Crocs me
ueden seguir afuera. Lo siento por los que no
s tienen. Por favor vuelvan a sus asientos.

he turns on a Mag Light as she exits, speak-
g in Spanish and occasionally English.

CTOR 2: (DSC) Welcome to UNSTORIES,
d thank you so much for coming!

CTOR 3: (DSC) Benvenuti a
Unstories", e grazie mille di essere qui!

CTOR 4 opens curtains and enters to
odium CSL.

University of
California, Davis
Public research school
founded in 1905

What you will see tonight the result of a collab

All the language presented is

drawn from interviews, legal documents, media s

Because of the constraints of the play, women play men, men play women, adults play children, and racial

ACTOR 2: What you will see tonight is the result of a collaboration between theater and anthropology.

ACTOR 3: Stasera vi presentiamo il risultato di una collaborazione tra il teatro e l'antropologia.

ACTOR 2: All the language presented is drawn from interviews, legal documents, media sources, and theoretical texts.

ACTOR 3: Le parole del manoscritto vengono direttamente da interviste, documenti legali, media e testi teorici.

ACTOR 2: This is more of a thought piece to provoke dialogue than a narrative play.

ACTOR 3: Si tratta più di un pezzo per pensare e creare un dialogo che non uno spettacolo narrativo.

ACTOR 2: It's an experiment. And you will see the performers with script in hand.

ACTOR 3: È un esperimento. Come vedrete, gli attori hanno il manoscritto in mano.

ACTOR 2: We will be running our own technical support, like lights, props, video, and sound.

ACTOR 3: Siamo noi che faremo il supporto tecnico delle luci, video, suono e props.

ACTOR 2: Because of the constraints of the group, sometimes women play men, adults play children, and racial casting is rough.

ACTOR 3: Visto il gruppo limitato, a volte le donne interpretano il ruolo degli uomini, gli adulti quello dei bambini, e il casting razziale è un po' approssimato.

ACTOR 2: It is not an artistic choice, but we would like to alert you so that you are not confused.

ACTOR 3: Non è una scelta artistica, ma ci teniamo a dirlo per non confondervi.

ACTOR 1's instructions have been audible from ACTOR 4's phone throughout the introduction. ACTOR 5 enters from USR. ACTOR 9 enters from USL and ACTOR 4, ACTOR 5, and ACTOR 9 all follow ACTOR 1's instructions so they are mirroring the actions of the outside group on stage. The group outside returns after a few minutes, entering the theatre, taking their seats again, and keeping their Crocs. The phone call ends, and we no longer hear ACTOR 1's voice.

ACTOR 1: Por favor mantén los Crocs a tus pies. Welcome to Siracusa.

ACTOR 1's next lines here are also simultaneously translated in voice-over into Italian and Spanish creating a cacophony of languages.

ACTOR 1: Bienvenidos a Siracusa. You will need to find your way to processing. Tendrán que encontrar el camino hasta la cabina de identificación. Please be careful as you walk down the ramp from the boat. Tengan cuidado al bajar del barco.

ACTOR 7, wearing gloves, hands audience Crocs, and bottles of water. ACTOR 7 and ACTOR 1 exit SR.

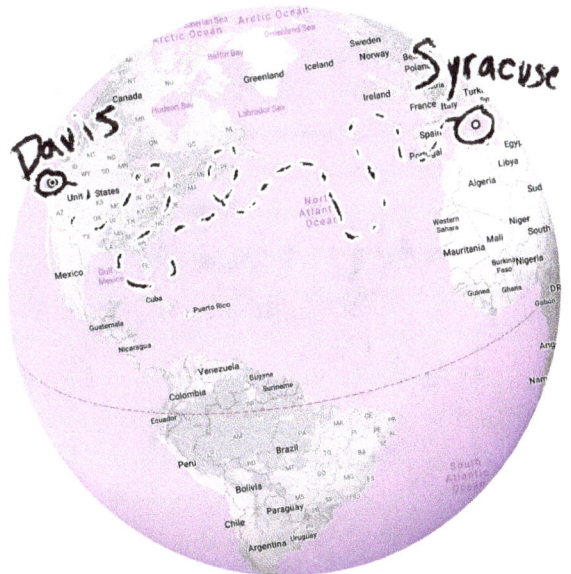

Stage directions for the reader:
float your paper boat in
your container.

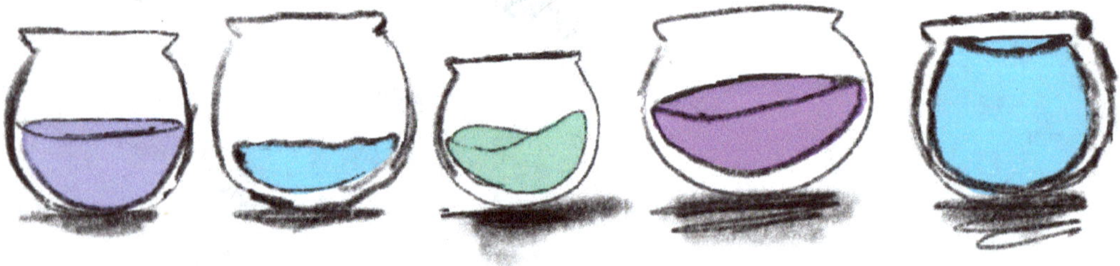

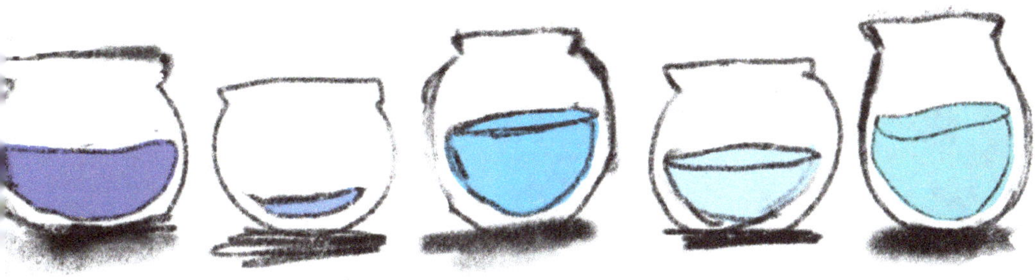

Episode ⛵ Research Boat

Stage directions for the reader:
check your boat. Is it still afloat?

ACTOR 4 as ANTHROPOLOGIST (*taking a
paper from the stack holds it up for the audience
and says*):

This is from field notes taken
at the port in Siracusa, Italy in the summer of 2016 where boats of people rescued at sea arrive.

STEPS
1. As people get off the bo they are given new crocs and water
2. They go through a medical Tr iage un

red cross tent.

3. They sit on the ground
   forming a rectangle
   encircled by policemen
   on the pier until everyone has disembarked.

*ACTOR 4 makes a paper boat demonstrating
how it's done for the audience. She walks DS.
She places the boat (Bowl #1) in it.*

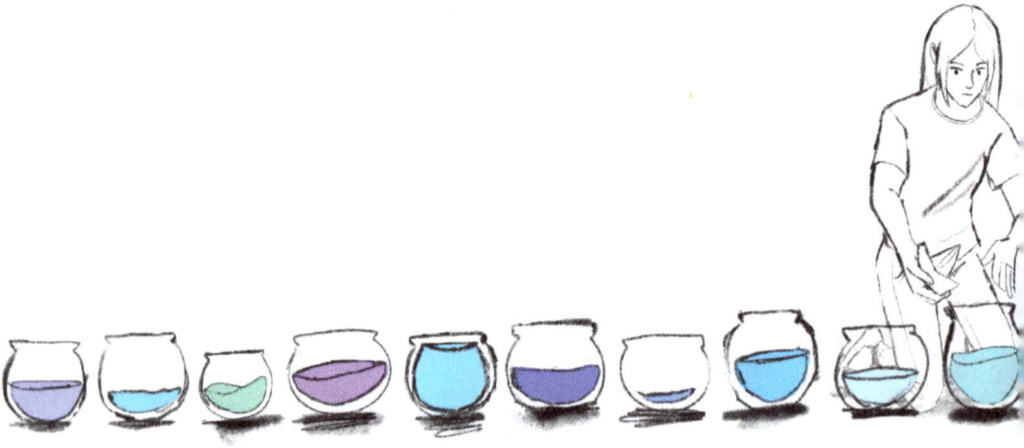

Stage Positions Are Always From Actor Perspective

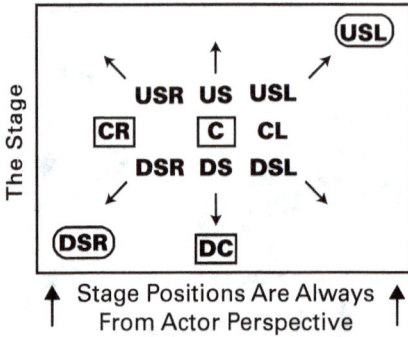

Three actors enter and form a row downstage. Three more dancers enter and form a row US, directly behind them.

ACTOR 2 crosses to the podium and opens a laptop.

ACTOR 2: This is from Favret-Saada's essay "About Participation." (*Reading*) "The Anthropologist claims to practice 'participant observation.' In rhetoric, it is called an oxymoron: to observe while participating, or to participate while observing, is about as obvious as savoring a burning hot ice cream."

Stage directions for the reader: we invite you to learn and perform the dance.

ACTOR 2 stops reading and watches as 3 downstage dancers perform a slow formal dance. The others in the upstage row study the movement of the downstage dancers.

ACTOR 2: (*Returning gaze to computer and reading*) "To accept to 'participate' and to be affected has nothing to do with understanding through empathy. I shall consider two principal meanings of 'empathy.' According to the first, to empathize means a person, 'vicariously experiences the feelings, perceptions, and thoughts of another.'"

(*He stops reading and watches again*)

DS row repeats their movement sequence. The US row now joins in the dance, copying or learning it as they move. This round they are very focused on the person right in front of them.

ACTOR 2: "By definition, this type of empathy presupposes some distance between the subjects: it is because one is not in the other's place that he or she tries to represent or imagine what it would be like to be there." (*He stops reading and watches again*)

Another round of learning the dance with both groups dancing simultaneously. This time the group in the second row seems to do the dance with less attention to the first row.

ACTOR 2: (*While he reads, the first row, who started the dance, exit.*) "A second definition o empathy - insists, on the contrary, on the fusion with the other by identifying. This definition says nothing about the mechanism of identification but insists that it enables (*Here the second row steps DS into the first group's stage* *osition*) one to know the effects of others."

He stops reading and watches)

he second group re-performs the dance as if it were their own.

ACTOR 2: (*As the second row exits*) "Now I ay that to occupy such a position gives us no nformation as to the other's effects; it affects ne, that is to say mobilizes or modifies my wn set of images without in any way nforming me about those of my partner."

urtains close. ACTOR 2 takes a paper boat Bowl #2) from inside podium and places it in he fishbowl. ACTOR 2 exits DSR.

Episode Fishing Boat

CTOR 5 as FIRST MATE and ACTOR 1 as ᵖANCER have put their lamps on. DANCER ᵃs an umbrella. During the following text ᵖANCER gets under the ladder, which she ᵃnd FIRST MATE have set up DSR. FIRST ᴹATE, climbs the ladder and onto the beams ᵇove the stage space, crossing USR on beam. ℂTOR 6 as ANTONINO enters with a book, ᵒlds it up, and starts reading.

ᴬNTONINO: This is from Antonino Audino's ᵒok: (*He puts a hat on to "become" ANTONI-ᴼO*) December 26, 1988. Late afternoon we set ᵃil from the Syracuse port: regular service, no ᵍnal, no warning. The sea was calm and flat. ᵛe came across some solitary fishing boats ᵃnd thoroughly checked them. Once we fin-ʰed the routine control, the captain suggested ᵛe broaden our route.

ᵒnar Sound cue fades in.

Stage directions for the reader: to play sonar sound cue scan the QR code.

ᵖANCER comes out from under the ladder to ᵉrform a dance solo to the music of the sonar. ˢ she dances ACTOR 2 as CAPTAIN enters ʰe edge of the USR playing space and ACTOR as FISHERMAN enters directly across from ᶦm in the USL space.

ᴬNTONINO: The sun had already set, and our radar signaled an echo. What we call a target in technical terms. There was a boat 27 miles from the coastline sailing toward Malta. We reached it. It was a simple fishing boat, the Valentina. We came up beside the fishing boat. Everything was by the book.

CAPTAIN: Coast Guard. We have to board. Who is the captain of the fishing boat?

ANTONINO: The fisherman replied:

FISHERMAN: The captain is in his cabin… He doesn't feel very well....

CAPTAIN: What happened?

FISHERMAN: It's not a big deal! When we left from Porto Palo, he already felt unwell… now we are going back!

CAPTAIN: Anything to declare?

FISHERMAN: There's nothing in the hold… nothing worth declaring!

ANTONINO: We tried to light up the fishing boat as much as we could with our torches.

(*CAPTAIN moves his light across FISHER-MAN'S face, which is obscured*)

ANTONINO: Our attention fell on the fishing nets: they were perfectly dry. [That was suspi-cious. The captain said to me]:

CAPTAIN: Get on board.

ANTONINO: [We got on board] We expected the usual routine: smuggling cigarettes, weapons or drugs. After some minutes we heard our colleague screaming.

ACTOR 8 as CUSTOMS OFFICER: Captain! There are many people with strange faces. There are a lot of Christian souls down here… (*CUSTOMS OFFICER starts to Cross to SL side of beams*).

ANTONINO: There were forty people clumped in the hold. What were they doing there? [It was 1988]. We did not know what it was all about. Nowadays we would have explained all this with two words: illegal immigration.

DANCER *performs another minute of dance*

solo, CUSTOMS OFFICER drops down from the beams, the sonar fades out. DANCER's dance also resolves. CUSTOMS OFFICER an DANCER exit USL.

ANTONINO walks into the lit part of the stage and talks to the audience.

ANTONINO: A journalist later interviewed me about that detention. At the end of the inte view, he looked me in the eyes and said: "Get ready for an invasion of a size that no one can imagine. This is just the beginning."

ACTOR 6 who was playing ANTONINO removes his hat and changes to the costume o, AHMED's DAD.

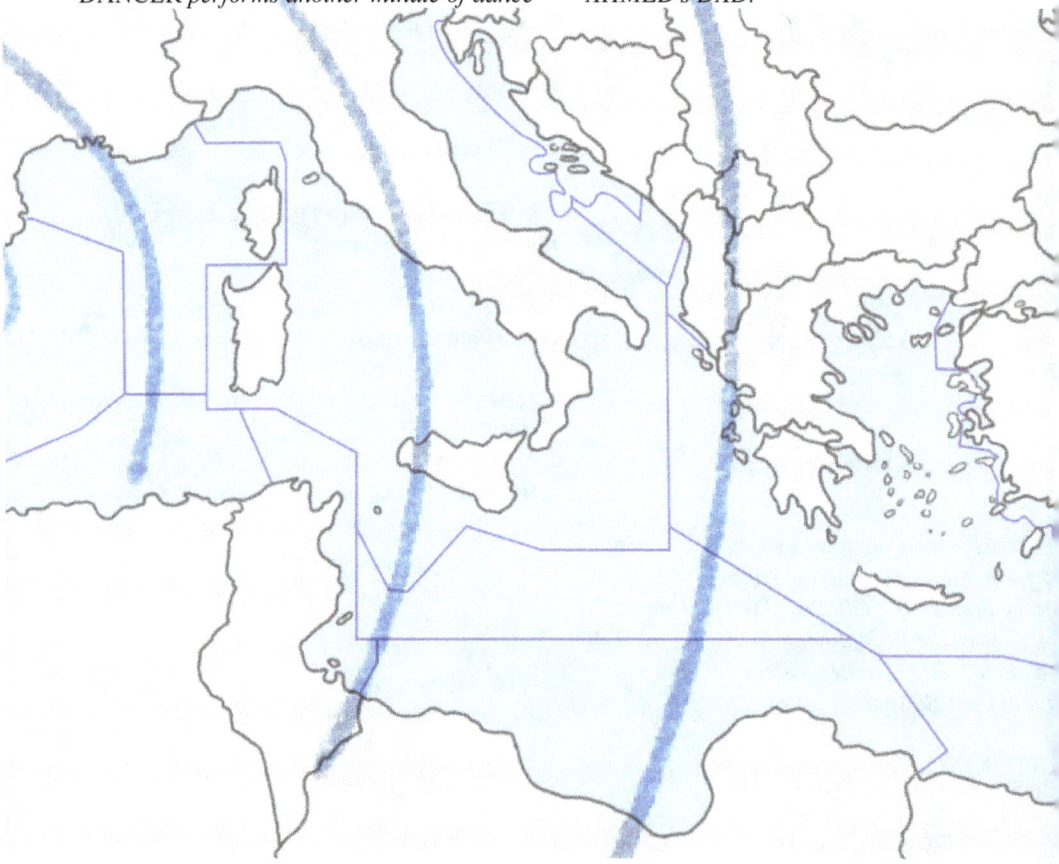

Episode 🌀 Magli Ocean Video

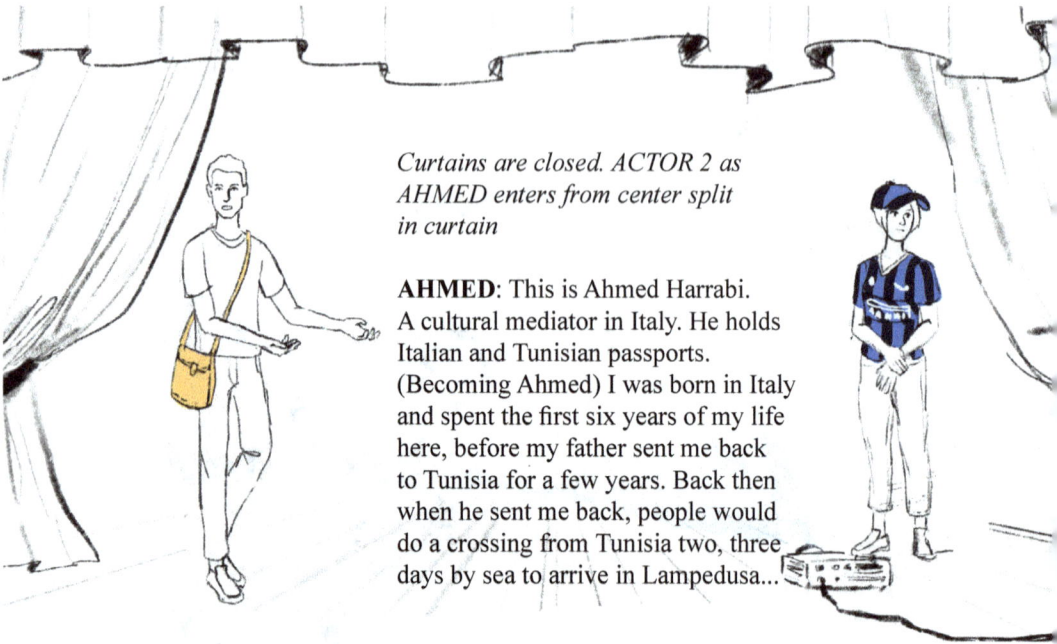

*Curtains are closed. ACTOR 2 as
AHMED enters from center split
in curtain*

AHMED: This is Ahmed Harrabi.
A cultural mediator in Italy. He holds
Italian and Tunisian passports.
(*Becoming Ahmed*) I was born in Italy
and spent the first six years of my life
here, before my father sent me back
to Tunisia for a few years. Back then
when he sent me back, people would
do a crossing from Tunisia two, three
days by sea to arrive in Lampedusa...

...Some stayed there, others were repatriated.
In my city, in Tunisia I had a lot of friends
who left, not just for the sake of it, but because
there was a strong presence of Italian TV in
Tunisia. You would see, like, the good life...
the concerts, the nightclubs... you would see a
lot of prosperity, no? And people thought going
to Italy could change your personal story, or
the economic path of your family.

One of my best friends, Magli, decided to
leave, no?

*AHMED opens the curtains to reveal ACTOR 1
as MAGLI. A video of a stormy sea running on
the back wall.*

And he proposed to me to leave with him. He
was a child, 14, 15 years old. We were peers.
He goes:

MAGLI: Why don't you leave with me? Since
your dad's there, your family

is there. They will give us a place to sleep an
your dad can help us find a job...

AHMED: I told him, "I don't know, I have t
call my dad first." So when I called my dad h
told me

AHMED'S DAD (*pops in from DSR*): What
the fuck are you doing? Your situation is by
the book.

You have documents. You need to come by
plane (*He pops back out - off stage*).

AHMED pauses. MAGLI crosses downstage of the table and picks up projector during AHMED's next line; MAGLI walks in a U down to center stage enlarging the projection and then slowly walking upstage shrinking it. The wind sound from the video clip is extremely loud. MAGLI floats the projection of the ocean back and forth across the back wall and then slowly walks towards the wall in the direction of the sea, and the projection becomes smaller and smaller.

AHMED: But Magli decided to go. He didn't make it… they never fished them out of the sea… a lot of years have passed. It's very likely that the ship sank and he died as a result, because, usually, as soon as they arrive in Italy they would call their parents to say, "we're in Italy." (*10-second pause - AHMED turns to watch as MAGLI crosses above curtain. And then the curtain is closed*).

Curtain closes.

AHMED: But the call never came…

Five more seconds of wind sound after curtain is closed and then MAGLI turns off projector. AHMED exits USR. ACTOR 7 as BUREAUCRAT enters USL and crosses to rolling file cabinet.

Stage directions for the reader: using the QR code, take five minutes to watch and listen to the sea. Continue listening to the sound of the sea, and slowly re-read this episode.

Stage direction for the reader:
print an image of a child in your life,
and glue it or tape it to this page.

Episode Crocs Categories

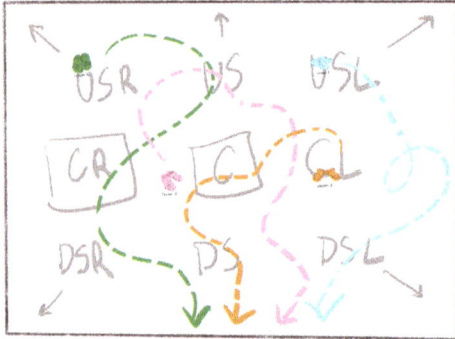

ANTHROPOLOGIST crosses to podium. BUREAUCRAT #1 is rifling through files. When ANTHROPOLOGIST arrives she hands her the first of a number of documents. BUREAUCRAT #1 stands by as ANTHROPOLOGIST speaks. ACTOR 1, ACTOR 3, ACTOR 5, and ACTOR 9 enter from split curtains each carrying a pair of Crocs. They place Crocs on stage and form a line USR facing ANTHROPOLOGIST. While this is happening ACTOR 2 as BUREAUCRAT #2 enters USL in Bureaucrat jacket and joins BUREAUCRAT #1 at rolling file.

ANTHROPOLOGIST *(picks up a document from a pile of paper and holds it up to show the audience)*: This is a copy of the Geneva Convention on Refugees. *(Reading)* According to the Geneva Convention on Refugees, a "refugee" is a person who is outside her country of citizenship because she has a well-founded fear of persecution because of race, religion, nationality, gender, or membership of a particular social or political group. Such a person may be called an 'asylum seeker' until granted the status of 'refugee.'"

ANTHROPOLOGIST points a Mag Light at the first pair of the category 1 Crocs. *ACTOR 1 crosses and steps into them. ANTHROPOLOGIST hands BUREAUCRAT #1 the documen she was reading. BUREAUCRAT #1 hands it t ACTOR 1. ACTOR 1 starts folding it into a pa per boat. As BUREAUCRAT #1 brings ACTOI 1 the first document, BUREAUCRAT #2 hands the next document to ANTHROPOLOGIST, who reads again.*

ANTHROPOLOGIST: According to the United Nations Protocol as part of the Palermo Accord, a "victim of human trafficking" is a person who was recruited, transported, and transferred by means of a threat or any other form of coercion and forced into different forms of exploitation, sexual or not. They are granted the right to temporary and renewable residence permits on the condition that they participate in a rehabilitation program. The firs step of the rehabilitation requires filing criminal charges against her traffickers.

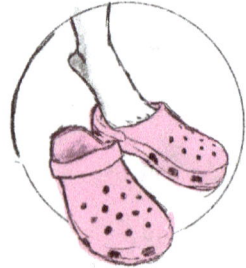

ANTHROPOLOGIST points the Mag Light at the second pair of the category 2 Crocs. *ACTOR 2 crosses and steps into them. AN-THROPOLOGIST hands BUREAUCRAT #1 the document she was reading. BUREAUCRAT #1 hands it to ACTOR 2. ACTOR 2 starts folding it into a paper boat. As BUREAUCRAT #1 brings ACTOR 2 the second document, BUREAUCRAT #1 hands the next document to ANTHROPOLOGIST, who reads a third time.*

ANTHROPOLOGIST: According to the United Nations, a "migrant worker" is "someone who migrates from one country to another to seek employment and improvement in living standards because of economic turmoil in the home country. Economic migrants are not entitled to the provisions granted to victims and refugees, and are more thoroughly screened and required to provide proof of employment before entering the host country."

ANTHROPOLOGIST points the Mag Light at the third pair of the category 3 Crocs. *ACTOR 3 crosses and steps into them. ANTHROPOL-OGIST hands BUREAUCRAT #1 the document. BUREAUCRAT #1 brings ACTOR 3 the document she was reading. ACTOR 3 starts folding it into a paper boat. As BUREAUCRAT #1 brings ACTOR 3 the third document, BU-REAUCRAT #2 hands the fourth document to ANTHROPOLOGIST, who reads a fourth time.*

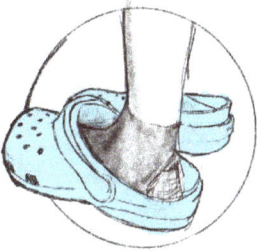

ANTHROPOLOGIST: According to the United Nations committee on the rights of the child, an unaccompanied foreign minor is "someone who has been separated from both parents and other relatives and is not being cared for by an adult. The convention provides the right to special protection against all forms of physical or mental violence, abuse, neglect, or exploitation. And if seeking refugee status the right to benefit from social security."

ANTHROPOLOGIST points the Mag Light at the fourth pair of the category 4 Crocs. *AC-TOR 4 crosses and steps into them. ANTHRO-POLOGIST hands BUREAUCRAT #1 the doc-ument. But this time BUREAUCRAT #1 hands ACTOR 4 a premade boat. BUREAUCRAT #1 exits USR. ANTHROPOLOGIST lowers the Mag Light. ACTORS 1, 2, 3, and 4 all step out of their Crocs and cross slowly downstage.*

ANTHROPOLOGIST: These categories exist because there are national borders.

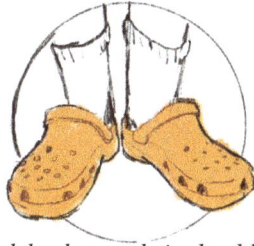

The four look back over their shoulders at AN-THROPOLOGIST, hold a beat, and then turn back to look at the audience. They then place their boats (Bowls #3, #4, #5, and #6). They hold a beat and exit quickly.

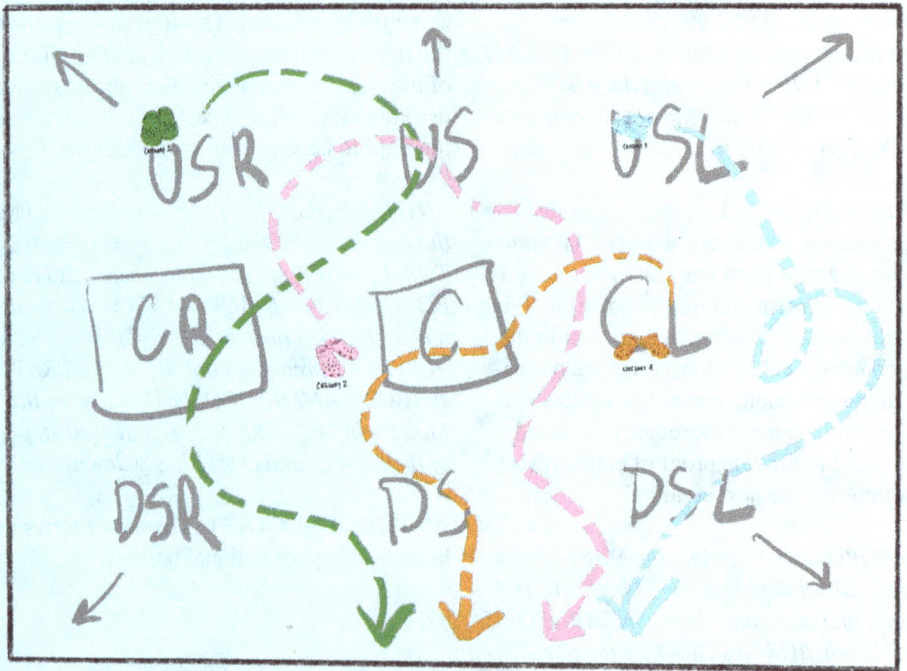

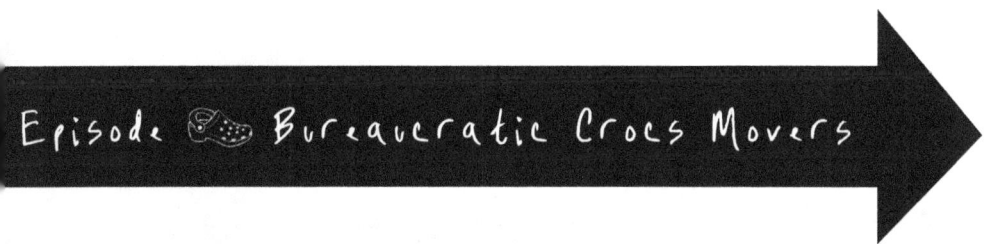

Episode 🩴 Bureaucratic Crocs Movers

ANTHROPOLOGIST: This is from field notes gathered at the port in Siracusa: (*BU-REAUCRAT #1 hands ANTHROPOLOGIST one more paper. ANTHROPOLOGIST reads*) The boat was full of African men, some families, a few women, and many minors. They disembarked the men first, the rest later, to keep them out of the sun, we guessed.

BUREAUCRAT #2, now also in a Bureaucrat jacket, joins BUREAUCRAT #1. They walk downstage center and address the audience.

BUREAUCRAT #1: Welcome to Siracusa. You will need to find your way to processing.

BUREAUCRAT #2: Please be careful as you walk down the ramp from the boat.

BUREAUCRAT #1: We are going to need those Crocs back.

BUREAUCRAT #1 and BUREAUCRAT #2 split up. BUREAUCRAT #1 goes and gets Crocs from the audience, while BUREAUCRAT #2 picks up Crocs from the pile USL. They both distribute Crocs and water bottles around the stage.

ANTHROPOLOGIST: Steps:

1) As people get off the boat, they are given new Crocs and bottles of water.

BUREAUCRAT #3 and BUREAUCRAT #4 enter and join in the distribution of Crocs and water bottles. Their frantic choreography runs underneath the Anthropologist's next lines.

2) They go through a medical Triage under the Red Cross tent.

3) They sit on the ground forming a rectangle encircled by policemen on the *banchina* until everyone has been disembarked.

4) Once everyone has gotten off the boat…

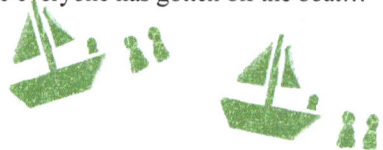

5) …They all march outside of the protected area of the port and move to where all the organizations and institutions have their stand.

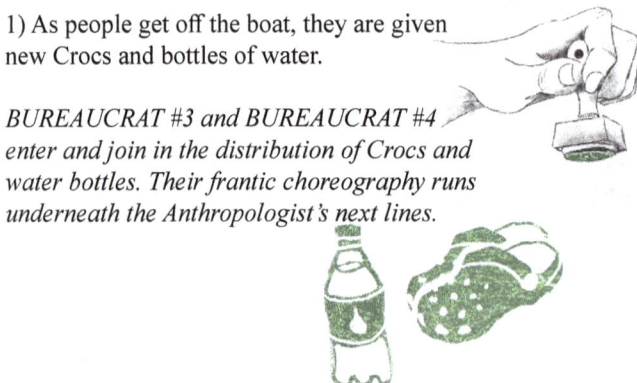

BUREAUCRAT #1 and BUREAUCRAT #2 pull the curtains, revealing BUREAUCRAT #5 and BUREAUCRAT #6 sitting at a table in fluorescent light performing "bureaucratic" activities – reading, stamping, filing documents, etc. On the table: coffee pot, cups, paper, file box, and stamps. They are rubber stamping and filing lots of papers. BUREAUCRAT #1 and BUREAUCRAT #2 return to the frantic collection of Crocs.

ANTHROPOLOGIST:

6) They form another rectangular group in front of the immigration office stand where they get registered by giving their name, date of birth, and nationality. Here they are finger-printed. They are now given a number written on a piece of white paper and their photos are taken.

Nome: _____
Data di nascita: _____
Nazionalità: _____

7) They can now go rest in the big tents where there are camp beds in rows.

BUREAUCRAT #1 and BUREAUCRAT #2 exit USR. BUREAUCRAT #3 and BUREAUCRAT #4 remain and begin clearing Crocs and water bottles into the bucket and then exit SR.

8) Protezione civile now gives out a plastic bag with food in it: an apple and a cheese sandwich.

9) Protezione civile gives out some clean clothes, soap, and shampoo if asked for. They can take a shower.

10) After lunch, UNHCR officials give out information about laws and norms to people who want to apply for political asylum.

11) Those who need medical assistance can go see the doctors at the NGO Emergency clinic or are transported to the hospital.

BUREAUCRAT #5 and BUREAUCRAT #6 exit the table USL.

12) At around 6 pm, the same meal is served: apple, sandwich, and water. People form a long line in front of supermarket cart where there are white plastic lunch bags.

When ANTHROPOLOGIST, now alone onstage, says this last line, ACTOR 9. HOMIEX enters.

13) Some do laundry and hang their clothes in the tents or on the fences surrounding this part of the port.

HOMIEX and the ANTHROPOLOGIST hang a white sheet over the "clothesline."

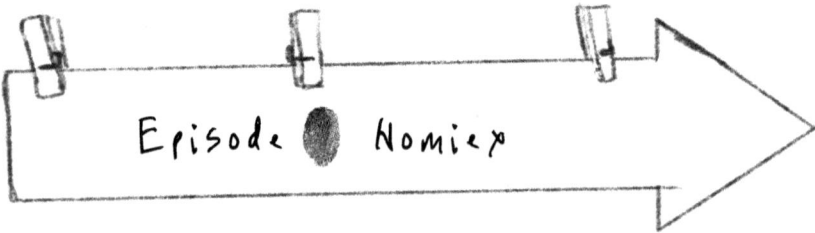

ANTHROPOLOGIST: This is Victor, a young man
from Nigeria. His artist name is Homiex. According to
the state, he is classified as an "unaccompanied foreign
minor." (*Homiex's artwork is projected onto the sheet*).

ANTHROPOLOGIST:	What inspired you to paint it? 1:06 AM
HOMIEX:	I makes my art with my present mood. I woke up in the morning with so much anger 1:07 AM
HOMIEX:	And I decided to put in in an image form. 1:07 AM
ANTHROPOLOGIST:	Bravo!! 1:07 AM
	I want to chat mor abt your art! More

Victor
en today at 11:04 AM

Can I ask you about
some specific one?
1:44 AM ✓✓

Like: the one you use
for your profile: the
injury...what did you
want to convey?
1:45 AM ✓✓

The guy is said to be
suffering internally
1:47 AM

I have showed the
suffering in form of
xray view
1:47 AM

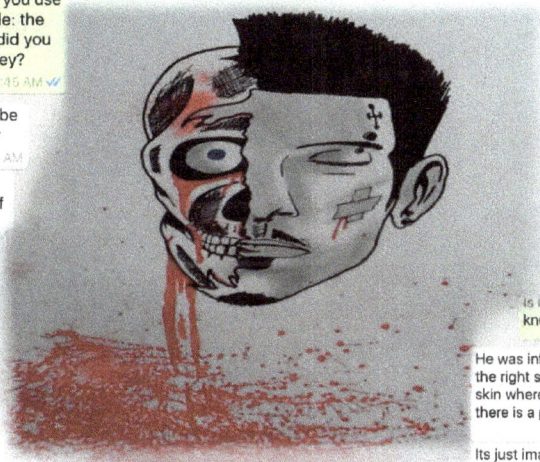

Is he someone you
know?
1:47 AM ✓✓

He was infected On
the right side of the
skin where the where
there is a plaster
1:48 AM

Its just imagination
1:48 AM

It's about suffering?
1:49 AM ✓✓

Yea. It is a sorrowful
art

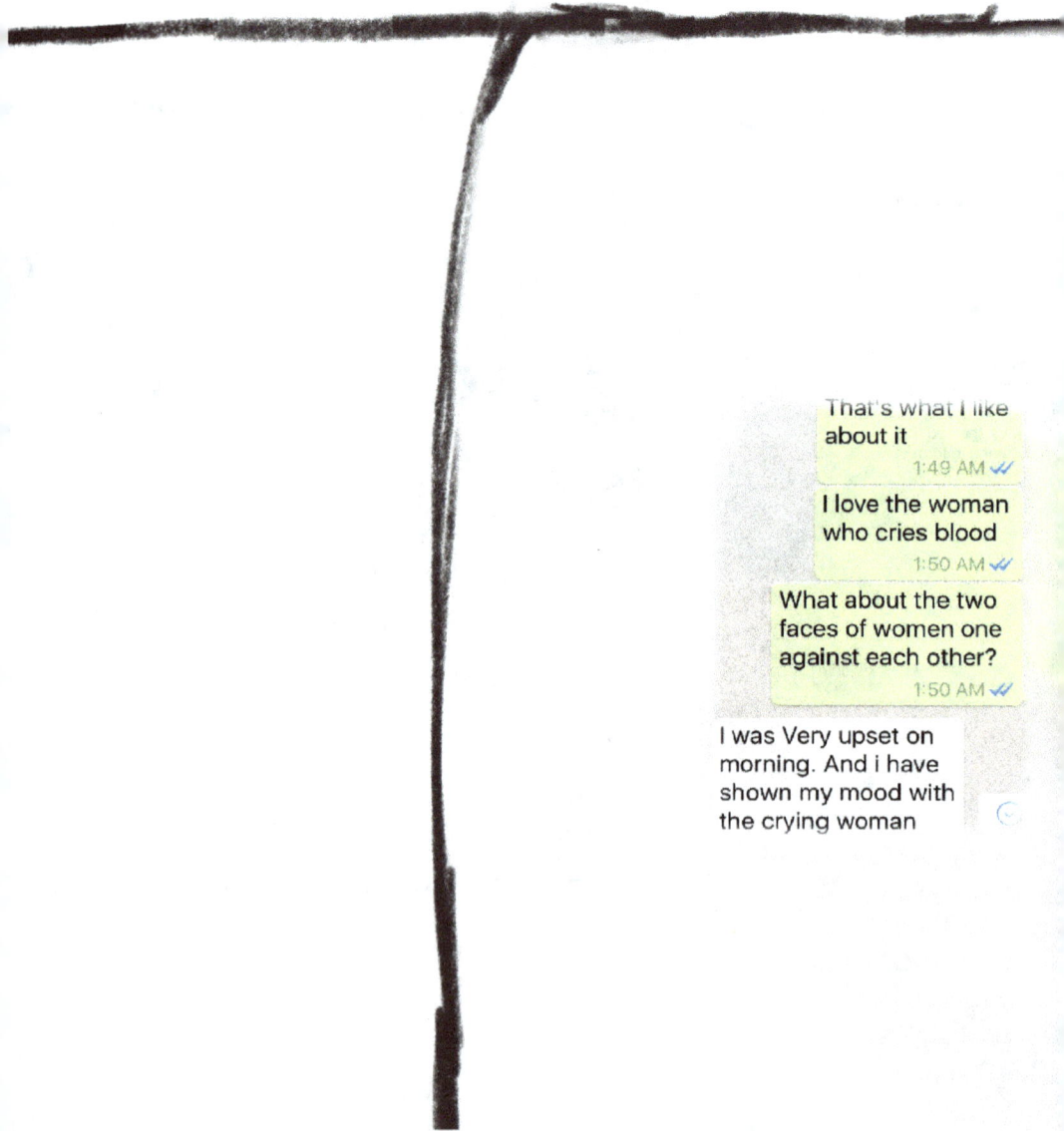

That's what I like about it
1:49 AM

I love the woman who cries blood
1:50 AM

What about the two faces of women one against each other?
1:50 AM

I was Very upset on morning. And i have shown my mood with the crying woman

The two lips are just kiss
1:51 AM

The red lip is a female and the brown the malle
1:51 AM

Male
1:51 AM

Oh I see
1:54 AM

Is there a story there? Or any emotions in particular?

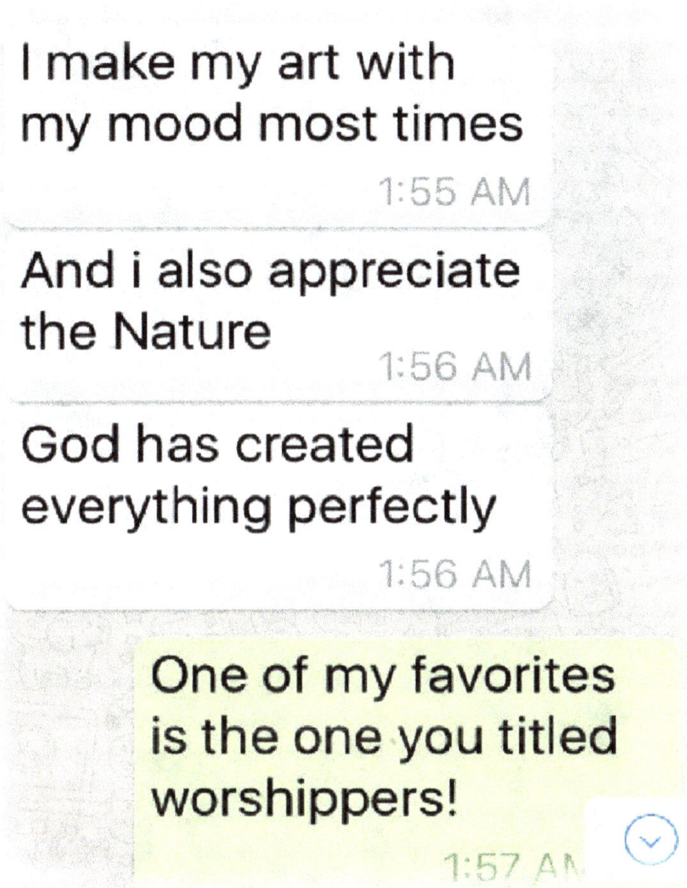

I make my art with
my mood most times

1:55 AM

And i also appreciate
the Nature

1:56 AM

God has created
everything perfectly

1:56 AM

One of my favorites
is the one you titled
worshippers!

1:57 AM

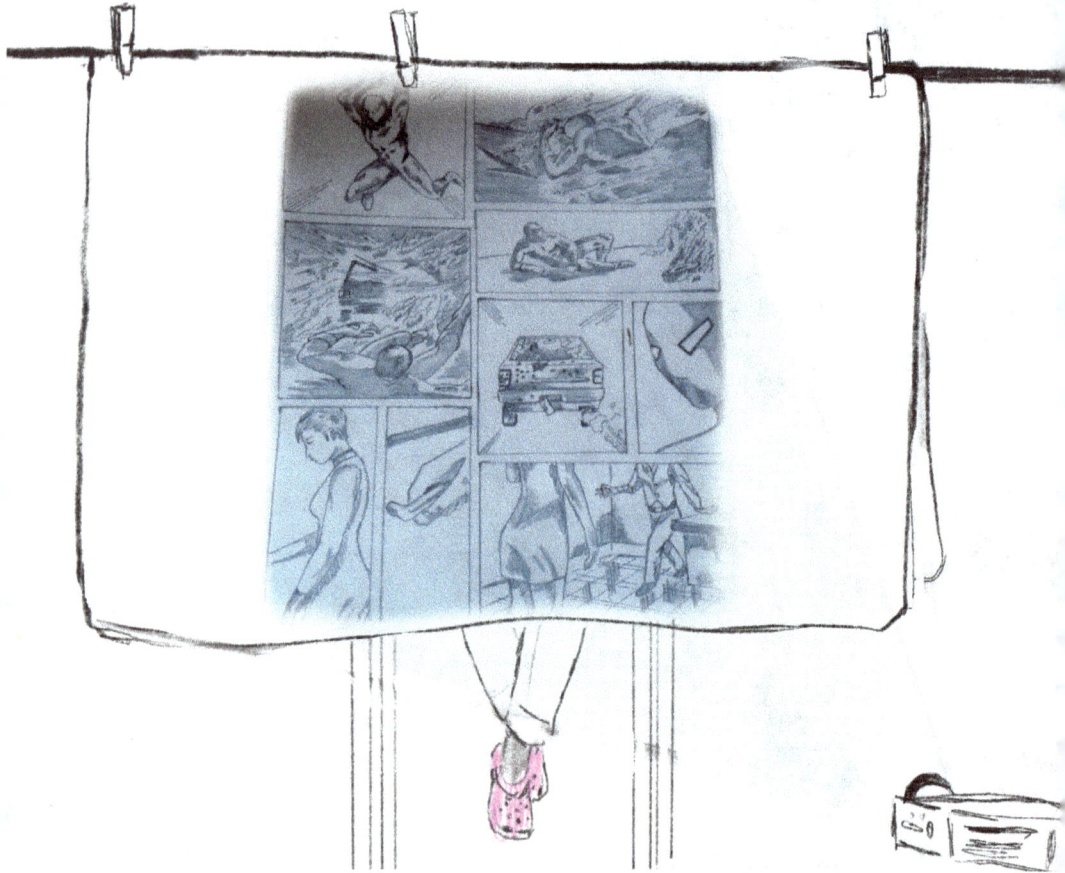

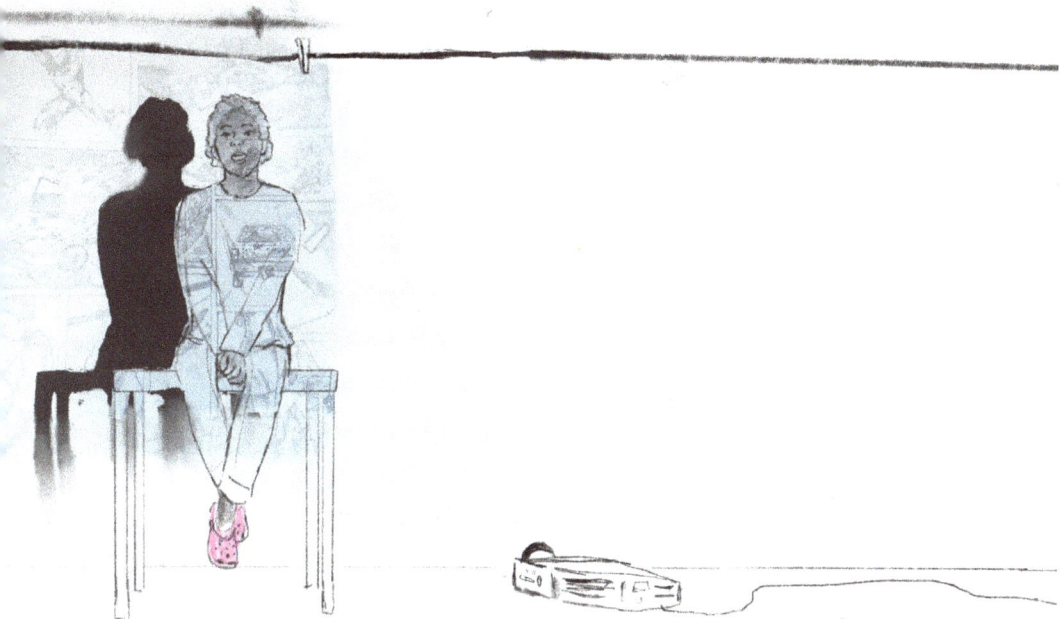

ANTHROPOLOGIST *pulls the*
sheet open like a curtain revealing
ACTOR 5 *as* MARY *sitting on the*
DSL *corner of the bureaucratic*
table. She wears pink Crocs. *After*
a few more seconds of cartoon on
back wall superimposed on Mary,
she speaks in sotto voce yawning.
HOMIEX *exits. Anthropologist*
continues:

Episode △ Mary (Monosyllabic)

THIS IS MARY, FROM NIGERIA. ACCORDING TO THE STATE SHE QUALIFIES AS A "VICTIM OF HUMAN TRAFFICKING." I MET MARY IN TURIN IN THE FALL OF 2014. SHE HAD BEEN IN ITALY FOR THREE YEARS. SHE HAD TWO CHILDREN AND WHEN WE SPOKE SHE TOLD ME:
IN NIGERIA I WANTED TO STUDY MEDICINE AND BECOME A DOCTOR.

AT THE TIME WHEN I MET HER, MARY WAS GOING
THROUGH THE STATE'S REHABILITATION PROGRAM
FOR VICTIMS. WHEN MARY HAD HER INTERVIEW, THE
CULTURAL MEDIATOR WAS COMPLETELY IN CHARGE.
A CULTURAL MEDIATOR IS SOMEONE WHO TRANS-
LATES NOT ONLY LANGUAGE BUT WORLDVIEWS
FOR THE VARIOUS STATE INSTITUTIONS.

DENUNCIA

My name is Mary Ogbomo. My story begins in
September of 2008. My mother was sick and
medicine was too expensive for my family. It was
not I who requested the certificate of nationality
from the Nigerian Embassy, but my "madame,"
who had control of me. I entered Europe with a
passport issued to Joy Owie but that had my picture on it. It was my godmother Momy who, un-
beknownst to the rest of my family, invited me to
her house and introduced me to Mike. He assured
me he could help me go to Holland to continue my
studies. I had completed the first year of medical
school in Nigeria. They added that I should keep
the offer a secret. I told Mike that my family could
not afford the cost of the trip. He replied that he
would take care of it and that once in Holland, I
could study and look for a part-time job and pay
him back later. I affirm that in Nigeria I never
heard anything about girls being brought to Europe who were forced into prostitution.

*Anthropologist folds the denuncia into a paper boat and places
the boat in a fishbowl (bowl #7)*

ACTOR 2 as SILVIO[1] and ACTOR 7 as PAOLA enter from USR, pick up the costumes off chairs in the cafe set up. They put on their costumes as SILVIO speaks.

SILVIO: This is Silvio and Paola. They live in public housing in a town in the North of Italy.

They sit down, coffee cups in hand, and speak direct address to the audience as if the audience were the anthropologist interviewing them in a café.

SILVIO: I'm from the south. I was also discriminated against at school… I've been through this myself…my classmates teased me for years, saying I was a *terrone*…southerner. It was difficult. So, we don't discriminate against people. Italians here in the neighborhood are not racist, they're not intolerant. But they get mad at all this weight that gets put on their shoulders. It's the system.

PAOLA: Take housing, for example. There are points awarded for public housing. Having a kid gives you more points. The more children you have the more points you get. The immigrants have large families, they get points. They give them the house because they have more kids than we do. This is the kind of thing the system does.

SILVIO: It's obvious, if the law protects you, you use it, of course. So, to get the right amount of points… one is the number of kids, and you have to have a low income, but not zero.

PAOLA: For disability – one point. For every minor – one point.

SILVIO: (*To Paola*) No, the minor isn't one, it's half a point, I think.

PAOLA: (*To Silvio*) No, it's one point. And then you have to have a certain income.

SILVIO: So… say I'm a foreigner, can I apply for public housing even if I'm here illegally?

PAOLA: (*To Silvio*) No, if you're here illegally, no.

SILVIO: But here is what they used to do. If you're illegal, you come here and you go to someone you know, and say, "Will you take me in as a guest?" Of course, they say yes, right? And then they go to the Popular Housing Agency and they say, "This man wants to come live with me, he's my cousin," and they integrate me. The Agency couldn't care less.

PAOLA: And all it takes is to sign some papers.

SILVIO: And then another comes along and they become really full, and what do they do? They apply for public housing, you also get more points for overcrowding, a point for this a point for that…

PAOLA: And 90% of foreigners – including my colleagues – tell you, "I have a house back home. When I retire, I'll go back," and they go to their warm houses. And you say, "Shit, I have to stay here waiting for retirement, getting old. And you in the meantime are building a villa. You take your ass to the warmth, and I stay here rotting after having worked my ass off."

SILVIO: And in the meantime, they cut in

front of everyone else. Right? By the state creating this system, they're taking away from their own population, their homeland, to help foreigners. Italians who are already struggling feel that. They say, "Come on, you're in my homeland, you're taking away from me now?"

PAOLA: Yes, there is a feeling here in the neighborhood. "You take from us to give to them."

SILVIO: But what are you going to do?

PAOLA: Well, this summer, the mayor of Arezzo changed the criteria for points for public housing to give more points for residency. So, if you were born and grew up here, for every 15 years you get nine points! So, now Italians, obviously, have more possibility to get into public housing, even if they don't have a lot of kids.

SILVIO: Now I have the law on my side. You arrived later, so I'm first. And whatever's left over you grab it. Of course, it's right to help them out too, but our people first.

PAOLA: He's from the Northern League the mayor who changed the criteria. I used to vote for the Democrats, all my life, but this past election, I voted for the conservatives. There were a lot of evictions of Italian families 150 families in 2013. That was because of the democrats.

SILVIO: Now, I do think the democrats wanted to invest in immigration, but I don't think the evictions were caused by the growing number of immigrants. It's the laws that need changing. So, I never take it out on the refugees. The laws need changing. But the more

trouble you're in the more you take it out on people that in some way seem better off than you.

PAOLA: Yes! You see these people playing soccer all day… maybe dressed nicely…

SILVIO: See them with their cell phones.

PAOLA: And you say, "Geez, I'm killing myself working all day."

As SILVIO speaks his last line, PAOLA folds a paper boat from one of the newspaper sheets.

SILVIO: And it's there that the war between the poor begins. Everyone defends their own culture, their own mentality… Those cultures aren't as open as we are, their religion, their day to day, how the woman is viewed… we're more "simple," open… we have a big feast, we all eat together; for them, trouble…it is really a clashing of cultures and mentality. Not just the economic factor. We are all poor here.

SILVIO hands PAOLA the boat. PAOLA places the boat in a fishbowl (Bowl #8). PAOLA exits USR. SILVIO changes from Silvio costume to bureaucrat jacket.

---

1. Silvio was actually Silvia but we needed a male actor to play the role because of the casting and technical requirements at this moment in the piece.

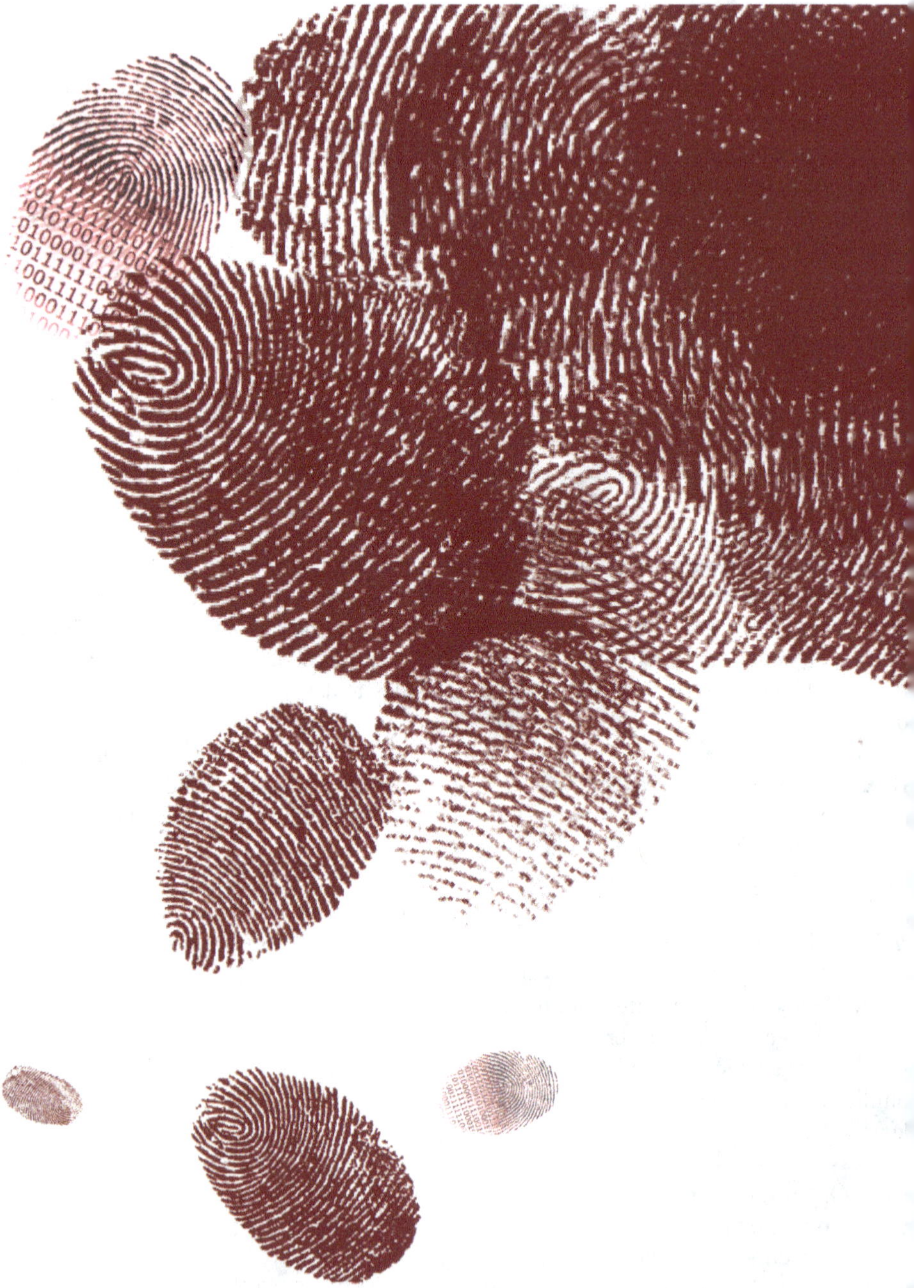

Episode ● Legal Doctor

ACTOR 2 brings chair from cafe to USR.

LEGAL DOCTOR enters in lab coat from USR and crosses to CL below the podium. She opens the computer on the projector table. Three MEDICAL HELPERS enter, surround the chair, and take turns talking sotto voce to the empty space.

SHELTER COORDINATOR: They take fingerprints at the moment of disembarkation, when they first arrive in Italy, in order to identify them.

LEGAL DOCTOR: ...which is what you're supposed to do upon landing in Italy, but never gets done.

SHELTER COORDINATOR: And then, they take fingerprints again every time the boys apply for a document, such as the residency permit, and again when they turn 18, and they have to convert their residency permit. In all these passages fingerprints are taken.

LEGAL DOCTOR: I am a forensic doctor. I work for the Immigration Office. We attempt to give the most certain estimate on immigrant patient's age. There are many methods.

There are all these foreigners who avoid being kicked out of the country, "Ah no, look we're minors." And so the objective is if we show that we're checking on them then they know that it's not so easy to declare anymore... let's say I tell them: "In fact your age is unclear, but it's between 17 and 18." Then you know? when you enter the United States at immigration: they do wrist, hand, eyes, fingerprints they do all this. If you do this at the border, then that's the end of discussion. Why don't we do it here, it's not so impossible. Let's say I tell them, "Actually, I'll check your digital fingerprints, etc.," which is what you're supposed to do upon landing in Italy, but never gets done.

FOREIGN MINOR enters with a large roll of paper. MEDICAL HELPERS turn and see her. They run to her and embrace her, covering her up. They freeze in this position and FOREIGN MINOR freezes in the midst of them. Start video projection that plays through the end of the episode. The video shows the progressive sketching of an image. More and more lines are added which finally accrue into the sketch of the wrist bones below.

LEGAL DOCTOR: One is an x-ray of the left hand. In young bones, there's an interruption called the accretion cartilage, which allows for elongation. But as you grow more and more, this cartilage turns more and more into bone. It's like a little accordion

FOREIGN MINOR unfreezes and slips out from amongst the MEDICAL HELPERS who remain frozen. She unrolls the paper and lays down on it drawing.

LEGAL DOCTOR: The bones complete their ossification in adulthood. And so when it's retrieved, one can deduce this is someone under 18 years old.

When the LEGAL DOCTOR stops talking, MEDICAL HELPERS unfreeze and notice FOREIGN MINOR has moved. They cross to get her, pick her up and carry her away from the paper placing her DC, directly in front of the audience, and stand her up like a marionette. As LEGAL DOCTOR speaks, they examine her, checking her pulse, looking in her eyes, ears, and mouth, touching her forehead, while the doctor continues talking.

SHELTER COORDINATOR: As far as that wrist exam is concerned - the auxological exam - it is not a doctor that orders it but the magistrate from the tribunal of minors because it is the magistrate that authorizes the procedures to verify the person's exact age. Of course, there is always a 6 months range of error, more or less. In any event, if a boy has just turned 18 or he is almost 18, there is always the presumption that they are a minor.

LEGAL DOCTOR: Obviously there is no complete certainty. We can give a range: 16 to 18 years, 18 to 20. The results are sent to the police headquarters, or the prefecture. The magistrate knows this is the most imperfect of situations. They even ask me to give some sort of probability curve, as long as it's established that they're a minor.

Again the group freezes. FOREIGN MINOR slides out, returns to unrolled paper, and continues drawing.

SHELTER COORDINATOR: (*Simultaneous with the LEGAL DOCTOR's following line*) By the way, the exam attesting the real age also includes an exam of the hip. In case the person tested is an adult, they enter the age range of 25-27 or 20-22, and they have to leave the shelter for minors and enter one for adults.

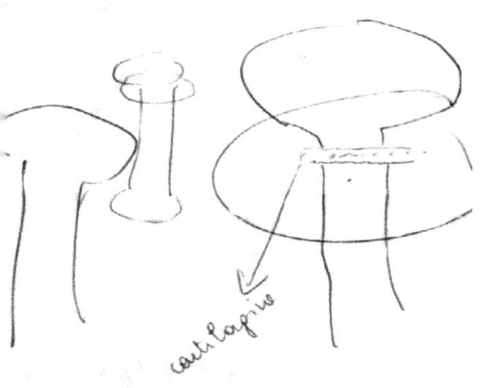

island

ridge ending

crossover

delta

core

cartilagine

LEGAL DOCTOR: *(simultaneous with SHELTER COORDINATOR's preceding line).* So it's a reception for minors or a reception for adults. If it's for adults, it's three days and then you go home: I wash you, I dress you and then you go back to your country. If you are a minor I can't do anything, I have to maintain you, I have to help you.

Again, MEDICAL HELPERS notice that she is gone and go get her again. They carry her to the chair UR and sit her down and resume the positions they started out in. They take turns asking her questions in sotto voce.

LEGAL DOCTOR: *(finally winning out over SHELTER COORDINATOR's voice he speaks this last line alone).* The minor has a cost, those who are of age can be shipped back to their home country. I need to establish wheth-er or not the person is of age. You can't expel migrants if they are minors.

Obviously profiteers say they're minors even though in reality they're thirty years old. And if I say I'm a minor and you say I'm not, well......

prove it... prove it!

MEDICAL HELPERS freeze and FOREIGN MINOR escapes again. She picks up her paper and exits. SR. MEDICAL HELPERS notice FOREIGN MINOR is gone and race out after her USR. Fingerprints appear projected on the drawing of the hand on the wall US. The image blurs.

LEGAL DOCTOR removes the medical chart from her clipboard, folds it into a paper boat, and places it in a fish bowl (Bowl #9)

Curtain closes. End Projection.

Episode — Anti-Crisis Assemblage

The Anti-crisis Assemblage episode begins with ACTOR 3 reading some theory quietly at a podium then builds: First, to one loud clear MEDIA PERSON and then to layers of others. MEDIA PERSON on top of MEDIA PERSON in a steady build until finally the stage is filled with a cacophony of MEDIA PERSONS talking over each other and eventually becoming indecipherable one from the other.

The parts of the media texts that are not underlined are the primary text that is heard by the audience at that moment in the episode. The parts that are underlined are spoken sotto voce. They are not heard distinctly by the audi-ence but become a bed of sound over which the next MEDIA PERSON that enters must shout to be heard.

ACTOR 3 enters from USL. She stands at the podium and picks up a copy of Janet Roitman's Anti-crisis, and holds it up so the audience can see its cover.

ACTOR 3: This is from Janet Roitman, An-thropologist (*She opens the book, places it on the computer and reads*): "[When speaking of history] one might ask: What sort of narra-tive could be produced where meaning is not everywhere a problem?"

Stage directions to the reader: scan on QR code to add the voices and continue to read the following lines out loud.

MEDIA PERSON #1 enters through the split in the curtains. He holds up a folded newspaper and starts speaking loudly.

After MEDIA PERSON #1 has spoken for a few moments then MEDIA PERSON #2 enters and stands next to MEDIA PERSON #1 he also holds up a folded newpaper. After a few more moments MEDIA PERSON #1 starts to speak in sotto voce as MEDIA PERSON #2 begins speaking loudly over her.

ROME — Hundreds of people were feared dead on Sunday after a ship crowded with migrants capsized

(*MEDIA PERSON #1*'s Sotto voce text) and sank in the Mediterranean, as the authorities described a grisly scene of bodies floating and submerging in the warm waters, with the majority of the dead apparently trapped in the ship at the bottom of the sea. The fatal shipwreck may prove to be the Mediterranean's deadliest migrant disaster ever and is only the latest tragedy in Europe's migration crisis.

ISTANBUL —This Year we have seen a record number of refugees trying and too often dying to get across Europe's Mediterranean frontier.

(*MEDIA PERSON #2*'s Sotto voce text) propelled by brutal wars, the collapse of Libya and other states, environmental disasters and grinding poverty that both cause and feed on this human misery.

After MEDIA PERSON #2 has spoken for a few moments as MEDIA PERSON #3 enters and stands next to MEDIA PERSON #2. He also holds up a folded newpaper. After a few more moments MEDIA PERSON #2 joins MEDIA PERSON # in sotto voce as MEDIA PERSON #3 begins speaking loudly over both of them.

After MEDIA PERSON #3 has spoken for a few moments MEDIA PERSON #4 enters and stands next to MEDIA PERSON #3. She also holds up a folded newpaper. After a few more moments MEDIA PERSON #3 joins MEDIA PERSON #1 and MEDIA PERSON #2 in sotto voce as MEDIA PERSON #4 begins speaking loudly over all of them.

BUDAPEST —In Hungary, hundreds of migrants surrounded by armed police officers were tricked into boarding a train with promises of freedom, only to be taken to a "reception" camp. In the Czech Republic

(*MEDIA PERSON #3*'s Sotto voce text) the police hustled more than 200 migrants off a train and wrote identification numbers on their hands with indelible markers, stopping only when someone pointed out that this was more than a little like the tattoos the Germans put on concentration camp inmates.

BERLIN — There is a direct correlation between the number of immigrants entering the country and the rise in crime rate.

(*MEDIA PERSON #4*'s Sotto voce text) a recent study conducted by the Confcommercio group on the statistical connection between crime and immigration found that in a determined area, if the number of immigrants increases by 1 percent, the crime rate in the same area goes up by 0.4 percent.

*When MEDIA PERSON #4 says the words
"crime rate," ACTOR 1 as DANCER enters
from USR. She wears all white and wears
five headlamps: one on her head, two on her
elbows, and two on her knees, which are illu-
minated on the steady setting. Over the next 30
seconds, everyone's sotto voce text gradually
drops to a whisper then to silence. The Sonar sound cue from the beginning of the play
begins and rises as the voices fade. DANCER
begins dancing and the four MEDIA PEOPLE
are pushed off stage one by one by her energy.
As she dances and the intensity of the dance
increases, we begin to hear her breath becoming more and more labored.*

ACTOR 3 *(After watching the dance in silence for a few moments ACTOR 3 reads again from Roitman):* "How did crisis come to mean a protracted historical condition? The very idea of crisis as a condition suggests an ongoing state of affairs. Can one speak of a state of enduring crisis? Is this not an oxymoron? [And yet] crisis is the defining category of our contemporary situation." *(After watching the dance):* "There is no politics without crisis because we have no language for it. *(Closes the book and exits)*

Sonar sound continues to build. DANCER continues dancing for several minutes with no other musical accompaniment. Lights slowly fade so spectators eventually see nothing but the moving headlamps. The headlamps change from solid white light, to solid red light, and then eventually to flashing red lights. DANCER continues to dance. By the time the stage lights have completely faded, spectators see only the whirling flashing red lights on her body and hear only the sonar and her heavy breath. Eventually she slows down and stops moving altogether. Spectators continue to hear the heaving breath. They experience this image for another few moments. Finally, the flashing red lights are turned off one by one, leaving the stage in darkness.

End of performance.

Stage direction for the reader:

TO END YOUR JOURNEY, PLEASE TEAR OUT THE FOLLOWING PAGE AND FOLLOW THE INSTRUCTIONS

1. Fold your paper in half on the vertical line and reopen the paper

2. Fold your paper again on the horizontal line

3. Fold the top corners in

4. Fold up the exposed edges on both sides

5. Grasp the center bottom edges and pull them away from each other and flatten into a square

6. Fold front and back layers up from the bottom to make a triangle

7. Grasp bottom edges from the center, pull apart and flatten

8. Pull top flaps outwards

9. You almost have a boat! Test your vessel in a bowl of water. Finesse the shape so it floats upright

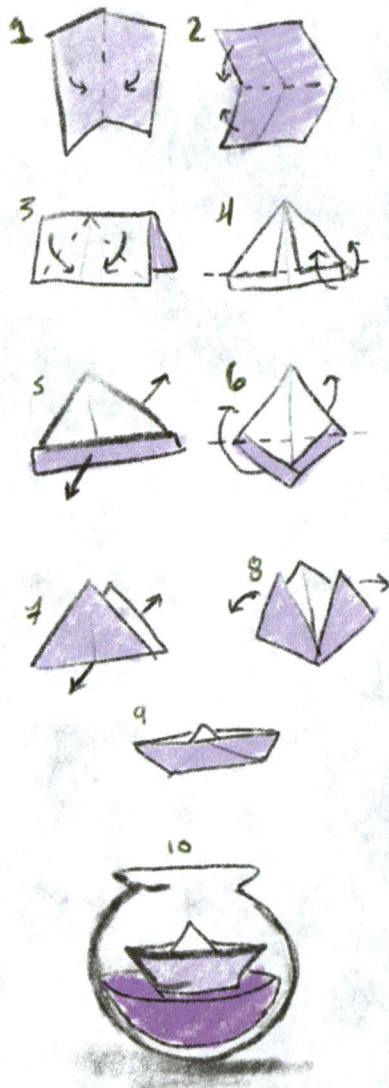

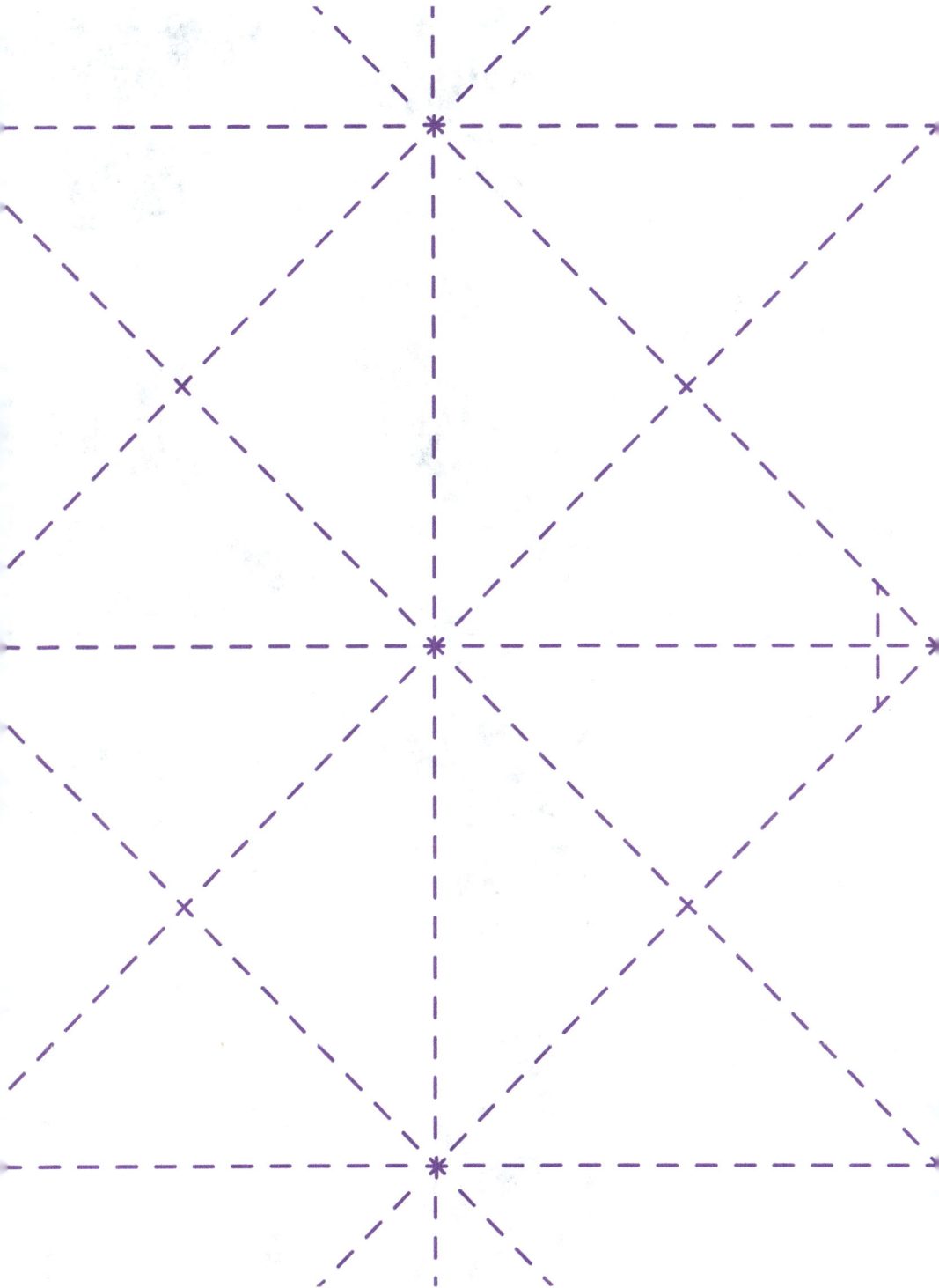

Stage directions for the reader: please remove your first paper boat from the bowl of water. Look at the faces you see in the picture on the boat. Now turn the page and make a second boat.

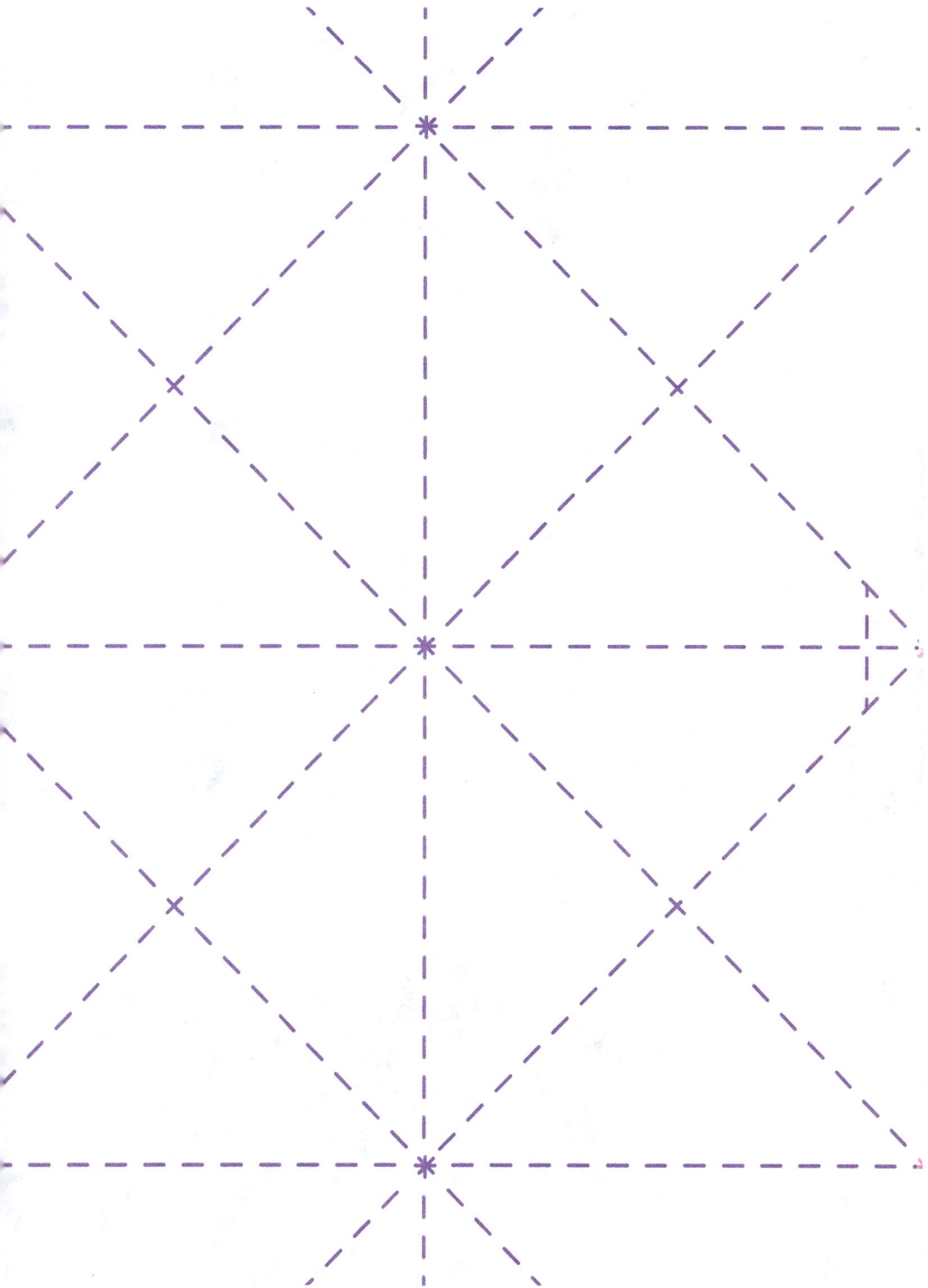

Stage directions for the reader: compare the two new boats you've made and make a decision. Set one of these boats afloat in your bowl of water

End of play...

Association #2

Post Scriptum: Translating Performance into Text

Cristiana Giordano and Greg Pierotti

To translate the performance score into a text for a reader, we knew a visual component was required. We enlisted the help of illustrator Tristyn Caneso. As the three of us worked, we found that the visual component could not be simply illustrative. We challenged ourselves with the same principle that guided the devising of the performance event. In theater making, we don't want to waste the theatrical power of the elements of the stage by using them to be simply illustrative—repeating or supporting what the text is already accomplishing. Instead, we strive to place the elements of the stage in more complicated and sometimes even dissonant relationships to the text, so that the audience can engage and square these discrepancies between design, staging, and text for themselves by creating their own associations, narratives, and meanings.

We found this to be equally true of the elements of design on the page. We needed to find ways that the text and design could create dissonances and resonances that might engage and draw readers into their own acts of analysis and interpretation. Feeling our way into what the piece did in the performance space and then attempting to convey that on the page, required yet another catching (Favret-Saada 1980), a reconsideration of how the printed text lived in relationship to its layout, color, image, formatting, blank space and digital media links. We wanted the interaction of text and design to add up to a larger affective experience for the reader.[1]

The rendering of the "Episode—The Legal Doctor," which appears toward the end of Chapter 2, is a good example. Most of the episode's text was drawn from an interview with a legal doctor responsible for fingerprinting and bone scanning migrants to determine their age. This medical exam allowed him to either categorize people as "minors," and move them into the system, or to categorize them as "adults," which allowed the Italian state to deport them. In the performance, the episode conveyed a rather complex and unresolvable set of contradictions. Without landing on a prescriptive analysis about what was acceptable or problematic for all the participants in the act of identification and classification, the performed episode addressed the complexities and paradoxes of these bureaucratic processes. Some of the conundrums that the episode highlighted were the difficulty of locating an empirical truth about people through scientific procedures, the problems and contradictions of the care and control of the state, and the ambivalence of biometric practices. However, when we put the words on the page, the printed text, which included descriptive stage directions, failed to convey the affective qualities of the episode. It read as if the actor performing the legal doctor was describing a complex and problematic identification process, while four other actors were pretending to represent what was being described in a playful way on stage. How could we convey the actual felt sense of the episode on the page, as we had on the stage?

Rendering the performance script for the page required yet another type of devising. The fingerprints, for example, were images that appeared as an illustration of the identification processes enacted by legal doctors on foreign minors. We had projected slides of fingerprints against the back wall of the playing space. In that context, the fingerprint was not a dramaturgical form in the same way the fishbowls had been, but were more a design element used to embellish the visual storytelling in the episode. As we started revising the script for publication, we discovered that these same images could become more performative than they had been in the stage event. We gave them a central position on the page. The thumbprint emerged as a form that required the text itself to follow its curving lines. As text collided with image, it slowly became less and less legible, understandable, discernible. Therefore, visual forms were not merely decorating the script but interacting with text to perform not only the process of identification but also the obscurations that arise from these same identification methods. This is the idea of a performative text where words bend and follow the form and lines of the fingerprint. The form impacts the empirical material, which gets written in a different shape, color, and order. In other words, design can guide content as easily as content usually guides design.

This formal discovery also re-engaged us with our research material in two important ways. First, we realized that now we needed more material about the function of fingerprints for the state. We conducted more interviews, including one with a shelter coordinator, which turned out to be enlightening. We also reexamined the legal doctor's transcripts to find the specific parts most suited for this formal leap. This clarified the important event of the doctor's text: he was struggling with a border, the one between what can be empirically proven about the body of the migrant, and what can only exist in an opaque range of probabilities.

This illegibility mirrors the paradox produced by the relation between a biometric form that tries to represent the transparency of identity and biography, and the text that gets inscribed in it. For us, the dissonances between text and form/design also performed how, lacking legal identification, bodies in movement were actually able to obscure their realities to the state in ways that benefited them. For other readers, this text may perform different associations. This is what we hoped to convey with new forms on the page, but here again each reader will create their own associations. This is the point of our writing and research experiment, Affect Theater. We do not aim to create a shared understanding in the audience of specific meanings or linear narrative arcs, but to create a space of associative thinking and feeling.

Stage direction for the reader: *The current order of the episodes is only one possible way of organizing the material at hand. The dramaturgy we proposed in Chapter 2 is as follows:*

Episode 1—GPS head
Episode 2—Research Boat
Episode 3—Participation Podium
Episode 4—Fishing Boat
Episode 5—Magli Ocean Video
Episode 6—Crocs Categories
Episode 7—Bureaucratic Crocs Movers
Episode 8—Homiex/Mary
Episode 9—Mary (Monosyllabic)
Episode 10—Neighborhood People
Episode 11—Legal Doctor
Episode 12—Anti-Crisis Assemblage
The end

Play with this order and come up with your own montage, or dramaturgy, rearranging episodes and experimenting with the (un)stories that emerge from it. For examples, read Episode (11)—Legal Doctor, as the opening of the entire sequence, followed by Episode (4)—Fishing Boat, and see how the rest of the montage comes together. Re-read the episodes in your new order and see what different associations emerge.

Your dramaturgy:

Episode 1—
Episode 2—
Episode 3—
Episode 4—
Episode 5—
Episode 6—
Episode 7—
Episode 8—
Episode 9—
Episode 10—
Episode 11—
Episode 12—
The end

Part II

Minor Stories

Making Strange in Theater and Anthropology

Cristiana Giordano

Scenes of Arrival

In the summer of 2016, I joined a group of doctors working for the Italian humanitarian NGO Emergency, which, among other services, provides primary care at ports of entry in Sicily where boats of people rescued at sea arrive.[1] I became part of their team, first as a researcher doing fieldwork at the ports, and later as a consultant for a book project on the medical conditions of foreign workers in the agricultural fields in various regions in southern Italy (Puglia, Campania, and Calabria).[2] On an early morning in July, I left Siracusa, Italy, with the NGO's medical team to drive to the commercial port where their mobile clinic was stationed. They had called me late the night before saying, "Domani c'è sbarco, incontriamoci presto" (Tomorrow there is a disembarkation, let's meet early). We drove for half an hour to reach the port entrance in Augusta, where two policemen checked our badges to make sure we all had clearance to enter the fenced areas. The team was composed of two doctors, a nurse, a psychologist, a cultural mediator,[3] and a freelance photojournalist who had joined to document the procedures at the port.

The morning sun was unforgiving. When we arrived, the mercantile boat that had rescued several small boats at sea the night before was already there. Those rescued sat on the boat in the sun. We stood on the pier for at least three to four hours waiting for the disembarkation process to start. The rumor among the various humanitarian groups operating at the port was that 600 people were getting ready to be disembarked. We later learned from a Cameroonian man who was among them that six small boats had been rescued the night before in the stretch of sea between Libya and the Italian coast. From where I stood, I could observe the standard procedures of this kind of *sbarco* (disembarkation), while Emergency's medical team was getting ready to receive the newly arrived at their mobile clinic parked in another area of the port, approximately half a kilometer from the pier.

The doctors of the *Uffici di sanità marittima, aerea e di frontiera*, USMAF (Offices of Maritime, Aerial, and Border Health), dressed in white uniforms and wearing masks over their mouths, were on the boat conducting a first round of medical triage, making sure no one needed immediate attention. On the pier, waiting for people to disembark, were members of various organizations.[4]

People finally started to get off the boat in a straight line, one by one. As soon as they touched the ground, they were asked to take their shoes off, and they were given a pair of fake Crocs of all eye-catching colors: orange, green, red, blue, pink. The man handing them out was shouting the shoe size as he saw the next person in line approaching from a distance: "Forty-six!" "Forty-three!" "Thirty-eight!" I was standing right behind him. He turned to me and said, with a hint of pride in his voice: "I know all their shoe sizes! I have been doing this for the last three years and have gotten used to guessing!" People also wore an orange bracelet with a number that was assigned to them at sea, right after being rescued.

The boat was full of African men, a small number of families, African women, some children, and many young men, presumably minors. They disembarked the men first, the rest later, to keep them out of the sun, I guessed. After disembarking, people were asked to form a line and, one by one, to go through another medical triage under the Red Cross tent placed right in front of the boat. They were then asked to sit on the ground on the pier until everyone was disembarked, forming a rectangle, encircled by policemen who kept the group in place. Once disembarkation was over, everybody stood up and marched outside the protected area of the port, passing through the narrow gate that separated it from where all the organizations and institutions had their tents. Everyone was asked to sit on the ground, forming another rectangle in front of the Immigration Office stand. People were asked their name, date of birth, and nationality; then, they were photographed and fingerprinted, the usual process of identification. At this point, everyone was given another number on a piece of paper. They were now directed to the big tents where camp beds were lined up, one next to the other, so people could rest. At around 1 pm, volunteers from local NGOs pushed supermarket carts overflowing with small white plastic lunch bags near the tents. Lunch consisted of one apple, a cheese sandwich, and water. Soap, shampoo, and some clean clothes were distributed for people to shower. Some did laundry in the public restrooms and hung their clothes on the fences surrounding the port. After lunch, UNHCR officials gathered small groups under the tents to discuss the different laws and procedures to apply for asylum or other statuses. Those who needed medical assistance went to the NGO (Emergency) clinic; those in critical condition were transferred to the nearest hospital. In the late afternoon, people formed another long line in front of a supermarket cart, just outside the tents, and another food bag was distributed with the same meal for dinner: one apple, a cheese sandwich, and water.

Passages and the Funnel Effect

Since 2015, the expression "the funnel effect of immigration" has often appeared in mainstream discussions to describe the drastic increase in numbers of people arriving at Italian ports. The peninsula has functioned as one of the main gateways to Europe, where people often get stuck waiting for documents to be issued. These images of funnels and never-ending bureaucratic procedures are reminiscent of what Dipesh Chakrabarty has called "the waiting room of history" (2000)—in other words, a representation of humanity as divided among those who make history (the west) and those who wait to be admitted into it. The expression "funnel effect" also points to the contradictions at the heart of the European Union's decisions on how to manage the increased numbers of incoming foreigners. While fostering liberal inclusion and multiculturalism, various EU member states advocated for not admitting any migrants and reinstating strict border control at different moments in the last seven years.[5] Shifts in routes and political leaderships[6] since 2015 have impacted the number of people landing in Italy, with peaks of over 100,000 in 2017, 2020, and 2022.[7] The Covid-19 pandemic added another layer of complications and border closure that has impacted the flows of incoming people in Europe.[8] For their geographical configuration, Spain and Italy have remained among the top five European countries most impacted by arrivals by sea, and the Mediterranean route to Italy the deadliest one.[9] In this context, the Italian government and civil society have often played a frontline role in managing the so-called "refugee crisis" in the Mediterranean.[10]

According to the Dublin Regulation III (2014), an undocumented person entering Europe must apply for asylum or humanitarian protection in the country of first arrival. This implies that once people arrive in Italy, they must start the process to receive legal status and go through a series of bureaucratic phases to obtain a permit to stay, even if their intended destination is another European state. The Italian asylum process, often stretched out by appeals, can take more than two years, thus clogging the various institutional structures aimed at receiving and maintaining asylum seekers. Hence the expression "the funnel effect."

The application for asylum may start at one of the ports like the one near Siracusa, where I did research in the summers of 2016 and 2017. The port itself is not just a physical site of reception and identification, care and control. It is, in the words of one of the doctors I collaborated with, a "non-place," a line of demarcation between the sea and the land, international and national borders, lawlessness and legality. As such, it is a highly bureaucratized and anonymous site that operates through an excess of administrative procedures (Augé 1992). It is a physical harbor and a set of practices that different actors refer to as *sbarco* (disembarkation), but it also occupies an imaginary line between friend and enemy, the familiar and the stranger. In Italian, the word *porto* (port) shares the same root with the word *porta* (door). It refers to a passage through which people and objects move, crossing a blurred zone of categorization. There was something literal about the port functioning as a funnel that channels bodies through various phases of identification and recognition, and regulates the flows of people, stories, fingerprints, numbers, and documents.

Here, the word *sbarco* comes to signify a complex and layered process of medical, bureaucratic, legal, military, and humanitarian screening and evaluation that involves numerous actors and institutions, and a very compartmentalized approach to reception.[11] The images of multitudes of people disembarking from boats and being rescued at sea have colonized our social imaginary and understanding of the most recent movements of people, and have reduced migration to the moment of the crossing and, eventually, arrival (Pinelli and Ciabarri 2015). In media representations, the *sbarco* has become a synonym of migration itself, and of the "invasion" and "crisis" it has caused. But the *sbarco* reverberates well beyond the fenced area of the port, encompassing an assemblage of sites, rules, techniques, and processes that go beyond the disembarkation itself. This includes shelters, camps, documents, offices, waiting, categories, archives, fingerprints, and signatures that exist in temporalities other than the one allowed by an emergency. As Laura Y. Liu observed: "Points of entry complicate the imagined linearity of the border, its presumed edge" (Multiple Mobilities Research Cluster 2017: 32). The *sbarco*, then, exceeds the stories enabled by the grammar of crisis; it includes sites outside of the field of quick intervention such as reception centers, clinics, schools, social services, and immigration and police offices, which offer forms of recognition and care (Giordano 2014). The *sbarco* as an assemblage also expands into sites left unmapped by the state and through stories left untold.

In an essay on the role of discovery in anthropological research, Ugo Fabietti reflects on the importance for anthropologists to wander into bordering fields of knowledge and to be guided by what may at first appear as "insignificant information," or an "error" of sorts, to discover uncharted territories and new ways of thinking of our ethnographic sites (Fabietti 2012: 16). He uses the Italian verb *errare*, whose Latin origins means both to wander and to err. Drawing from Carlo Ginzburg's famous article on the *processo indiziario* (evidential process) as the typical mode of enquiry of the human sciences (Ginzburg 1980), Fabietti reclaims the importance of minor details and things serendipitously discovered while doing research. For Ginzburg (1980), the *processo indiziario* is a mode of reasoning and knowing that attends to small details, or to what appears to be an insignificant fact. He compares the work of the art historian, the detective, and the psychoanalyst to argue that their forms of knowledge originate from paying attention to minor clues. While they each operate in a different register (the aesthetic, the forensic, and the therapeutic), they concur in their method of prioritizing that which is deemed to be insignificant at first glance. To discover a fake copy, for instance, the art historian must look for the tiny details with which ears or hands are rendered. The painter betrays himself through them, not in the overall style of the painting. Ginzburg provides the example of art historian Giovanni Morelli who, at the end of the nineteenth century, wrote a series of articles about the correct attribution of original works of art. He also draws a parallel with Sigmund Freud who, as a psychoanalyst, was able to "see" his patients' pathologies by observing their symptoms, minor unusual signs that led him to an underlying problem.[12] Sherlock Holmes (Ginzburg's third example), like the art historian and the psychoanalyst, follows clues that risk going unnoticed to solve the mystery of a crime. What is seemingly irrelevant turns out to be central in the resolution of a riddle.

The collaborative process of Affect Theater has taught me to think and observe details in more associative ways which have shifted not only my way of relating to empirical material, but also of wandering and erring in the field (Fabietti 2012). What catches my attention, or triggers my curiosity, what evokes a reflection, or an insight (and eventually the making of an episode) may not necessarily be the most obvious or visible scene, or the most literally related site to the issues at hand in any given research project. Things are often related in oblique ways, their relations often silent and improbable to the logics of the institutions charged with the task of monitoring migrations and identifying individuals. In ports of entry and other sites of migrant reception, for instance, I was frequently reminded of the minor, not only because of the generative nature that Ginzburg and Fabietti identify in it, but also for its political valence (Deleuze and Guattari 1983). With its sensationalist accounts of migration, its emergencies that the media and political actors constantly produce and circulate, the crisis narrative foregrounds an idea of emergency and state of exception that only partially accounts for the contemporary moment. While this way of narrating the real fosters the illusion of redemptive interventions that may fix the current crisis, it also forecloses the possibility of accounting for events that fall outside the emergency paradigm. There are many details that go unnoticed in the official crisis rhetoric but that tell different stories and broaden the scope of the contemporary moment by showing glimpses of new worlds/forms of life in the interstices of state institutions and practices. These details emerged in the performance *Unstories*, through the mobilization of mundane elements of the stage (trash bags, fishbowls, or the gesture of bighellonare), allowing the empirical material to resonate in a minor note. As Erin Manning wrote: "[The minor] has a mobility not given to the major: its rhythms are not controlled by a preexisting structure, but open to flux" (2016: 1). In this sense, the minor works from within the major discourse of crisis and questions its dominant standards. While I was thinking with institutional modes of reception and identification of foreigners at the very moment of the *sbarco*, I was also aware that most practices and processes exceeded themselves into zones that were merely hinted at in the very context of the port and that unfolded beyond the port's fences.

In observing the procedures of disembarkation, I was struck by how well the figure of the funnel captures both an engulfed situation of bodies passing through narrow zones of identification and reception, and the fundamentally split nature of power and sovereignty (Foucault 1991): on the one hand, power functions as a form of custody and control (of foreign bodies and borders) and, on the other, it rescues and cares for those who make it under its sovereignty by fitting its categories of recognition (Giordano 2016). The expression "the funnel effect of immigration" points to the complex nature of power that observes and categorizes, excludes and discriminates, while protecting and taking care of those who make it within its purview. From a distance, the *sbarco* seems to follow a step-by-step linear process (from disembarking to medical triage to biometric identification to more medical examinations, etc.). There is a rational organization that clusters different organizations and institutions to fulfill the task of reception, identification, and care. Experienced from within, though, the port and the *sbarco* are blurry and labyrinthine: the roles of various humanitarian organizations and police forces often overlap or are reversed. It is not uncommon to witness a humanitarian actor denouncing the presence of "human traffickers" among the people who have disembarked to the police. Or, to see members of the police forces referring people in need of medical attention to the mobile clinics or the Red Cross tent. Power's porous and shortsighted nature goes hand in hand with its split and opaque character. It is from this blurriness and pervasiveness—that Foucault taught us to see so well in the workings of institutions and population (Foucault 1991)—that power derives its effectiveness and strength. Such force lies in the fact that power cannot be localized in one single institution and practice, nor be identified as always working in a particular direction.

While the *sbarco* provides a space of governmental and humanitarian surveillance that moves people through techniques of care and control, it also allows for other practices to occur. Some people *refuse* to be fingerprinted or find ways to escape from the port and go off the radar of institutional gazes; others get identified at ports, are transported to shelters, and disappear shortly after to travel North, or enter a parallel world of squatted homes and unmapped shantytowns. This refusal may function as an alternative political position in critical relationship to the state (Simpson 2017: 2), or an appeal to the "right to disappear" (Sanyal 2017), and a desperate attempt at a different kind of recognition. People burn their fingerprints and stitch their mouths as a refusal to be recognized through the logics of the nation-state.[13] The funnel describes a spatial configuration of bodies moving through narrow zones of identification to be inserted, or squeezed, into the register of the law. The "funnel effect" is also the expression that the media, the nation states, and various political actors use to emphasize, and create, a sense of engulfment caused by the presence of foreign others. Yet, this figure only partially captures the complexity of these scenes of arrival. Institutions work more like porous apparatuses that often fail to "funnel" or process objects and people through the bureaucratic system. These very practices work and re-instate themselves through what *escapes* institutional procedures. What falls outside of the legal jurisdiction of the state constitutes a lawless land that law itself produces, but that state discourse represents as outside of it. As Veena Das and Deborah Poole put it, "Margins are a necessary entailment of the state, much as the exception is a necessary component of the rule" (2004, 4). Something similar could be argued for what eludes the purview of the state, and thus becomes marginal and minor in relation to it.

In the non-place of the port, the *sbarco* also presents the opportunity to pass through the fence that separates the port from the fields, and to go undetected. Many of the people entering Europe under the paradigm of humanitarian emergency become part of a growing unrecognized workforce in the seasonal agricultural industry throughout Italy. They enter a lawless system of exploitation that, while violent, also provides shelter from state monitoring (Giordano 2016; Peano 2017). As a funnel, the *sbarco* simultaneously enables forms of legal identification that can lead both to papers and access to services and rights, and to ways to escape into alternative forms of life.

In Part II of this book, attending to minor details beyond the port and the *sbarco* allows me to resonate with these other forms of life and possibilities in the midst of dominant discourses and grammars. I think with those experiences and sites that fall outside the official grammar of the state, and that the paradigm of political emergency fails to capture. Attuning to the minor in its various valences estranges common discourses around migration and borders, un-storying anthropological ways of writing them. In some instances, I follow the tonality of the minor in Ginzburg's sense of the "tiny details" and errors; in other cases, the minor is a site where different stories form adjacent to the master narrative of history and the state archive, and the taken-for-granted story of one-way progress (Tsing 2015).[14] I create a tension between the different ways of working with and through the minor by thinking with details, objects, and debris and how they can open other ways of narrativizing the world (Giordano and Pierotti 2020, Stewart 1996). Curating this material for the page in a more associative way is something I learned in the workshop where we mix elements of the stage with empirical material. The playful, intuitive, and affective creation of theatrical episodes in Affect Theater (Chapter 1 and 2) reverberates in this second part of the book. I ask how anthropology can tap into theater's power to make the familiar strange so we can decenter overarching narratives of crisis and create the possibility of imagining encounters and accounts otherwise, where seemingly contradictory stories and apparently opposite worlds exist simultaneously. This is a way of un-storying monolithic accounts: by decreasing the power of their truth claims and making it crumble so that the crumbs themselves, not the whole, can start telling stories in other ways, without resolving or explaining the content of their telling.

On Power and Its Grammars

Let me take a short detour to explore the concept of grammar in relation to dominant and minor discourses. The grammar of power mobilizes specific categories—crisis, asylum seeker, and refugee, among others—that elicit specific stories in order to grant different forms of humanitarian protection, or to enforce repatriation. By grammar here, I don't mean merely the set of abstract rules for correctly speaking a language, or the syntactic and semantic use of words and sentences. I draw from Ludwig Wittgenstein's work (1958) a broader and more elusive understanding of grammar as a set of norms—what he calls "language-games"—that are used and practiced when we speak a language and, in so doing, produce and sustain forms of life. Such norms are interwoven with the fabric of life, and they don't merely guide the abstract use of language but the practice of everyday life as well. According to Wittgenstein, "The term 'language-game' is meant to bring into prominence the fact that the *speaking* of language is part of an activity, or of a form of life" (1958: 23), and the relation between grammar and language is like that of the rules of a game and the game itself. For him, games are not arbitrarily ruled by norms that could, in another context, be substituted by other equally arbitrary rules. In other words, they don't just provide an interpretation of any given world, like the cultural explanation of a custom or ritual, but they constitute the essence and very existence of that world (and its customs and rituals).[15] In this idea of grammar, rules and norms are practices that produce worlds. For Wittgenstein, "Grammar tells [us] what kind of object anything is. (Theology as grammar)" (1958: 371, 373). That is, theology is a grammar wherein God figures as one of the objects of contemplation and knowledge.

Similarly, one can argue that sovereign and bureaucratic powers, as well as other forms of knowledge, are grammars that translate experience into their language-games, which, in turn, sustain specific worlds/forms of life. In the context of contemporary migrations, for instance, different state apparatuses and laws translate people crossing borders into specific categories of legal recognition that correspond to predetermined subject positions. Grammars make object and subject positions intelligible; some entities become objects while others are constituted as subjects. What falls outside a form of life and its grammar belongs to the realm of the untranslatable, thus exceeding the very syntax that makes certain objects, subjects, and actions recognizable. I am here interested in what remains unexpressed in a grammar, specifically that of crisis.

To think about crisis as a form of life with its own specific language-game, implies approaching it as a set of rules and norms that organize the ways in which events become understandable and knowable.[16] Within the grammar of crisis, movement, borders, and the events attached to them become specific kinds of objects of knowledge, with specific trajectories and outcomes. For example, the movement of people crossing the sea and other national borders becomes a form of "migration," and those who move become known through various subject positions and categories that make up such grammar: "asylum seeker," "refugee," "economic migrant," "victim of human trafficking," "clandestine," "trafficker," and "unaccompanied foreign minor" (Giordano 2014). Italian government agencies and NGOs working in the field of migration are often invested in eliciting victim stories from asylum seekers or people who might qualify as victims of human trafficking. In doing this in and through these language-games, people are asked to tell and to speak their stories in a specific victim register eliciting specific types of recognition (Giordano 2015). In this way, the grammar of crisis tells us what kind of subjects and objects are represented through these categories and what disciplinary practices are needed for their management. In the story one tells before the state, there is little room for opacity (Demos 2009); one of the characteristics of the security regime is its emphasis on visibility and capture (Sanyal 2017: 21). The stories that belong to a minor register remain unrecognized and unheard; they fall outside what the crisis language-game can verbalize.

Minor Stories

There is another way in which minor stories matter to the overall project of this book and the ways in which ethnographic theater devising may create a space for them to be heard, experienced, and performed. Gilles Deleuze and Felix Guattari developed an important reflection around Kafka's writing as a form of "minor literature" that emerged and thrived from within a dominant language, German, which was for Kafka (a Czech Jew in Prague) an acquired idiom. For them, a minor literature has three main characteristics. First of all, it is not "the literature of a minor language but the literature a minority makes in a major language" (Deleuze and Guattari 1983: 16). In this sense, Kafka's German is a "deterritorialized" tongue employed for minor use, *with* a somewhat rearranged syntax that destabilizes its common use. It is a language that opens a space for *minor perspectives* from within a major language. This is a tongue spoken in accents that are audible in oral as well as written form. The second characteristic is that everything in a minor literature is "political" (Deleuze and Guattari 1983: 16). By existing in what they call "a narrow space," a minor literature's relation to the question of the individual becomes indispensable because it conveys a different story. Its third characteristic is the collective value of such a story and literature (Deleuze and Guattari 1983: 17).

Unlike the minor detail of Ginzburg's *processo indiziario* (Ginzburg 1980), Deleuze and Guattari's minor has nothing to do with the question of evidence and revelation of a truth. Instead, it is a process through which a different language is formed from within an official one and coexists with it. While the error, the clue, and the symptom reveal the existence of a displaced story, a minor language creates a different perspective, a "deterritorialization" that makes something familiar unfamiliar. The two ways of approaching the question of what counts as minor are in part connected, and in part disconnected. They both highlight different potential views from an unusual (minor) angle. In Kafka, the minor perspective is a position from which one speaks and writes in a dominant language, and, in so doing, remakes it anew. It is a mode that makes a language sound estranged; it is the effect produced by an accent, which is not just a question of pronunciation and sound, but a matter of making a grammar one's own by accentuating it in unique ways, turning it into a new idiom and experience. For Ginzburg, the error, the clue, and the symptom are anomalies and interruptions that point to a hidden reality; they, too, incarnate a different story and provide a new perspective, but with the assumption that they may also reveal an underlying truth (something my work is not engaged with).

To explain the effect of estrangement produced by a minor language, Deleuze and Guattari write about the *deterritorialization* of the mouth that occurs when a minority speaks a dominant language (1983: 19). In learning a foreign language, the mouth, teeth, and tongue need to adjust to the movements required to produce new unfamiliar sounds. Different muscles are needed to speak different languages. This physical readjustment also requires an estrangement in perspective that affects written as well as spoken language. We hear an accent in Kafka's writing. Accents, then, are moments of interruption, or variations on a theme told through a minor view.

Kafka's deterritorialization of language resonates with other forms of estrangement. When we, as researchers, think through minor details, we shift our focus and attention to what may appear marginal and unimportant yet holds the potential for a different perspective (Ginzburg 1980). In the case of current migration flows and border control in the Mediterranean, as an anthropologist I attend to events and experiences in ways that are different from how the nation-state represents and categorizes bodies (Scott 1999), nor do I follow the urge to make an argument or truth claim. Instead, the task is to experiment at the margins of dominant grammars, exploring the stories that the crisis discourse erases or judges unimportant. Robert Brinkley, editor of Deleuze and Guattari's article on minor literature, notes: "The desire to evade interpretation is not a desire to be against interpretation, to negate it. To do so, after all, would be to continue to exist in its terms. The desire is rather to affirm an alternative which is simultaneously uninterpretable. Experimentation, Deleuze and Guattari suggest, is an alternative to interpretation" (Deleuze and Guattari 1983: 13–14).

In line with this experimental mode, creating a performance and a workshop is the alternative space where I have learned to combine a taste for language with a desire to draw from nonlinear and non-textual ways of knowing that are often occasioned by a minor perspective. I don't mean "knowing" as a synonym of "understanding." We often know without understanding, and vice versa.[17] In Affect Theater workshops we engage empirical research material without needing to understand it or make meaning out of it. The question of interpretation is turned upside down, not because we learn new ways of interpreting ethnographic material, but because we unlearn them. I started to approach my work, as an anthropologist and a writer outside the workshop, as a process that delays interpretation, plays with associations, and remains intrigued by the practice of making strange (deterritorialize), something that both ethnography and performance are engaged in.[18]

When we worked on the *Unstories* performance events, we experimented with a form of deterritorialization of narrative guided by a taste for details and an interest in decentering text. Stories and narrative are the usual mode of making sense of the world of movement and borders in many of the contexts in which I conduct my research, and, more broadly, in anthropology (Taussig 2009, McGranahan 2015).[19] It is often the mode of attention that anthropologists bring to their field sites, whether these are cities, archives, villages, biographies, institutions, households, clinical records, objects, and so on. In the specific context of contemporary migration, there is an urge—on the part of institutions and the press, but also academia itself—to know the story of the migrant other. It is the desire to reach a true testimony that fuels the production of accounts considered "official" and produces a saturation in the ways of telling and listening, to the point that stories of migration are not about what they tell (literally) any longer and are often split from the reality they attempt to account for. For instance, in my previous work with foreign women who qualify as "victims of human trafficking" in Italy and took part in the state-funded rehab program to achieve legal status, I argued that the *denuncia*, the document that testifies their victim status before a court of law, while not entirely truthful is not a lie either (Giordano 2014: 160). This document chronicles the story of the "victim" as the state conceives of it; it does not necessarily testify to the actual experiences of discrimination, violence, and "victimhood" people face in their own day-to-day reality, or that may have forced them to migrate.

In the stories conveyed through the *denuncia* a lot remains unsaid because it cannot be verbalized through the form of the state document (Giordano 2014).[20] These verbalized stories—like most stories—become the repository of a certain degree of silence that is at the heart of mainstream discourse, and that cannot be accounted for through language alone. The unspoken falls outside institutional discourses. It resides in and animates the contradictions of stories: it is heard in what is not told, and it always eludes mainstream discussions. It doesn't belong to the register of the sensational or to the rhetoric of emergency and crisis. As Kathleen Stewart observes, "There is always something more to say, always an uncaptured excess that provokes further questions, new associations that just come, and fresh gaps in understanding. Rather than complete or 'exemplify' a thought, narratives produce a further searching" (1996: 32). It is to this uncaptured space that my work with performance and Affect Theater turns. This is also the space that Lisa Stevenson has called the "ethnographic unconscious,"[21] which makes itself thinkable/feelable through what may seem like an anomaly, or a slip of the tongue, a minor perspective of sorts. If linear stories lose their elocutionary power (as in *denuncia*), the task is to work with more associative and affective ways of telling and listening, outside the argumentative register. I join Michael Jackson when he writes: "Anthropologists sometimes turn to literature . . . to unsettle that which social science has considered settled and to make good what science has left unexplored and unspoken." He calls the unexplored "penumbral domains" (Jackson 2017: 92), areas that lay in partial shadow.

Associations

I listen to the "penumbral" invoked by Jackson as a series of sites, objects, and moments that may escape logical thinking, and the cognitive impulse to clarify them through narrative. Over time, *Unstories* the performance became the antidote to this urge; it turned into a broader project of un-storying narrative, telling stories in an associative rather than a linear way, through evocative forms rather than rational plots, so that the penumbral could linger and affect the reader/performer/spectator/researcher, rather than being brought to light and disappear behind clarifications. An attention to the minor—whether in the sense of details, traces, and clues (Ginzburg 1980), or in the sense of a minor perspective (Deleuze and Guattari 1983)—goes hand in hand with the associative as a mode of affective knowing that doesn't locate meaning only in linear reasoning. What I call the associative resonates with Kathleen Stewart's "logic of digression and accidental" (1996: 80). This logic suggests a form of fidelity to the real (McLean 2017: 47) that acknowledges that "it will always exceed the accounts we are able to give of it" (Pandian and McLean 2017: 23). To me, the associative is an oscillation between the literal and the evocative, the symbolic and the real, between signifiers and signified in a floating movement that resembles a swinging of affects, images, and thoughts. Associations estrange our usual way of thinking, shaking our taken-for-granted connections of cause and effect, linear argumentation, or logical reasoning.

In working with the associative, I am inspired by psychoanalysis, but not only. The practice of free associating is often linked to the psychoanalytic method of speaking and making connections counter to the rational activities of the Ego and the Super-ego. It is a method to estrange the working of the conscious mind, "an ever-sophisticated pathway" for the articulation of the unconscious (Bollas 2009: 14). While "[c]onscious reasoning is a highly favored form of thought," as Christopher Bollas writes, "within the fields of consciousness alone there are hundreds of ways to think. And when we include unconscious thinking in the mix, the doors open to an astonishing variety of thought systems" (2009: 58). By introducing an element of surprise and foreignness, free association is one way of thinking that undoes our usual way of meaning-making.

I also turn to minor details that provide a perspective not *about* things in the world, but *adjacent* to them. When we associate, we put one thing beside another, one thought along another, in chains or whirlpools of relations. This form of attention, though, is not only directed to the language that makes up the text of stories. When Greg and I talk about decentering text, we refer to a process in the workshop and performances that creates spatial associations between words, objects, light, sound, space, and smell. What is being deterritorialized is not just the mouth, the tongue, and the teeth that vocalize a language (Deleuze and Guattari 1986), but also the eye that sees objects and lights in the workshop space in a way that makes them resonate with parts of texts; the ear that associates a sound to an object, a ray of light, and later to a sentence; and the hand and the entire body moving in space, through objects and lights, accompanied by sound. Everything is part of an experiment in estrangement and decentering, so that a different account takes shape in a way that spins mainstream discourses around, reshuffling them so that the unspoken can resonate. In this sense, through associations one can rework the material that is made available by dominant languages and discourses (and grammars), rearrange it, and create a minor language of sorts capable of letting different aspects of the realities conveyed by a major "language" be experienced. While some may think of free associations as a genre of speech (which occurs within the psychoanalytic setting), in our process we propose extending association to moments of academic and performative creations, and to pose it alongside a minor language that offers a different account, with an accent. In this sense, *Unstories* belongs to a minor register.

The kind of associative thinking we practice in Affect Theater is similar to the work of dreams and dream interpretation, as mentioned in Chapter 1. What matters in dreams is not their literality, but the net of evocations and loose connections that are set in motion by the dream's images and sounds. If we approach dreams literally, we kill the message they convey. What is generative in the dream content is the allusiveness of its visual and sonic components, and their fragmented manifestation. There is a process of displacement that takes place in dream work: unconscious material (what Freud calls "dream thought") gets displaced during sleep into the "dream content" (the actual dream we dream at night) not in a direct linear way, but through processes of distortion, condensation, repression, and omission. What we see in dreams is an oblique and distorted rendition of unconscious material (Freud 1899) that becomes estranged from itself in the dream—in a way, it is deterritorialized—so that it can be experienced through the images the dreamer sees in dreams. The dream is the accent in which the language of the unconscious is spoken when we are asleep.[22] In this light, the dream can be listened to as a minor perspective, as a site where another language makes itself heard through a distortion or a peculiarity which "disrupts our conventional sense of mastery" (Kondo 2018: 114). In dreams, as in Affect Theater, such language is not only made of words and/or sentences, but it is also composed of objects, symbols, smells, light, signs, and so on. Dreams force us to listen associatively rather than literally.[23]

What does it mean to listen associatively? How do we practice this kind of listening more broadly when working with empirical research material? And how does this apply to the process of Affect Theater and its reverberations outside the workshop and on the page? While the associative usually refers to a nonlinear practice of speaking and imagining mental links, in my current work I expand its analytical potential to "genres of listening" (Marsilli-Vargas 2014) and relating to the material world. I turn again to Bollas, who writes, "When we walk about in our world, we are poised at the intersection of two evocative objects: one purely internal, arising out of desire or affect, the other consisting of actual things we encounter in the real. . . . [O]ur encounter, engagement with, and sometimes our employment of, actual things is a way of thinking" (2009: 58). In our workshop, this translates into a corporeal way of associating (thinking *and* listening). By "corporeality" I don't mean what pertains to the body only, but a way of being present to the empirical material and collaborations in ways that include various senses and modalities of relating.[24] Our practice of Affect Theater engages with a way of making associations that involves thinking, moving, affecting, and being affected by different kinds of bodies. As Jane Bennett reminds us: "Spinoza's conative bodies are also *associative* or (one could even say) *social* bodies, in the sense that each is, by its very nature as a body, continuously affecting and being affected by other bodies" (2010: 21). The associative and the affective, then, are similar modalities of resonating with (and listening to) reality in ways that evoke not another reality altogether, but different aspects of it that exceed logical and commonsensical modes of making sense.

What about an "associative anthropology," then?[25] Stuart McLean, writing about anthropology's critique of the comparitivism of its father figures, proposes an intriguing recuperation of the old practices of creating encounters and connections between worlds that appear to be distant and disconnected from one another. Since Boas, comparativism has been denounced as producing a series of "speculative flights" only partially grounded in the empirical reality of the specific sites of fieldwork. In the history of the discipline, ethnographic specificity was meant as an antidote to the risk of universalism inherent in comparisons, relegating comparisons to a past to be dismissed. But, McLean writes, some comparisons and examples "suggest not only a multiplicity of possible human worlds but also the prospect of unpredictable and mutually transformative encounters between spatially and temporally disparate people, things, and places" (2017: 151). He further articulates: "Comparison shows us that there is more to reality than we previously thought. . . . Descriptive fidelity to the actual is routinely prioritized over poetic invention, which is, in contrast, denied any direct purchase upon the real" (McLean 2017: 153).

Associations—like comparisons—produce new combinations of elements. The associative is an engagement with the world that produces new encounters, tensions, and disjunctures by tapping into the poetic/poietic in a way that resonates with the comparative. Associations evoke something of reality that's been overshadowed by commonsense and logic. The fact that they cannot be empirically verified does not mean that they are not anchored in reality, but rather that the reality that they weave together exceeds the actuality of any given specific site and time, just like comparisons. I join McLean in his reclaim for comparison in anthropology in so far as it is a way to claim the associative as an analytical and creative engagement with the worlds we inhabit and possible unforeseen realities.

The associative process—whether in thinking, listening, moving, or affecting—allows for a nonlinear relation to empirical material beyond the workshop and the making of performances, and it can shape other renderings and forms of writing the real. In what ways does experimental ethnographic theater provide an excursion through the associative that can impact writing, not only for the stage but also for the page? This is one of the challenges I have set up for myself through my collaborations in Affect Theater and my writing, within and outside the workshop space.

Making Strange

In the summer and fall of 2018, I spent four weeks with Odin Teatret and its founder, Eugenio Barba, for a workshop and theater festival in Holstebro, Denmark, where the company resides, and for a series of laboratories in Albino, Italy. In 1964, Barba founded his company and started what he called Theater Anthropology, an exploration of performance and presence through different theater traditions. In the mid-1970s, he coined the expression Third Theater to describe a phenomenon that was taking place in the theater scene and that described his experiment with Odin Teatret.

> A theatrical archipelago [third theater] has been forming during the past few years in several countries. Almost unknown, it is rarely subject to reflection, it is not presented at festivals and critics do not write about it.
>
> It seems to constitute the anonymous extreme of the theatres recognized by the world of culture: on the one hand, the institutionalized theatre, protected and subsidized because of the cultural values that it seems to transmit, appearing as a living image of a creative confrontation with the texts of the past and the present, or even as a "noble" version of the entertainment business; on the other hand, the avant-garde theatre, experimenting, researching, arduous or iconoclastic, a theatre of changes, in search of a new originality, defended in the name of the necessity to transcend tradition, and open to novelty in the artistic field and within society.
>
> The Third Theatre lives on the fringe, often outside or on the outskirts of the centers and capitals of culture. It is a theatre created by people who define themselves as actors, directors, theatre workers, although they have seldom undergone a traditional theatrical education and therefore are not recognized as professionals. (1986: 193)

Barba's Third Theater occupies the position of a minor language. Like Kafka's use of German, Third Theater is not the theater of a minor technique, but the theater a group on the fringe makes from within dominant traditions and practices, at the margins of infrastructures and in spite of capital and professional recognition. Third Theater emerges in the interstices between mainstream theater and the avant-garde, and it thrives by being at the edge of both theater traditions; it produces a deterritorialization of what we commonly understand theater to be, living outside of the usual matrix of success and visibility. It also resonates with the idea of a minor language insofar as Barba's theater is by its very nature political and collective, aiming at entering society to create an interference with dominant languages and discourse.

From the perspective of this "fringe," Barba also talks about the great potential of theater to produce something that written accounts and stories cannot: simultaneity on the stage. By "simultaneity" he means the coexistence of different story lines, plots (or the lack of thereof), languages, and temporalities in a montage of juxtaposed elements in resonance or/and dissonance with one another. It is an art aimed at disrupting the unity of the text (Kondo 2018: 49) and at confusing the divide between the linear and the associative, the real and the fictive. In *On Directing and Dramaturgy*, Barba explains: "A story through words, both written and oral, must necessarily organize events one after another, following the vector of time. A story which takes shape in theater can on the contrary show two or more different events at the same time and in the same place" (2010: 102). Simultaneity does not mean symmetry; on the contrary, in Barba's dramaturgy the creation of asymmetry is crucial. All of Odin Teatret's performances juxtapose scenes from different times and places, different genres (poetry, songs, fragments of novels, segments of articles, original texts from the actors, archival material, etc.); they use different languages that are assembled simultaneously on the stage, creating a cacophony of sounds and a sense of linguistic estrangement. This sense of disorientation is never only linguistic; the very idea of estrangement is the main force at the heart of their performances and permeates all senses: of space, smell, vision, and touch.

Barba's theater is deeply influenced by Bertolt Brecht's practice of *Verfremdung*. The term refers to the experience of alienation, defamiliarization, and "making the familiar strange"—all imperfect translations of *Verfremdung* (Barnett 2014: 76)—that theater may produce. David Barnett, writing on Brecht, explains it as "the ability to perceive reality without collapsing it to fit particular agendas," so that old assumptions are not taken for granted and new understanding is possible (Barnett 2014: 77–8).

How does estrangement work in actual practice, training, and productions of the Odin Teatret ensemble? How do they produce estrangement for the stage?

They start from the premise that any form of art is an operation of transformation from one reality into another. Any form of creation is a process of estrangement. Painters, sculptors, and poets estrange images, materials, and words so that the viewer, reader, and listener are introduced to a different way of experiencing reality. In acting, the actor has to estrange/transform her own body. One of the main techniques Barba teaches is to learn to do things in the opposite way in which the body is conditioned to do them. For example, one simple exercise we did during one of the laboratories was to walk very slowly in a perfect straight line while the musicians were playing fast music; or the opposite, walk very fast at the sound of slow music. This is not an action, which in Barba's parlance refers to the set of movements we are pre-programmed to do. It is a *re*-action: it doesn't follow a preconditioned way of doing and moving; it resists the impulse to do things automatically. In *re*-acting, the body learns to explore the broad range of movements it can perform, and the actor is estranged, in a way awoken to a whole new reality of her body, and old habits are undone. Similarly, in Affect Theater when we explore objects or other elements of the stage, we do so to experiment with their phenomenological potential, not their literal and common use. We are interested in the element's full potential and not to its pre-assigned functions.

In this process, the spectator's expectations are also estranged. Barba's plays create a series of oxymorons in action, of contradictions in movement and speech, like when words don't correspond with what the actor does with the body, or when the body doesn't follow the rhythms of music. In this way, Barba said, "The actor makes the spectator hallucinate because they see something other than the reality they are used to." This work of estrangement of reality pervades the entire production of a play. When Odin Teatret actors begin working on a performance, they don't start from the interpretation of a text. Julia Varley, one of the company members, said: "We don't start from meaning, even if meaning may arise in the process." Just like in our practice of Affect Theater, what precedes the writing of a text/performance is a series of exercises and practices away from the literality of words, or from text all together. For example, in working with the text (it can be a random excerpt the director assigns his actors as a starting point for rehearsal), Varley first departs from the literal meaning of words: "I go on a journey away through associations, into personal experiences, historical references, giving life to the people present in the text, or to an element. I forget what words are saying. . .; when I come back to the text, I understand it in a different way." Creating a labyrinth of associations is crucial to the creative process; it opens up the literal meaning of a text and makes it resonate with other realities, words, and worlds, becoming other than its original signification and simultaneously expanding its scope. This resonates with my earlier reflections on comparisons and associations and the ways in which they expand reality. One word can say different things at the same time, simultaneously meaning one thing and its opposite; this is the magic of theater. Like in a dream, someone who is dead in real life may become alive again on the stage; or the image of a cat may signify a pet, the horror of superstition, or both things at the same time. Because the relationship to text doesn't occur through the register of literality, what actors do is create a relationship to the words and sentences that is only partially about text itself. The relation between a physical score (sequence of actions) and a text is about the wild set of associations that the written text inspires in the actors' bodies, minds, senses, and memories.

To sustain the alienation effect, things shouldn't be all clear by the end of the performance, either. The spectator needs to understand some of the information conveyed by the play, but clarity is not the purpose of this kind of theater. The actors and director resist the temptation to convey a message through the performance. It is the spectator who makes meaning through their own projections and associations, and the relations that are created on the night of the performance. Each spectator feels, sees, perceives, and connects with something that they don't really understand, "hallucinating" something that did not exist prior their encounter with the play. What matters is not meaning per se, but the connections that spectators make viscerally. It is a process of *relations/ associations* being made at different levels: between actors and director, actors and their techniques, texts and bodies, spectators and performance, spectators and actors, and elements of the stage and performers. The layers of relations that make up the event of the play are infinite, and they follow nonlinear, simultaneously parallel and intersecting paths occurring in the rehearsal and on the stage. In Affect Theater, we follow a similar associative process that slows down textual interpretation and multiplies the associations between empirical material, collaborators, space, and elements of the stage (Chapter 1).

The practices of breaking the actor's—and the spectator's—automatism in search of a different range of movements and relations are similar to the effort of speaking a minor language from within a dominant one. They resemble the process of breaking the rules of a dominant idiom and speaking it with an accent. The actors look for a "minor" language of the body and the mouth (often acting in different languages simultaneously, with accents), made of gestures, actions, and reactions, learning to re-act rather than act, creating various effects of deterritorialization, estrangement, and un-storying. As a form of theater of *dissonance*, Barba's teachings have come to bear on the kind of anthropology I experiment with in this part of the book, and on the practice of Affect Theater that Greg and I share.

Unstorying Anthropology

How is estrangement, as a practice of making associations that defamiliarizes and creates new minor perspectives in performance and theater, related to an anthropology of un-stories, or a process of un-storying anthropology? If the task of performance, as we practice it, is to estrange reality, to surprise the spectators through the senses and not through meaning-making, how can anthropology derive from it the power of making strange that allows the unthought of our research to be felt, and the worlds around us to exist in all their simultaneous potentialities? How can this form of estrangement create an occasion "to be caught again" (Favret-Saada 1980) or to be caught *anew* in the realities of our ethnographic experiments, so that our writings become more visceral and woven into the worlds we, as writers and researchers, re-present anew?

In *Walter Benjamin's Grave*, Michael Taussig writes: "Anthropology is blind to how much its practice relies on the art of telling other people's stories—badly. What happens is that those stories are elaborated as scientific observations gleaned not from storytellers but from 'informants'" (2006: 62). Anthropologists often use stories to interpret and explain, to make a point, or to point to something else for which the story is instrumental. It is this pretense of "pointing to" that Taussig is critical of when he argues "not for masterful explanations but for estrangement" (viii), a form of writing from within, "instead of standing outside pointing" (vii). In Walter Benjamin's famous essay, the storyteller was the conveyer of eternal counsel and moral message, never arguing through abstract statements, but through the story's "ability to exchange experiences" (1968: 83). He compared storytelling to the novel and the news, and argued that, unlike stories, news information draws its power from what is nearest and sensational, verifiable and understandable; it thrives with what can be shared and dispensed quickly. A piece of information doesn't sustain itself through the same kind of slow repetition that weaves together and envelops storytellers and listeners. Its temporality is fast, and its spatiality is contained. For these reasons, "It proves incompatible with the spirit of storytelling," which "preserves and concentrates its strength and is capable of releasing it even after a long time" (90). Its temporality is slow, and its spatiality the world and beyond. It borrows from the "miraculous" while information relies on the "plausible" (1968: 83).

If stories, then, are not instruments used to argue or demonstrate something else, if they do not point to anything in particular, then they become the end in and of themselves, the manifestation of experience conveyed through a fusion of words, hands, ears, bodies, and minds. Stories don't just convey information, but they transport the teller, listener, and content of the story to the place where the story takes place.[26] They are the means through which we get caught again in the intensities of fieldwork (Favret-Saada 1980). In them, experience is not represented as a product of the past that is retold, but it is presented anew as something occurring and repeating itself in the here and now, each time in a renewed fashion.

If "anthropology is a storied discipline" (McGranahan 2015), let me reiterate: how do we then un-story our discipline in a way that allows for different forms of writing and telling *from within* and not *about*? To un-story the usual representation of worlds is a task already familiar to anthropology, a discipline that has, though, often fallen into the same trap of being storied by "bad stories" itself, or by too many stories *about* rather than *around, of* others rather than *adjacent* to them. In a long-term effort to decolonize anthropology, scholars have initially emphasized the importance of reclaiming our interlocutors as intellectuals with stories and voices of their own and taking their forms of life and theories seriously. This is still a commitment we need to renew over and again, and that has fostered generative debates around reworking anthropology (Harrison 1997), or an anthropology other/wise (Elliott and Culhane 2016, de la Cadena and Blaser 2018), remaking cultural analysis (Rosaldo 1989), and creating an alternative anthropology (Buck 2016).[27] Since the beginning of these engagements in the 1980s and 1990s, decolonizing anthropology has also become a project of creating new methods across disciplines that allow for new epistemologies and commitments with reality to emerge, beyond the academic canons and the taken-for-granted forms of single-authored ethnographic writing (Conquergood 2013, Madison 2018, Hartblay 2020).

In Affect Theater, we decenter text and the author. We also blur disciplinary boundaries, not knowing exactly what kind of knowledge we create, but with the intent of inviting others (collaborators from and beyond the field) into the process of making the empirical material of life and research speak for itself, letting the voices that populated fieldwork continue to resonate in space and through bodies, and not only on the page. This is an experiment with cross-pollination— or contagion—of the usual genre of ethnographic writing where we aim to deterritorialize (un-story) anthropological practices through performance, but also to produce a new space for writing, understood more broadly.

Let me now return to the tensions between master narratives of crisis and minor stories of life experienced otherwise in the context of migration, borders, and what gets foreclosed from narration. If we follow Benjamin's distinction between storytelling and information, and if news information produces stories that don't tell but make noise—like in the coverage of the "refugee crisis" in the Mediterranean (Fernando and Giordano 2016), and of crisis narratives more broadly (Roitman 2014)—then the task is to think of an anthropology that reclaims storytelling. To further echo Benjamin in a somewhat provocative way, I wonder whether anthropology should be concerned with what would count as "dis-information," meaning that which is slow and tortuous, somewhat hidden from a first sight, not commensurable, minor in its nature, marginal in its doing, resembling waste but in fact amounting to a precious unusual angle from which to attune with the novelty of relations, conversations, silences, and ambiguities. This implies un-storying the usual ways in which anthropology produces knowledge through its own stories *about* difference.

In this book, we are engaged in a process of rethinking forms of writing that involve techniques drawn from theater and performance, and that allow for the hand, the ear, the mouth, space, and objects to tell along with words, sentences, and narratives. We are interested in ways of telling where words and language may fall aside—or be suspended or go side by side—while stories unfold through and with other elements of the stage, in all their ambiguities. Working with the performances of *Unstories*, for instance, implied both acknowledging the reality of borders and "crisis," while also capturing the elusiveness of lived experience and cutting through the public's saturation with violent images and terrifying statistics about migration. In this sense, dramaturgy and performance became both a heuristic method and a way to estrange anthropological ways of writing. The spectators of *Unstories*, just as the readers of this book, can associate with the research material. Associations are ways of knowing not through certitude, but through affective intuitions, and surprising montages.

In the remainder of this part of the book, I engage minor details that fall outside, beyond, or to the side of the scene of arrival at the port and of the *sbarco* that opened this chapter. They don't stay "in place" or, rather, they don't stay in the place of master narrative or the linear story of progress and recognition that the nation-state, the media, and political actors assign to the figure of the migrant and the function of borders. I attend to the humans and materials that don't find recognition at ports of entry, nor in institutional settings, with a taste for that which official discourses on migration and borders usually ignore or damn as irrelevant. As we do in our performances, here too I follow the traces left by objects, holes in the fences, and paintings, I listen to tiny details as ethnographic sites that show the existence of other worlds outside the grammar of crisis. I explore the ethnographic and political valence of the minor, and the realities that live one beside the other, or one on top of the other, but that often remain overshadowed, or create a shade over the other. To attend to minor clues, to dream through associations, to create connections between different elements of reality, is not a way to provide a truer account, but to produce a confusion in the linearity of stories about movement, and to imagine other accounts.

In the following pages, I think with the art installation of a Tunisian artist who collects debris from the shipwrecks at Sicilian beaches, creating relations with those who didn't make it to the official ports of entry after the crossing. I converse with the paintings of a young Nigerian man who resists identifying with the category of the refugee and victim. I walk through foreign seasonal workers' shantytowns and attempt to take the perspective of the debris and waste that get repurposed to create a home. Just as the artist who reassembles the debris of the shipwrecks, and the seasonal workers who repurpose waste to make an alternative abode for themselves, as a writer and an ethnographer, I re-assemble pieces that fall through the cracks of institutional discourses to imagine an account that is attuned to the presences and absences of bodies, words, and objects. As I write, I am the one associating and montaging. But there are layers of association other than my own that populate this text: the reader's associations, our collaborators' making relations with the research material when we created *Unstories*, and the spectators' projections. The author(s) of this book are the directors of a first layer of associations, the dreamers of the dream, but hopefully in a way that allows the reader to roam through and around the material as well, dream their own book, and dramaturg their own performance.

4

The Force of Objects

Scenes of Loss and Creation

Cristiana Giordano

The Dump

In the late summer of 2016, my friends and collaborators Ramzi, a Tunisian artist and educator, and Antonino, an Italian retired coast guard, invited me to join them at the old port of Porto Palo, an hour from Siracusa. They wanted to show me a cemetery of boats where many of the relics of vessels used to cross the Mediterranean and confiscated by the state now rest (Figure 6). In the early 1990s, people fleeing

Figure 6 Cemetery of boats. Lampedusa, Italy, 2014. Photo by Cristiana Giordano.

Africa and the Maghreb used to arrive directly at small ports like Porto Palo. There were no bureaucratic or medical procedures to follow at the ports. As Antonino explained to me, people in the village would come out and open the ovens to bake bread and other goods for the newcomers. All the identification processes happened at police offices and hospitals in town, not at the commercial port.

On that windy morning, we went hunting for the objects and fragments of boats that had been abandoned at the dump. Many things cross with humans and sneak onto the shores of Europe, escaping the screening procedures of the *sbarco* (Chapter 3). For an art installation, Ramzi had been collecting things that once belonged to those who crossed. He also collected remnants of the boats themselves: rusted nails, slats of rotted wood, and engine parts. For several weeks that summer, he and other local artists exhibited their work in an empty, unconsecrated church, the Chiesa di Gesú Maria, in old Ortigia. Entitled "Uprooted," the exhibit displayed artwork that resonated with the experience of movement and borders (Figure 7). Ramzi showed his paintings

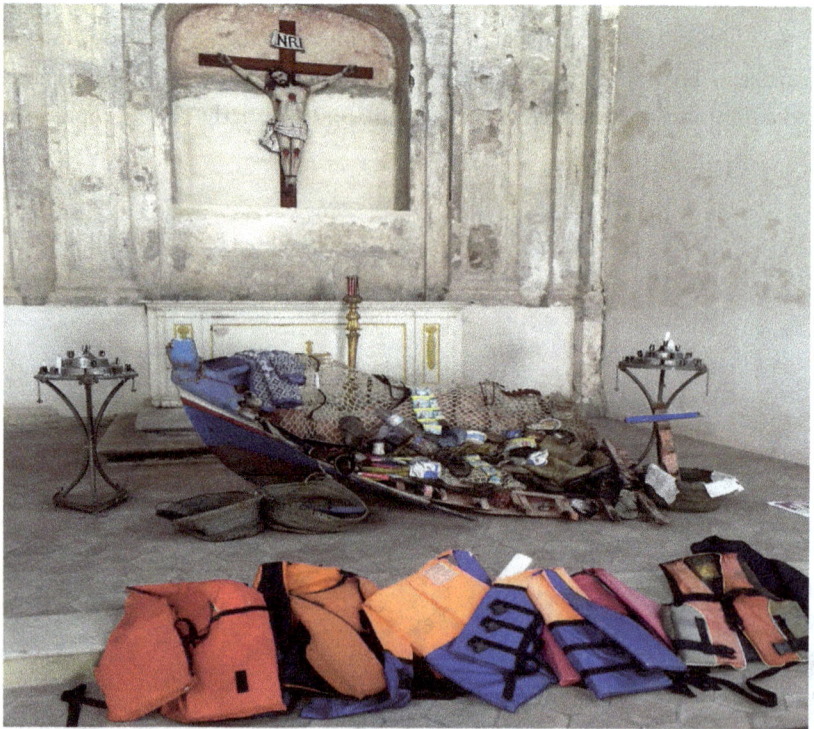

Figure 7 "Museo dei sogni frantumati," by Ramzi Harrabi. Siracusa, Italy, 2016. Reproduced with the permission of Ramzi Harrabi. Photo by permission of Cristiana Giordano.

of boatloads of people crossing seas (Chapter 5), and his installation, "Museo dei sogni frantumati" (Museum of fractured dreams), made of shoes, belts, hats, water bottles, photos, books, empty cans, faded documents, life jackets, and backpacks recuperated at ports, beaches, and boat cemeteries. François Koltès, a French artist and collector and a Siracusa resident, contributed an installation entitled "La marche de l'abysse" (The walk by the abyss) composed of *papier mâché* bodies hanging from the ceiling and forming a disordered line of what resembled walking corpses (Figure 8). Through this artwork, Koltès envisioned a museum of the future that hosted the bodies—or the ghostly remnants—of those who died during the crossing of the Mediterranean. Elisabeth Atkinson, a British artist based in Sicily, had a series of silk scarves painted in abstract tones hanging throughout the Church, adding a poetic and soft touch to the event. The entrance to the exhibit was free, with a basket for donations placed on the floor by the main door of the Church. The money collected from donations and the selling of art went to fund projects that Ramzi was running with migrant youth, especially those hosted in shelters for unaccompanied minors where he worked.

Ramzi is an educator, cultural mediator, artist, activist. He is a citizen of Siracusa who moved from Tunisia over twenty-five years ago. He runs an

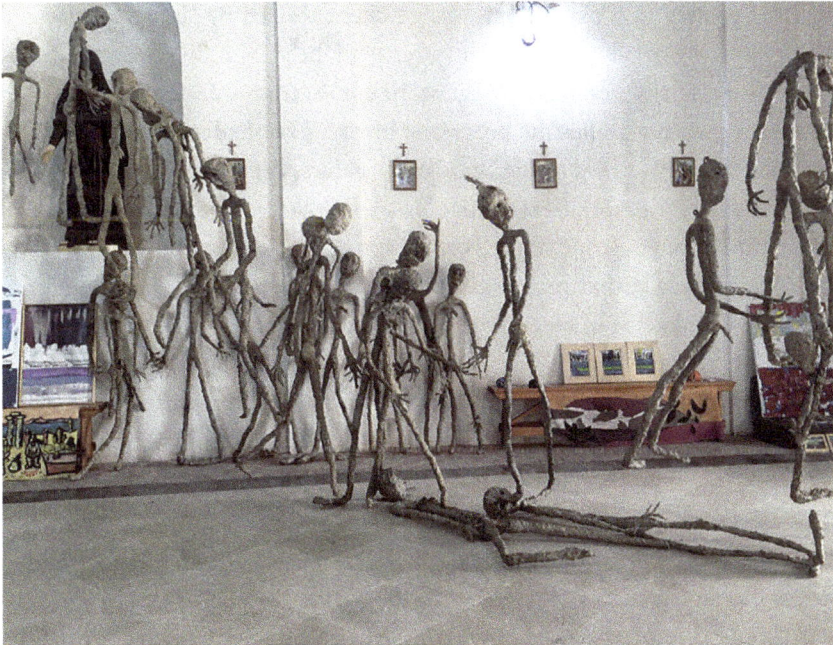

Figure 8 "La marche de l'abysse," by François Koltès. Siracusa, Italy, 2016. Photo by Cristiana Giordano.

intercultural and interfaith center and works for different institutions as a translator and social worker around issues of immigration and integration. We met on an early morning in August, 2015, as I was walking around the old part of town, Ortigia, and he was setting up the same art installation in the square in front of his center. We became fast friends and started thinking together about projects around movement and borders. The following summer, we decided to do a theater workshop with a group of young African men, and I was there to develop it with him.

Before that summer morning in Porto Palo, I had visited other boat cemeteries. There are several of them scattered throughout Italy. In Lampedusa, a few years back, I walked around the fenced area of the dump—or cemetery, as the Lampedusians call it—where confiscated boats are kept. For a moment, I felt I was part of what has been described as "dark tourism" (Horsti 2019: 56), wandering through sites associated with the "refugee crisis" and relating all sorts of images of precariousness and violence to what I glimpsed through the fences.

At Porto Palo, the debris of the shipwrecks that Ramzi and I explored made me think of what novelist Elena Ferrante, in a completely different context, calls *frantumaglia*. For her, *la frantumaglia*—a Neapolitan dialect word—describes a sense of loss and uncertainty enveloping the mind and body at certain moments in life. It refers to a psychological state characterized by "bits and pieces of uncertain origin [that] rattle around in your head not always comfortably" (cited in Ferri and Ferri 2015). The word comes from *frantumazione*, a noun in Italian, which signifies the process of breaking or shattering, and *frantume*, another noun, referring to the shards themselves. Although Ferrante uses the term to evoke a sense of existential loss, a labyrinth of emotions one can be caught in without escape, there is something very material in the root of the word *frantumaglia* that makes it evocative of the enmeshment of things and emotions, fragments of objects and the affects that emanate from and stick to them. Ferrante says more: "The *frantumaglia* is the storehouse of time without the orderliness of a history, a story. [It] is an effect of the sense of loss, when we're sure that everything that seems to us stable, lasting, an anchor for our life, will soon join that landscape of debris that we seem to see" (Ferrante 2016: 100).

The Church

From the landscape where Ramzi collects debris for his art, we moved back to his studio at the Church, where he was working on the "Museo dei sogni frantumati."

He reassembled everything in an installation that staged the fragmented and deadly nature of the crossing. He scattered the collected objects—or what remained of them—on the wreck of a boat: an unpaired shoe, ripped documents, a torn Koran, unopened cans of food, a fish net, life jackets, empty water bottles, a necklace, prayer mats, a flip-flop, some straw baskets. The whole installation was meant to perform the traces of the crossing, a testament to what doesn't make it into news headlines or political debates on border crossings. To me, it also resonated with the impermanence and performativity of materials, the ways in which waste can be presented to people as their own discarded material turned into art, and how objects and things in performances and installations can be active players "along side rather than behind" their human collaborators (Schweitzer and Zerdy 2014: 6). In the midst of what looked like waste and garbage, apparently unimportant details (Ginzburg 1980, Fabietti 2012), or a *frantumaglia* of things that had lost "the orderliness of a history" and the coherence of a story (Ferrante 2016), his installation also provided a holding, or a sort of shelter, of the absence of those who died during the journey and did not make it to the port. It displayed that which cannot be funneled through the official channels, and doesn't get translated through the various phases of the *sbarco* into one of the state's categories of recognition ("asylum seeker," "refugee," "victim of human trafficking").[1]

In the context of current migrations to Europe, corpses are often left unburied and unnamed, or abandoned in what is becoming a cemetery at sea. The debris and the corpses remain uncaptured by the logic of state recognition (Stoetzer 2018); as traces, they evoke an absence that stays open to meaning (Derrida 1967); as objects, they are "the material expression of death that eludes our ultimate knowing" (Bollas 2009: 33). In this sense, Ramzi's installation differs from the fixity of the museum. As waste, on the other hand, the debris is represented as that element of dirt and savagery that is supposed to lie outside the state's jurisdiction but that also threatens it from within (Das and Poole 2004). Ramzi's curation recuperates it from its disposable state, and positions it as a full living object that conjures the living and the dead. The debris comes to matter as a remnant and, in this sense, it is cared for. Ramzi's intervention is in tune with the disposition toward minor details—that Ginzburg attributes to the *processo indiziario*, and that Fabietti poses as a research posture—because he knows that the debris of the shipwreck conveys a different story, usually untold through official discourses.

Official discourse about migration revolves around statistics, sensational accounts of the crossing, images of masses on the move, of wired walls, of definite boundaries, and the dichotomies that go with them (legal/illegal, victim/criminal). It is to counter the tyranny of literality and its failure to account for what falls outside official discourse, that Ramzi's art takes shape. By the tyranny of literality I mean the language of sovereign power that dictates the conditions under which certain categories of people are legal or not, desirable or not, deserving protection or not, based on stories that the state hears only in a literal way. His installation and his paintings of boatloads of people are both opaque and evocative; they work as antidotes to the violence of the media and the documentary. The elusiveness and poignancy of the remnants from the shipwreck are at odds with the literality of the state, while also evoking its blind spots, the things and accounts that are overlooked, pushed aside, of those who died or remained undetected, and whose presence resonates in the literal as well as in the fiction of both documents and art. The debris interrupts the linearity of official narratives. Visitors and passersby at Ramzi's exhibit often commented, in writing or spoken comments, how the paintings and installations transported them into an emotional and affective field. What they had only apprehended, up to that moment, through journalistic commentaries or news footage as a harsh but somewhat distant reality had become an experience through art.

In his work on history, memory, and the work of the unconscious, Michel de Certeau understood traces as the leftovers of histories (1992) that don't fit into the master narrative of the present (Napolitano 2015). The installation consigns the traces of those who survived and those who died during the crossing to another order of possibility. Lost objects bear witness to those whose stories of life and death are not documented in the state archive, which translates them into manageable categories and erases the traces of the shipwrecks. Ramzi's assemblage becomes a different kind of harbor, or point of arrival of the dead, which attends to the wrecks in the fullness of their scattered presence. It provides an affective archive that shows the limits of linear representation (Navaro-Yashin 2012). In some ways, his installation re-stories the remnants, restoring an order (the installation) where they have a place. The decayed objects are delivered in the language of art, which stages absence. Telling a story through the debris is a way of accounting for the humans they are/were a part of. Debris, as trace, is imbued with an uncanny doubleness; it is presence and absence simultaneously; it performs a story in the partial absence of its object/subject/content. Debris differs from the archeological remnant or the archival document in so far as the artistic framework wherein it is placed opens up its evocative power rather than fixing it in a sanctioned and institutionalized meaning, something the museum or the archive may aim to do.

Ramzi's work resonates with Affect Theater. His installations are series of associations of objects, space, light, and the humans (e.g., artist, visitors, curators) who interact with them. In our workshop, when we play with elements of the stage to make theatrical episodes we search for their theatrical rather than narrative potential, their evocative rather than literal force, to explore their sensorial qualities rather than to make them function in the ways they commonly do. The "Museo dei sogni frantumati" is akin to an Affect Theater episode, a performative moment made of different elements and their affective interactions.

Displaced Objects

In the last ten years, an emerging art inspired by the "refugee crisis" has increasingly drawn from the aesthetics and materiality of objects left behind during the crossing. Objects similar to those Ramzi collected and curated in the Church populate art exhibits, installations, sections of museums and galleries, films, and performances by prominent and less-known artists and activists around the world (Barry 2019). While it appears to be a new genre in and of itself, the use of objects and debris to represent the humans who once used them has characterized art at other critical moments and in other contexts.[2] In all these instances, objects stand for the resurrection of a remnant so that their anonymous owner can be committed to memory (Sanyal 2017: 11), and the dead can be conjured into the present.[3]

In the context of the contemporary, objects such as lifejackets, shoes, documents, clothes, belts, and boat parts have become symbolic of borders and their violence; they evoke feelings ranging from compassion and sympathy toward those on the move to rage and disgust toward the systems that sustain forced migrations and the necropolitics of borders. Scholars have questioned to what extent, for instance, these artworks create a sense of empathy and compassion toward those who migrate in order to counter populist discourses and interventions that intend to build new walls and forms of exclusion (Barry 2019), or whether they contribute to the "image fatigue" produced by the visual overload surrounding the "refugee crisis," and to the emotional exhaustion of being interpellated into sympathy for the victim again and again. Critics have noted that this kind of art—some call it "humanitarian art" or "refugee art"— may in fact generalize the experience of mobility and suffering at the expense of individual specific stories, universalizing an idea of humanity that sidesteps the recognition of political, social, and cultural difference (Kirtsoglou and Tsimouris 2016, cited in Yalouri 2019). In other words, this emerging artform can have different paradoxical and contradictory effects on the public: it can humanize the refugee while also erasing their individuality; generalize and memorialize the plight of those on the move, while also problematizing it; activate a sense of civic and political responsibility while also numbing and saturating the public with images of death (Khoo 2017 cited in Yalouri 2019). As Dorinne Kondo asks in relation to theater productions and identity politics in the United States: Does this kind of installation re-inscribe a humanist subject, producing the danger of empathy? (Kondo 2018) Or rather, I ask: Are these artworks a different kind of documentary project that is not necessarily about the human, but about a form of presence and agency that is human and nonhuman simultaneously? Perhaps the anonymous and generic quality of these material objects allows the spectator "to live in the visual, not the verbal, order" (Bollas 2009: 37), and to rest with the nameless and spiritual potential of materials.[4]

These questions deserve reflection. In Ramzi's installation, I see his use of objects—or what remains of them—as a form of translation of scattered materials into memory, a crossing from being an isolated object to an event interwoven with other events, people, movements, agencies. In memory and through artistic metamorphosis, the object is part of an assemblage of materials, intentions, audiences, discourses, people, practices, and places (Yalouri 2019, see Yalouri 2019). The remnant is not only used to humanize the refugee, but to highlight something more complex that problematizes the centrality of the human, and the usual dichotomies of subject/object, human/nonhuman. That is, an assemblage has an agency of its own that is constituted by the ways in which "people, animals, artifacts, technologies, and elemental forces share powers and operate in dissonant conjunction with each other" (Bennet 2010: 34). It operates through a "distributive agency" (Bennett 2010: 21) where all the materialities that shape a piece of art are agents and the artwork itself performs through the relations of a variety of elements affecting one another in a continuum (Barad 2003, Jones 2015).[5] Unlike the assemblage of the *sbarco* at the port, which is mostly articulated through practices of state recognition, Ramzi's art moves the lost objects to an order different from the law and its politics of identification, reinscribing that which exceeds the funnel (the dead and the lawless) within a curation—or assemblage—that resonates with a minor language.

His art unfolds from within a dominant grammar of crisis and migration, but with an "accent" that is incarnated in the debris he recuperates, the wreckage of the shipwreck that holds them, and the choices he makes on where to install the exhibits. Ramzi uses the material that state discourses on migration discard and relegate to the order of waste; he recuperates it—and cares for it—as a "language" that tells a story otherwise. However, his re-storying is not a restoration; he reshuffles objects, shows their disorder and chaos, and thus breaks them again, or simply shows their brokenness and loneliness. He operates from within an official idiom that frames the question of movement and borders in terms of migration and crisis, and through clear-cut categories of recognition ("the victim," "the migrant," "the refugee," etc.) and he re-stories it.[6] His work displaces a story from the underworld to the unconsecrated altar, from the order of waste to that of art. It reverberates through affective and associative forces, assembling materials, spaces, humans, and emotions. Objects as traces and minor details (Ginzburg 1980) reveal a story that could not otherwise be unveiled. What I call traces and "minor" are so from the perspective of the state and its languages. From its minor position, the debris has the power to reconfigure and deterritorialize the very discourse that has positioned it as minor.

In Ramzi's work, the debris creates a shift in points of view, an estrangement. The installation at the Church of Maria e Gesù is not a way to restore the humanity of the refugee, but to re-story movement in relation to the tyranny of the state's single story of migration and borders, to locate the story in the complexities of relations of which it is part. It doesn't completely un-story migration and borders, but it challenges the sensational crisis narrative of the state by foregrounding the force of objects and the spaces where they perform, a wordless and evocative narrative imbued with the silences of material traces.

Evocative Objects

The "Museo dei sogni frantumati" made me think of Italo Calvino's *Invisible Cities* and the imagined encounter between Marco Polo, the Venetian explorer, and the Kublai Khan, the emperor of the vast Mongol Empire, during Marco's travels in the East. In Calvino's rendering, Marco describes fifty-five cities to Kublai through poetic prose; he accounts for cities and their sounds, smells, lights, and moods. What is most compelling in this book, though, are the interruptions in Polo's descriptions. Every five to ten cities, an interlude about the conversations between Marco and the Khan makes the reader reflect upon the nature of communication, the work of the imagination, and the production of knowledge. Kublai wants to hear about the cities that Marco explores and that belong to his empire but that he himself has never visited. But Marco doesn't speak the emperor's language, nor does the Khan speak Marco's. The Venetian explorer uses everything he has at his disposal to tell.

> Newly arrived and quite ignorant of the languages of the Levant, Marco Polo could express himself only by drawing objects from his baggage—drums, salt fish, necklaces of wart hogs' teeth—and pointing to them with gestures, leaps, cries of wonder or of horror, imitating the bay of the jackal, the hoot of the owl. The connection between one element of the story and another were not always obvious to the emperor; the objects could have various meanings: a quiver filled with arrows could indicate the approach of war, or an abundance of game, or else an armorer's shop; an hourglass could mean time passing, or time past, or sand, or a place where hourglasses are made. (Calvino 1974: 38)

The emperor understands and sees his empire through the explorer's performance and the objects he utilizes. This mute, wordless commentary is Marco's way of telling stories about memory and loss, death and beauty, streets and canals, buildings and fields. Despite the lack of words, his accounts carry the force of a real story that is capable of lasting over time (Benjamin 1968). Such force also derives from the silence that pervades Marco's narration: "[W]hat enhanced for Kublai every event or piece of news reported by his inarticulate informer was the space that remained around it, a void not filled with words" (Calvino 1974: 38).

This "space around," devoid of the verbal, allows for a wandering that is not a way of understanding and interpreting a story; it is a space of physical wandering around objects, in their materiality and evocative force. Ramzi does not interpret the objects, but brings them together in a way that can mean different things or nothing. Just as Calvino's Marco Polo uses his own imagination to narrate cities through objects, space, and gestures, Ramzi performs a free association in space through objects and the very setting of the square, the unconsecrated church, or, the Strasbourg European Parliament, where he exhibited his artwork. What the objects themselves summon is in part determined by the public discourse on migration and borders, but they also reverberate other things, depending on the staging and the relations made possible by spectators and audiences that wander through them and imagine other scenarios and associations.

As mentioned in Chapter 1, Christopher Bollas's writing on the evocative world of objects extends the domain of free association from the dimension of ideas and thoughts to the world of actual objects, their materiality and affective charge.[7] Objects, like thoughts, allow us to create connections and associations that enable experience beyond the rational and the cognitive. In relating to

Ramzi's art and in my experimentation with elements of the stage in Affect Theater, I have found objects to be ways of thinking and experiencing, analytical tools and concepts in and of themselves. For Bollas, free association—as the psychoanalytic method of inquiry that is counter to what is represented as a logical and rational way of knowing—is not only the apparently illogical and subversive movement of ideas and thoughts (which the patient makes to access the unconscious), but also a "movement of action."

> Inner mental life and lived experience in the real are, of course, inseparable. Yet we can note how one's meandering in the real—moving from thing to thing—can in itself be a form of reverie that constitutes thinking in the real.... Thought that evolves out of lived encounters in the real—juxtaposed to thoughts arising purely from mind alone—bear the marks of life. (2009: 53)

Meandering through Ramzi's display of material things in the world—just like we meander in the workshop—is a form of free association which opens affective ways of "knowing" beyond the cognitive. Objects can act as processes, ways of thinking-by-action, and of experiencing the thing-ness of life. Marco Polo relied on the evocative power of objects when he lacked Kublai Khan's language to describe cities with words; he created assemblages of objects that came to signify or evoke things, in an endless associative performance of images.

The installation evokes through its form and the objects, an evocation that allows for aspects of the unthought of the "crisis" to be glimpsed or felt.[8] It takes form before making meaning, it reverberates before presenting, and it evokes before representing. Form blends with content. Assemblage communicates and allows visitors to associate. As Greg and I write in Chapter 1, when we devise ethnographic episodes with the elements of the stage, "we practice a form of associative thinking in space that brings to the fore aspects of the material that are not apparent if we interpret them through their literal meanings only" (p. 22).

Both Marco Polo's performances for Kublai Khan and Ramzi's installation share what Elena Ferrante calls *frantumaglia*,[9] the sense that things and emotions are enmeshed, that splinters of objects mingle with a blurred sense of self, that objects we are drawn to and that are drawn to us are forms of the ways in which we unconsciously "know." The associative is an oscillation of affects, images, thoughts, and things through which we access the "unthought known" of the empirical material, something that can only be experienced, not fully spoken about (Bollas 2009: 54). In making theatrical episodes, too, we oscillate between affects, elements of the stage, the spectators' imagination, and the empirical material of our research in order to perform a lived experience that may never be spoken about.

The European Parliament

Overall, I was intrigued by Ramzi's installation, not so much as an aesthetic assemblage but as an act of creation and invention. In his work, art becomes a form of *errance*, typical not only of our objects of inquiry that move around, but also of our anthropological endeavor (Fabietti 2012: 15). Ramzi literally transported objects from one place (the dump, the beach, the boat cemetery) to another (his studio, the church, the installation). For him, translation becomes an act of staging. This transposition allowed him to perform a scene where the dead could be alluded to, and the shipwreck acknowledged. It resembled an act of simulation where the dead are not literally displayed—as in a funerary ritual or a tomb—but are evoked by remnants of objects. The installation staged the undocumented and the dead so they can be mourned, and attended to, even though unnamed. As a whole, it re-signified the debris and moved it from the status of disposable waste to what Cassirer called "organs of reality" (Cassirer 1946: 8). For Cassirer, symbols don't mimic the reality they stand for; they are themselves organs of that very reality. The "Museo dei sogni frantumati" is not symbolic because it stands in place of the dead, but because it becomes the reality of the shipwreck itself that can be apprehended only through an oblique act of creation, a nonlinear story line, and the materiality of what remains. The materiality of the shipwreck is not a metaphor for the dead, but it is the way in which the dead stay among the living in a transformed way—a metamorphosis of sort—as a ghost, as a story, as a fragment of reality.[10]

As it erred elsewhere, the installation performed something else. In the fall of 2015, Ramzi was invited to bring it to the European Parliament in Strasbourg. A delegation of Italian congressmen from the Italian Democratic Party sponsored his travel and the setup of the installation in the plenary session hall. Renato Soru, the European congressman who organized the event, framed it as a testimony of the shipwreck that is often eclipsed in its tragic consequences. Alarmed by the numbers of deaths in the Mediterranean, he linked the current "migration crisis" to a "new Holocaust" occurring in the middle of the sea. To him, the scattered objects of Ramzi's installation recalled the mountains of shoes and random objects amassed in concentration camps. Soru's idea was to bring awareness of the violence of migration to the heart of European politics.

In his words, "Bringing these objects inside the plenary session means that the shipwreck has arrived right here. We hope this will force people to take responsibility for it."[11]

The Strasbourg installation performed yet another translation, in a literal and symbolic way. It continued to perform what Ramzi had intended: bearing witness to those who didn't make it to the other side of the sea, and to those parts of their stories that cannot be rendered in an official archive. Yet, using the European Parliament as a stage allowed a different kind of statement. It raised the question of the relation between aesthetics and ethics (Yalouri 2019), of how the installation relates to the traces of the shipwrecked. But it also begged for a deeper reflection on aesthetics and the law. How to welcome into the law those who have remained lawless and lost at sea? In Strasbourg, the installation consigned these traces to the sphere of international law, in an attempt to challenge law's self-understanding as punitive. On the one hand, it staged an ethics of hospitality and its potential to disrupt the law from its biopolitical distinction between the living and the dead. On the other hand, the installation implicitly stated that it is the very law that produces death, and the debris that is damned to be forgotten and disposed of. It is also on the grounds of this forgetfulness that the law is constituted and sustained.

There is another way in which I think with Ramzi's work. It relates to the question of heterotopias and difference that institutional grammars produce within their own cracks. If we understand heterotopias as spaces of radical otherness that disturb shared discourses, where categories no longer hold, and institutional languages are shattered and unable to name experience (Foucault 1994: xviii), Ramzi's urge to collect the traces of the shipwreck is a way to care for the unnamable of the crossing. His installation is occasioned by the bodies and objects that the *sbarco*—as an assemblage of practices and places that regulate the arrival of people—doesn't detect, or simply cannot account for. Ramzi recuperates the debris that makes up this form of heterotopia and reorganizes it into an installation. He rearranges the heterotopia by staging it so that it can be apprehended by a European audience, be that the European Parliament or the passersby on the streets of Ortigia who are surprised to see the remnants of the crossing on what was once the Church's altar.

Ramzi's art does not create another world/reality. He relocates a *topos*, moving it from the underwater to the surface, from the garbage pile to the altar, from the Southern port to the heart of European political power, so that it can be witnessed. This slip mirrors a difference (*hetero*), but it does not create a completely other place (*topos*). His work does not call for a radical invention of a new community which may emerge from a catastrophe (Giordano 2016). The museum of fractured dreams does allow for a different perspective on movement, where crisis is not the main lens through which events are understood (as it is for the nation-state), but another category that has left some details and stories at its fringe, to be picked up and cared for by a minor perspective such as Ramzi's.

In our friendship, I have listened to Ramzi's work in terms of traces recuperated and curated so that they can evoke the experience of the crossing or of what remains of it. It has taught me to listen to the debris as a minor detail that allows for an account of what crisis-grammar forecloses. The minor details that I follow in this chapter as ethnographic sites are also what exceed the port and the *sbarco*. They are an excess that falls outside the purview of the nation-state's politics of recognition; they are what cannot be translated through practices of identification, whether biometrical or confessional and biographical (Giordano 2015). They fall out of the master narrative of history, and they elude the official archive. They belong to an affective archive that Ramzi's installation collects and displays, and that the anthropologist curates into fragmentary stories that are more experiment than interpretation.

What are the other worlds that the *sbarco* sets in motion without capturing or controlling, like the objects Ramzi recuperates from the dump and end up on the altar? What falls through the cracks of the port of entry, creating other spaces of life and death? Spaces don't exist *a priori*; they emerge as effects of practices and the relations enabled by them. The *sbarco*, in all its complexity and layers, is a world-making process that exceeds itself and what it encompasses.

Association #3

A Hole in the Fence

Cristiana Giordano

One late morning at the end of summer, we left Foggia to reach one of the *ghettos* in the middle of the agricultural fields of this part of southern Italy where seasonal workers (mostly foreign men) live and work throughout the year. *Ghetto* is the name that seasonal workers and the Italian media use to refer to the encampments where workers live during the harvest, and often end up staying for lack of other living and working situations. Here, they are mostly involved in forms of exploitation also known, today, as *caporalato*: a system by which labor is paid below the national minimum wage through the black market, and people are put to work in precarious conditions that often lead to death. There is a larger economy in southern Italy—of which the *ghettos* are a product—based on centuries of landowners' exploitation of Italian peasants, low wages, lack of contracts, and control of the agricultural labor market by organized crime.

My traveling companions on that morning were another team from Emergency. Omar, Emergency's Senegalese cultural mediator, used to work on the mobile clinic that provided health care to those in need in this area twice a week up to when their project stopped operating a few years before. Laura and Greta—an Italian and a Bulgarian cultural mediators—had also worked at this encampment in the past and were now collaborating with Claudia, the project manager, to do follow-up research.[1] A year prior to our trip, they had asked me to supervise a book project about their medical interventions in this part of the country, where they used to run mobile clinics in areas mostly unserved by the national health care system, whether because they were too remote or off the institutional radar. The amount of clinical and statistical material covering the last ten years of their interventions lacked the more personal narratives of both care providers and patients, which they wanted to incorporate in their book project. We decided to do some fieldwork together, spending time in the sites where their clinics are or were operative, conducting interviews with policy makers and local stakeholders, and conversing with the people who live in the shantytowns and work in the agricultural fields.[2]

On that morning, we drove toward Borgo Creto, several miles from Foggia. Before arriving in the borough, I asked my traveling companions to describe the *ghetto* for me, and their impressions of the very first time they went there. I wanted to imagine this particular place through their memories before forming my own. Claudia remembered the café in the main square of the village where, as she put it, "The owner doesn't talk, he growls (*ringhia*)" to people, especially if they are black. Laura and Greta also remembered people from the village as fairly "racist and insufferable." The café owner's growl evoked a chilling effect, one produced by language becoming animal sound, and thus morphing how people are addressed and treated. It evoked a way of relating to others outside the symbolic power of language, through the collapse of meaning that leaves room for shameless and violent treatment. Does the owner mirror and repeat what he hears as the non-language of the other? In some places, people die from having this done to them.

With these images in mind, we drove through the center of the borough, where I recognized the fascist-style church on one side and the town café on the other. By the time we got there, it was early afternoon and people were indoors for lunch and siesta. Everything was shut down. The square had a deserted feel to it, except for a group of African men waiting at the bus stop. Just past the square, we took a fairly narrow, dusty road, following the sign *centro di accoglienza* (reception center). At the end of it appeared the C.A.R.A., the *Centro di Accoglienza per Richiedenti Asilo* (Reception Center for Asylum Seekers). Once a military zone with its airport and administrative buildings, the whole complex had been turned into a shelter.

This part of Italy is marked by a particular history. The countryside is punctuated by various *borghi* (boroughs, villages) that were built during the fascist era as part of a project of *bonifica*, of reclaiming lands. *Bonifica* was central to many discourses of fascist modernity. It started as a conversion of swampland into arable soil, unusable lands into agricultural fields, but it soon turned into the fascists' desire to purify the nation of all social and cultural ills. *Bonificare* saw human society as an organism that could be manipulated by means of a vast surgical operation (Ben-Ghiat 2001). According to Ruth Ben-Ghiat, "The campaigns for agricultural reclamation (*bonifica agricola*), human reclamation (*bonifica umana*), and cultural reclamation (*bonifica della cultura*), together with the anti-Jewish laws, [were] different facets and phases of a comprehensive project to combat degeneration and radically renew Italian society by pulling up the bad weeds and cleaning up the soil" (4).[3] The lands once reclaimed by the fascist regime are now left to their own demise, except when they are "reclaimed" anew by foreign seasonal workers or those who exploit their labor. Though, of course, reclaiming here has a different feel to it than the fascist project. It stands for occupying these fields for lack of other living situations, and for using them to house undocumented workers in precarious makeshift shelters.

We reached the end of the road and parked in front of the wired gate of the old military airport. We began walking along the fenced zone, observing the desolate landscape around us. I could see the old edifices of the airport, and behind them a series of new containers built to expand the capacity of the reception center. There was a marked difference between the two parts of the fenced area: the old buildings of the airport base housed those who had applied for asylum through the official channels. These buildings had bars on the windows and looked poorly maintained; clothes were hanging from the windows, which were for the most part closed or darkened. The containers, on the other hand, which also housed asylum seekers, were painted shining white and looked sparkling clean. Their almost-aseptic look contrasted with the piles of bicycle parts amassed outside on the concrete, along with piles of plastic, cardboard, and other waste. This contrast somehow suggested to me that the current use of the fenced area was foreign to its initial design, adding a layer of alienation to an already desolate scenery.

We kept walking along the dusty trail, flanked by broken glass, plastic bottles, and other sorts of debris, toward the countryside. Skirting the C.A.R.A., we found ourselves at a stretch on our right, and in front of us an expanse of shacks that had developed outside of the fenced zone, adjacent to it. After a few minutes of slow walking, we arrived at what we later came to refer to as *il buco* (the hole): a breach in the fence that surrounded the old airport (now a reception center), and through which a continuous flux of people passed in and out of the military zone. The hole was just a few meters away from one of the main gates to the C.A.R.A. where two armed policemen stood, knowing but indifferent. On the other side of the hole was a vast shantytown, bristling with activity of all sorts. People, bicycles, animals, merchandise, food, and objects of various kinds passed through the hole in the fence. The shantytown was immense and offered all sorts of access to goods, services, social interactions, and exchanges that the fenced and guarded area did not allow. It had developed along the three-kilometer-long former *pista* (landing strip) that once served for the general operations of the airport. The *pista* functioned as the primary arterial road around which the shantytown was being built.

The shacks were elaborate in that they were made from various recycled materials: beams of wood, doors, glass, tubes, cardboard, nails, planks, strings, bicycle parts. While we walked we saw men who were making new shelters, transporting materials in the trunks of cars, hammering and sawing, constructing with makeshift stakes found by chance. Some of the shacks were designated as restaurants and stores for clothing, shoes, bicycle parts, car tires, food, and hardware. All materials were recuperated from landfills, dumpsters, or perhaps from warehouses of charitable organizations, and were then resold and repurposed here. In some cases, the same kind of debris that ended up in Ramzi's art (Chapters 4 and 5) were used to build a shelter to live in, a grill to cook, or a bicycle to get around. But while Ramzi's installation reorganized a *topos* without creating a new one, here one had the feeling of entering a *topos* of another kind, one that thrived through a vibrant chaos or unruly logic, as if it was the negative of the image of the disciplined area inside the fence.

As we stopped by a shack that functioned as a taxi station for the *ghetto* (a banner said: "If you need a taxi, call here"), Omar explained to me that collecting construction materials had become a profitable occupation for the inhabitants of the shantytown—to the point that some didn't work in the agricultural fields any longer. Other commercial activities within the *ghetto* have emerged that are more lucrative than the seasonal harvests. The inhabitants of today's shantytowns find various forms of income beyond the harvest because of the pervasiveness of the black market, of which the shantytown is only a small aspect and product. People have been able to build an economy and infrastructure at the margins of the state that constitute an alternative world not yet mapped nor managed by it, but that operates alongside it and in its interstices.

Back at the *pista*, the landing strip, Laura, who used to work on the mobile clinic that served the *ghetto*, explained that the Muslims lived on one side of the strip, which was also where all the cats of the *ghetto* gathered. The Christians occupied the other half of the strip, where all the dogs settled. Each species running around their respective side of the *pista*—many skinny, a little battered—were making a life with the humans. In the middle of the *pista*, car seats functioned as traffic dividers, cars slaloming between them. From the *pista* itself, smaller alleys developed in asymmetrical and irregular forms, out toward the vast countryside. The state country road we had taken to get to the shantytown, bumpy and narrow, could turn hellish during the rainy season, with deep and wide potholes that made driving and walking a dangerous endeavor.

On this particular research trip to Borgo Creto, we met several people who had lived in the informal settlement for a long time and collected their reflections and frustrations on the conditions of life, access to health care, and work contracts. We met with the international group of activists running Radio Ghetto, a radio program of music, testimonies, and stories done in collaboration with the people of the *ghetto*. We also spent time just sitting and being there. This was the purpose of our time there, getting a sense of the general conditions of life so that we could share a series of reports with the larger public and improve the NGOs services to these communities.

When we retraced our steps back to the car, again we passed by the *buco*—the hole in the fence. Aside from the usual traffic of people that passed through, this time there was a sheep tied to the fence, in preparation for Eid, the end of Ramadan, a few days later. It was late afternoon when we started driving back to Foggia. The sky turned black. It started raining as lightning and thunder struck. From the car windows the countryside suddenly looked blurred, muddier, and dustier. Everything seemed to move slower: animals, humans, cars, and clouds, with the exception of the grass and trees, which were slapped by a wind that grew stronger by the minute.

When I revisited this walk through the *ghetto,* I started to think about the *buco* in the fence as one of the "tiny details" Ginzburg (1980) and Fabietti (2012) invite us to attend to, a minor detail that is deemed marginal—a defect in the fence—but that evokes something of the institutions and the *ghettos* that is not visible at first. As a site in and of itself, the *buco* also resonates with Anna Tsing's idea of the frontiers as "particular kinds of edges" that "are deregulated because they arise in the interstitial spaces made by collaborations among legitimate and illegitimate partners. . . . They confuse the boundaries of law and theft, governance and violence, use and destruction. These confusions change the rules and thus enable extravagant new economies of profit—as well as loss" (Tsing 2005: 27). Tsing further writes that frontiers are "imaginative projects" (32), zones "of not yet—not yet mapped, not yet regulated" (28). Following these reflections, the *buco* appears as a site that, despite being produced at the margin of the institution, and partially by the institution itself, is not yet mapped, not yet captured. It doesn't demarcate a here and there but creates instead a space of disorientation where the inside and outside of the reception center and the shantytown are blurred and unmappable. This confusion enables a certain kind of creativity that, as Deborah Thomas explains, is often "materialized through profound violence" (2011: 45), and can easily lead to destruction. It is a creation that doesn't follow the linearity of progress (Tsing 2015), nor of history, but that creates the worlds in which most of the people who are funneled at ports of entry and borders end up forging their existence.

While the *buco* is the product of a "collaboration" among the institution and the informal world, it also operates as a scene of flight through which uncharted places emerge and develop in unexpected and precarious ways. The shantytown itself is one of them, with all its commerce, cultural production, and political organizations. There are also political groups that formed inside the encampment that work for the rights and safety of seasonal workers and collaborate with Italian NGOs for fair treatment. These places take on a life-form of their own, while remaining intrinsically interwoven with the practices of state identification and recognition that, in Borgo Creto, are incarnated in the reception center within the fence. These worlds live side by side, implicated in one another by holes in the walls that allow people, objects, animals, waste, and debris to move in, out, and around. The *ghettos* are worlds that host undocumented foreigners and people who have been documented for a long time, have lost their regular jobs, and have moved near the agricultural fields to sustain themselves seasonally. These places resemble Ferrante's *frantumaglia* that has lost the orderliness of a history (2016); they often remain unrecognized because they do not fit into common categories of recognition. In the midst of great precarity, the waste and debris that would normally go unnoticed become not only world-making, but also a clue, or a symptom, of how laws and institutions work by producing their opposites—lawless and parallel worlds—as their excess.

Like the artist who reassembles the traces of shipwrecks, and the people of the *ghetto* who repurpose waste to make an alternative life-form for themselves, as an anthropologist I have reassembled pieces that fall through the cracks of institutions and pass through the holes of fences to attend to the presences and absences of bodies, words, and objects that disappear in major accounts. Resonating to and with that which occurs beyond and through the fences of the port and the old airport/shelter is not to provide a truer account, but to create a confusion in the linearity of stories about migration and borders. It is to think with the chaos that animates the holes that power simultaneously creates and is challenged by. This communion with waste and chaos is also a commitment to a minor perspective that is always political and challenges the violence of categories and the fixity of stories. It allows for a listening that is simultaneously attuned to what is uttered and what is kept silent, to the human who crosses borders and the nonhuman that keeps it company, to the literality of categories and the ambivalence of experience.

Ways of Drawing

Beyond "Refugee Crisis"

Cristiana Giordano

Enter the Artists and Their Paintings

On an unusually hot summer morning, Ramzi and I left Siracusa to drive to a shelter for unaccompanied foreign migrants located inland, an hour from the coast, where he worked as a cultural broker for the doctor on duty. The shelter was in an old hotel in the middle of nowhere: a reception structure that hosted foreign minors who were waiting to apply for papers or file for asylum. At the time, it hosted 136 young men. The site itself was pleasant. The surrounding fields of cacti and orange trees punctuated the otherwise desert-like landscape with dots of intense green. The location was isolated, with no public transportation available. To walk to the closest village, several miles away, one had to cross open fields in the full sun or walk along the same interstate road we had used to get there, also known as *la strada della morte* (the death road) because of the number of accidents that happen there. When we arrived, there were young men playing table football on the porch, others were in the big hall at the entrance watching TV, others were walking in and out of the back doors, aimlessly—some would say they were *bighellonando* (Preface). A police van was parked outside, surrounded by policemen chatting with one another. One of them approached Ramzi to ask him who I was. Without police clearance, I was not supposed to be there, but Ramzi "smuggled" me in, as he put it, by saying I was his driver. He enjoys doing this kind of thing, and so do I.

The doctor, a man in his late fifties, arrived exhausted and disoriented. It was his first day of work at the shelter. Ramzi led him inside his office and put some chairs in the corridor, so that I and those who wanted to see the doctor could sit and wait. Young men from Ghana, Gambia, Mali, Senegal, and Nigeria gathered outside the doctor's office. They were all talkative. They showed pictures and short videos of themselves rapping on their cell phones. One of them performed for us. They talked about the camp and how they didn't like being there. "It is too far from everything," they complained, and they had nothing to do during the day. They wanted to practice sports, play soccer. The only regular activity was Italian lessons a couple of hours a week.

The wait to see the doctor was long. I started showing them pictures on my cell phone. I had several photos of Ramzi's paintings and installation from Uprooted, the event at the unconsecrated church (Chapter 4). I spent several summer evenings in the company of his work and of the viewers who stopped to look at it. In his works, boats are a recurrent theme (Figure 9). The paintings are poetic in their simplicity and repetition, and his work is conscientious and skillful in the use of images that evoke the journeys on overcrowded vessels. His art engages the language of crisis—without necessarily questioning it—by translating experience into images of the crossing, with the awareness that there is a market for it. His playfulness with the grammar of crisis, though, is important

Figure 9 Uprooted series, by Ramzi Harrabi © Ramzi Harrabi 2016. Reproduced with the permission of Ramzi Harrabi. Photo by Cristiana Giordano.

because it opens up art's potential to exceed it, something I will return to later in this chapter. Ramzi knows that the "refugee crisis" has brought "academic and humanitarian tourism to Sicily," as he shared with me, and that it is "a great resource" for the island, and Italy at large.

As I showed my pictures, one of the young men started telling me about one of his friends at the shelter who was a very talented artist. He ran up to the room they shared and came back with several drawings of what looked like an elaborate graphic novel. We were all looking at them when Victor, the author, joined us and started talking about his work. Victor arrived in Italy in 2016, when he was seventeen, by boat, and had recently moved to the shelter for minors. He and I became involved in a very animated conversation about drawing, art, painting, and sculpture. I showed him photos of Alberto Burri's work and told him about *arte povera* (poor art) and the use of various materials—such as wood, tar, jute, and plastic—to make paintings. He told me about the graphic novel that he was developing; it was entitled "The Guardian Angel" (Figure 10). Set in northern Italy, his novel told the story of a spider-man-looking character whose main

Figure 10 "The Guardian Angel," by Homiex. Siracusa, Italy, 2016. Reproduced with the permission of Homiex.

mission was to protect and rescue an Italian woman who had been betrayed by her employer, kidnapped, and threatened with death. He already had forty pages of detailed drawings and was about to write the text in English to later have it translated into Italian. He was a very prolific illustrator, but his dream was to learn how to paint, he told me with a hint of shyness.

Later in the day, when the doctor's consultations were over, I introduced him to Ramzi, who was impressed by Victor's drawings. He asked him whether he was interested in drawing some images of his journey to Italy, the crossing from Nigeria to Libya, and of the Sicilian channel into Italy. He thought, as he later told me, that Victor could use his skills as an artist and his identity as a migrant to make some money, in the same vein of his own boat paintings and installation. He quickly envisioned Victor working for the tourists in the streets of Siracusa, making drawings of his migration, and thus capitalizing on his position as a foreigner. As an educator and cultural mediator with a long experience working with foreign youth, Ramzi saw the political potential of art to rework the categories of power to Victor's advantage. The art did not undo the very grammar that produced it; instead, the work resituated his relationship to its power. He could "game" the grammar, so to speak. Victor said that he really wanted to learn how to paint. Ramzi explained that he was willing to pay Victor some money if he made drawings that fit the exhibit on migration at the church. Victor was elusive and noncommittal. Ramzi insisted, but, in the end, Victor said he'd rather not draw his journey. After much back and forth, Ramzi gave up and agreed to teach him how to paint instead.

I was intrigued by Victor's refusal of Ramzi's invitation to draw his migration. The images of multitudes of people disembarking from boats, being rescued at sea, walking along railways, or cutting through walls of wire have completely colonized Europe's social imaginary and turned movement and borders into a media spectacle (Fernando and Giordano 2016). These images fit a grammar of crisis and catastrophe. By declining to represent his journey as a migrant, Victor took a position that, for me, partially resonated with the performativity of creation and the potential that is exemplified by Herman Melville's character, Bartleby the scrivener, who refuses to perform what he is supposed to do by saying, "I would prefer not to."

In this chapter, I reflect on experiences that don't fall within the grammar of crisis. They express a denial or, better, an interruption in how sovereign power translates the fluidity of experience into stable categories. I draw from a project on art and theater that I conducted from 2016 to 2019 in Siracusa, Sicily, with African youth who, according to the law, qualify as "unaccompanied foreign minors" and were waiting to be recognized as refugees in Italy.[1] This project focused on practices that form in the midst of other grammars, or respond to the lack thereof, outside the register of the eventful (Povinelli 2011). While the stories of selfhood that people craft to identify themselves before a court of law follow the register of the exceptional and the tragic (Ticktin 2011; Giordano 2014), many of the silent and affective responses of those who don't meet the requirements of the crisis narrative—and its categories—fall within the rubric of ordinary experience and diffuse suffering that cannot be rendered in any institutional or humanitarian language. A criminal-justice system that recognizes only scripted voices of human trafficking or asylum seeking tends to misunderstand those grammars that do not fit into the categories of recognition of the political lexicon of emergency.

Here I think with Ramzi and Victor, and consider the explorations that they do through art. I attend to their encounters through the register of the therapeutic. In this context, therapy does not refer to curing symptoms, but rather to an ethics—or an exploration of the potentialities of life—that takes form within or/ and outside the grammar of the nation-state and of humanitarian interventions. I depart from diagnostic reasoning to open a more psychoanalytic and existential reading of the ambivalence of movement.

In the context of the current refugee crisis in the Mediterranean and Europe, the routinization and bureaucratization of humanitarian interventions have produced a sense of chronicity. Procedures of rescue performed within the framework of a recurring state of exception (Agamben 1998) constantly translate the immediacy of the emergency into the long duration of a persistent condition. Within this grammar, experience needs to be reframed as "events"— as extraordinary, something that can be contained, as exceptional. As asylum seekers or refugees, people are required to present their experiences in the format of a life story of tragic events, ordered in chronological sequences, with causes for leaving and consequences to the journey—that is, in ways that fit the grammar of crisis. What happens, then, when the stories do not fit, or exceed, this frame?

Amadou, a young man from Gambia, told me after applying for asylum and being interviewed by the commission appointed to determine his status: "People like us don't have stories." I knew he had many compelling stories to tell because we had worked on a theater project together, sharing stories of different kinds. But the words he used before the commission did not appear to be eventful. They did not add up to an account worthy of the crisis archive. As an "unaccompanied foreign minor," he was automatically under the protection of the United Nations Convention on the Rights of Children, which prohibits any receiving states from deporting minors to their countries of origin. But to be granted legal recognition and access to services and rights after his eighteenth birthday, Amadou also needed the official status of refugee or of humanitarian protection, which would extend his legal status into adulthood. Hence, he had to appear before a commission that judged his specific case. He talked about being poor and hungry and wanting to continue studying; about being sad that his father had lost his job and couldn't provide for the rest of the family; about being seventeen with no prospect of finding a job and no school to go to. His words revealed fragments of ordinariness that didn't conform to the crisis-grammar. He did, indeed, lack the story that the state required to grant him refugee status. Rather than reading this as a case of omission and oversight, I want to ask how we can still relate to experience when it exceeds or simply refuses the crisis-grammars that are in place for people like Amadou. I turn to the aesthetic form, noting that not everything can—or should—be put into words. Or, in the spirit of Bartleby, what can be experienced or glimpsed when the only words are "I would prefer not to"?

Preferring Not To

Bartleby's character has been a source of interest for many who have attempted to interpret, understand, define, and capture his essence (Agamben 1999, Deleuze 1998, Hardt and Negri 2000, Zizek 2006). He is one of the scriveners employed at a lawyer's office to transcribe legal documents. He is quiet and efficient and attends to his tasks diligently and with precision until the day his employer asks him to run an errand outside the office and he replies: "I would prefer not to." Taken aback but intrigued by Bartleby's response, the lawyer doesn't fire him and instead becomes obsessed by his answer. Bartleby continues to work at the lawyer's office (one suspects he actually lives there day and night), but always replies he would prefer not to do whatever task he is asked to perform. His response disorients his colleagues and the lawyer, but they all gradually become affected by it, and start answering in similar ways. As a figure, Bartleby exceeds any definition (Beverungen and Dunne 2007). He stops performing tasks by stating "I would prefer not to," but he nonetheless continues to work at the office; he is a scrivener, even when he stops transcribing; he is not apathetic, even if he doesn't perform any of the duties and responsibilities attached to this position. His behavior creates an interruption not only in the usual flow of activities, but also in the sense of who Bartleby is. The statement—"I would prefer not to"—opens up the possibilities of other subject positions, experiences, and actualities. Bartleby dwells in the potential of what could be, wandering in the space in between categories and statuses.

By saying "I would prefer not to," both Bartleby and Victor produce an interruption, an abnormality in the grammar of power that potentially spoils its signifying force. Ramzi's idea of how to use experience to do art and simultaneously occupy an active subject position vis-à-vis the language of the state is caught within the same logic of the crisis and the kind of capital that is inscribed in it. The interruption produced by "I would prefer not to" suspends the biopolitical order, and something else unfolds in the in-between of pure potentiality. Victor's refusal to draw his journey is the occasion and source of creation. Or, at least, this is how I heard his reply to Ramzi's invitation.

In the weeks and months that followed that encounter at the shelter, Victor became Homiex, his artistic name. His African name in Edo is Eveshomane, which means "God is my creator," and Homiex is an abbreviated form of it, he explained to me. He started spending hours and days at the empty church in Ortigia, which Ramzi let him use as an art studio. When I saw him there, he was so immersed in painting and drawing that he would hardly raise his head to greet me. He looked focused and serious, tense and quiet. He seemed to inhabit another rhythm. Whenever we gathered with the other youth at the church to work on the theater project, he would never join. "I don't do that; I draw and now I paint," he once said. And he would keep painting instead or sit on the floor to observe us as we played with space, sounds, objects, and lights. He painted still lives, then city streets, squares, and buildings; women crying blood and men's disfigured faces; burning hands and sun-lit beaches; villages and birds. The range of his drawings revealed a breadth of urgent exploration, disciplined and excessive.[2] He rarely put things into words. Only when asked would he stutter a few comments, attempting at a description that failed to describe.[3] The drawings ask for a "looking" rather than a listening or a reading. They tend to be "a mute conversation with the thing drawn," where "[a] line drawn is important not for what it records so much as what it leads you on to see" (Taussig 2009: 269–70).

For instance, when he showed me the painting of "The Woman Crying Tears of Blood" (Chapter 2, Episode—Homiex), I asked him what inspired it. "I make my art with my present mood. I woke up in the morning with so much anger, and I decided to put it in an image form," he replied. Then, as he usually described his art, he added: "It's deep sorrow art." I wanted to ask what sorrow he was referring to but did not because I felt my questions had become loud and inappropriate before his drawings, as if his uncertainty in answering was starting to be mirrored in my hesitance to ask. There were no easy answers to my questions, and maybe there were no answers at all. When asked about what compelled him to draw in a certain way, he often replied, "I don't know." Instead of questioning, I began to "listen to/look at" images and their affects, noting how they refused to elicit a story or a narrative throughline. I was made to experience them through an immersion, to not succumb to the idea that they were descriptions of an experience. They invited a relation unmediated by the dominant migrant narrative.

A few days later, Homiex posted a painting of an injured man's face on his Facebook page, and he wrote me a text: "The guy is said to be suffering internally. I have showed the suffering in form of an X-ray view. He was infected on the right side of the skin where there is plaster. It's a sorrowful art." "What led you to paint it?" I tentatively wrote back. "I really don't know," was his reply. I let Homiex's not knowing linger in my experience of the paintings, creating cracks in my search for meaning, in my desire to read the painting as yet another iteration of the crisis and violence of borders. I heard his "I don't know" instead as a way for him to protect the intimacy of his paintings from the violence embedded in the language of recognition/interpretation (Chapter 2, Episode—Homiex). After all, as John Berger puts it: "A drawing is an autobiographical record of one's discovery of an event, seen, remembered or imagined" (2007: 3), and I was left with experiencing this trace, the absence of Homiex's experience appearing on the canvas.

Homiex is exploring a different relationship to experience and images, and the relation between them, than the one offered through the crisis-grammar. His language is made of fragments of speech-acts that have an oblique relationship to the figures he creates, just as his paintings have a free associative relationship to his experiences of the real world. They are affective engagements, relying on dream-like connections, unmediated by either signification or the demands of representation and explanation. He'd rather not explain them. They are untranslatable in the same ways that dreams—in their pictorial and fragmented form—are, interpretable only by way of a forged linear narrative.

When we dream, we apprehend the world through images rather than discursive modes of knowing; in this way, we glimpse the power of images that resist being rendered as singular and uncontested facts (Stevenson 2014). But dreams, like images, are not just ways of knowing. Binswanger (1993) argues that images in dreams are not indexes pointing to some other hidden meanings but are themselves manifestations of being. Dreaming and life are bound together, and the dream is the moment when existence happens in its translation into images. In dreams we encounter "a language that expresses without formulating" (Foucault 1993). Similarly, in paintings one can experience through image.

Homiex's art resists the allure of the event and its demands for narrative. His images are affective and express without formulating, making "sorrowful art" that refuses the teleology of crisis and response. It refuses the heroic eventfulness of the "migrant journey" that Ramzi suggested as a theme for his drawings, even while migration as an experience of movement and *errance* (Echeverri Zuluaga 2015) is not denied or repressed in his work. This theme traverses his paintings, echoing the archaic voices of the past and playing with the dangerous figures of witches and worshipers without being reduced to a discourse of African localism. He makes the figures "free" from the logic of the linear journey without abolishing the other grammars of power that come from elsewhere that he feels now interpolate him to draw. The illustrations of "The Guardian Angel," for instance, which he drew before his arrival in Italy, represent a hero-like character engaged in adventures of rescue, inscribed within and resonant with a grammar of Western heroism and economic fantasy, wealth, and redemption. When he showed me the painting (Chapter 2, Episode—Homiex) entitled "Worshipers," his verbal associations added more nuance to his own experience of the paintings:

> I don't know what those people are worshiping. I have showed a serpent's eyes as the gods which they are worshiping. The serpent is important in a village in Edo state, I was told many years ago, but I don't remember the village. They worship a python that only comes out once in years, and people make sacrifices to it.

I wanted to imagine that the painting gestured toward the power of magic and its force field, or that the serpent stood for other forms of power that could turn persecutory. But ambiguity in relation to the common tropes of movement, rescue, and salvation was built in. On another occasion, as we stood in front of the same painting, he said that he was scared by it: "It is as if the [serpent's] eyes are looking at you. . . . I look at the painting, and it's always looking at me! It keeps looking at me even when I look away. And at night, the color that I used in this place shines with the light."

Homiex's images resonate with a diffuse and generalized affect that exceeds the narrow logic of chronicity that commonly shapes crisis narratives. His artistic expressions of refusal may have something to do with the unbearable nature of certain unconscious memories—memories that cannot be represented in an illustrative way because they are intractable and can only be glimpsed obliquely, indirectly, and through what exceeds language (they also may have nothing to do with that). But this is certainly not to suggest, as a certain psychoanalytic reading would claim, that his images are merely symptoms or projections of a traumatic past (Recalcati 2016; Pandolfo 2018). As I mentioned earlier, what I mean by the therapeutic is not the care and/or cure of symptoms, but rather an ethics of creation, a disposition toward experience that allows for exploration and different experiences that exceed dominant grammars to occur. Homiex's "I don't know" allows for the possibility of not resolving contradictions and remaining suspended in the psychic and experiential space created in between them (Figure 11). It allows him to dwell in the ambivalence of his worlds without choosing a side to inhabit. After all, "drawing . . . is more about becoming than being" (Taussig 2009: 270).

In the space of his paintings, he is neither-nor: neither migrant nor refugee, neither foreigner nor Italian.[4] He could inhabit several state categories of recognition—"unaccompanied foreign minor," "refugee," "victim of human

Figure 11 "Enymies gone suicide," by Homiex. 2016. Reproduced with the permission of Homiex.

trafficking," "undocumented"—and make a profit out of these various pre-
assigned identities, but when he is interpellated to do so through his drawings,
he says he would prefer not to. His refusal is generative, and it produces a reveal
(McGranahan 2016, Simpson 2014).[5] Homiex relates his paintings to words in
ways that allow him to stay in-between categories of recognition. If he reduced
them to any specific event or narrative, he would dissolve the painting's very
force to create something new. This is similar to the potential that Giorgio
Agamben assigns to the figure of Bartleby, who would rather not follow his
employer's order. Victor's Homiex offers a refusal that enables him to operate
against the system with the force of a nonrational logic, an excess, "a question
without response" (1998: 83).

Ways of Refusal

The questions Homiex left unanswered (about identity, origins, life trajectory)
suggest that it is possible to live in the shadows of a grammar by enacting a
certain kind of refusal. In the space of this refusal, one neither belongs nor doesn't
belong to a grammar. This means that alternate stories may be told, and more
importantly, other presences felt.[6] This space of refusal resonates with Bartleby's
"I would prefer not to," while holding a certain tension with the idea of grammar
and the forms of life enacted through it which I explore in Chapter 3. Different
forms of power and knowledge are articulated through specific languages and
the subject/object positions they enable. I have offered an (analytical) montage
with Homiex's explorations, dominant languages, and spaces of creation because
the paintings he shared with me made me wonder when and how one could live,
or spend time, beyond or beside worlds, not being fully within or circumscribed
by a language-game.

   Different degrees of fluidity and transgression run through all forms of life,
and in-between spaces of creation enable experiences that are in the making,
whose form lacks fixed rules. In other words, it is a space that allows testing the
boundaries of what is allowed, playing with the suspension of categories and
the potential of experiencing otherwise. This does not mean one is completely
outside dominant worlds. It rather suggests that one can be in-between worlds,
in a playful space of invention.[7] The space in which Homiex creates images
resembles the experience of dreaming, constantly and simultaneously populated
by the external world(s) and by unconscious material (Freud 1899). In dreams,
rules are turned upside down, an image can mean its opposite, words can be

spoken backward, a dead person can be alive; yet, the dream content is only partially disconnected from "real" life, which gets reworked through the unconscious. Like in transitional spaces, in dreams worlds are suspended and rearranged, symbols are resignified in the temporary suspension of rational logic.

Homiex's art is an experiment. It resonates with the experimentation which "is an alternative to interpretation" (Deleuze and Guattari 1983: 13–14) that I introduced in Chapter 3. It gives form to the formless, affective, and elusive. When he links the image of the woman crying blood to his feelings of anger, he is connecting the figural to an affect that exceeds signification. The blood disturbs all relations of signification while staging an affect. His paintings and his ways of referring to them are not a window into reality and the world. They are "playing with reality" (Winnicott 1971). This process may lead to the creations of a new grammar-world, or not. Through them, he is producing an interruption in the grammar of power, and the logic of identity. Here, the potential of Bartleby's position is not the opposite of actuality, but it is closer to creativity as a field of affect in which force produces novelty, not the repetition of the same. This is the force of the therapeutic as an ethics that doesn't resolve contradictions and allows a painting to be simultaneously experience and image, story and the absence of narrative. This force is present in the interstices of the various grammars of power, and outside the language of symptoms and cure. Homiex's refusal to represent the "journey" doesn't signify a mere denial of history; instead, it precisely operates in the register of the performative, a "no" that enables a new kind of advent. It initiates, for him, a different process that separates experience from its representation, and allows him to dwell in a space of invention.

Association #4

What's in a List: The Affect of the Archive

Cristiana Giordano

Found dead: 25/05/12
Number: 1
Name: N.N.
Gender and Age: (±30, man)
Country of origin: Sub-Saharan Africa
Cause of death: body in advanced state of decomposition washed ashore off Lampione Island (Italy)
Source: FE/ANSA

Found dead: 08/10/12
Number: 6
Name: N.N.
Gender and Age: n/a
Country of origin: Africa
Cause of death: drowned, after boat of 24 migrants from Comoros capsized off the coast of Mayotte (F)
Source: VOA/UN/IRR

Found dead: 09/07/12
Number: 1
Name: Bernard Hukwa
Gender and Age: (man)
Country of origin: Zimbabwe
Cause of death: suicide, body found in River Thames (GB), he was waiting for asylum claim to be processed
Source: IRR/ZimEye

In 2012, a sixty-nine page, thick, relentless enumeration of 40,555 instances of people who died while crossing borders was released by UNITED for Intercultural

Action, a European network of 550 organizations against nationalism, racism, and fascism and in support of migrants and refugees.[1] The list, which gets updated yearly, documents the deaths of people "who have died due to the restrictive policies of Fortress Europe whilst trying to get into Europe" since 1993 (Media Release, June 20, 2020).[2] Between the time of my writing and the time of your reading, the numbers will have shifted, certainly increased. In June 2023, the numbers were 52.760. Drawing from the 1951 Refugee Convention, UNITED's list is intended as a tool to bring to the attention of leaders, policymakers, media, and the public at large the plight of those who died because of border policies. The list is also a way to shout out that "Refugee Lives Matter" and to "call on European leaders to scale up the work to keep refugees and migrants safe by providing access to lifesaving support, medical care, water, and sanitation." To further quote from the same media release, published in 2020 on Refugee Day (June 20):

> It is time to stop the dehumanization of refugees and asylum seekers not only via mass media and populist political statements but also by seeing them only as "numbers." **Refugees and asylum seekers are human beings** with families, backgrounds, and identities, **not just numbers**. We demand action on identifying personalities behind the numbers and informing families.
>
> **We demand that death by policy must come to an end!**[3] (Emphasis in original)

While searching the web for data and statistics on migration, I encountered many lists of people who died while attempting to cross into Europe. This one particularly struck me. It is organized into columns, each with a heading: date the bodies were found; number of corpses; name(s), if available, otherwise N.N. (no name) is indicated; gender and age; country of origin; cause of death; and source where the information first appeared. The format of the list is lines of names and numbers repeated over and again, but the content of each line changes, the detail of each incident may be different, or the same as the preceding line. It is a way of ordering material, of aesthetically presenting it in a clear frame. It is nothing to take for granted, but a style that allows a certain way of knowing. It is monotonous. It projects the world through numbers, places, destinations, symptoms, parentheses, evoked images of death, and disaster. It represents the catastrophe in a seemingly simple way, stripped of the chaos of disaster. It makes up for the absence of certain deaths from the register of the eventful. Some deaths just don't make news. But its simplicity and apparent linearity inscribes disaster in other ways.

180 *Affect Ethnography*

On the page and the screen, the list looks like this (Figure 12):

List of 48.647 documented deaths of refugees and migrants due to the restrictive policies of " Fortress Europe "

Documentation by UNITED as of 1 June 2022

Death by Policy - Time for Change!

UNITED racism fascism nationalism

Campaign information: Facebook UNITED Against Refugee Deaths, UnitedAgainstRefugeeDeaths.eu, Twitter: @UNITED__Network #AgainstRefugeeDeaths, Instagram: unitedlistofdeaths

UNITED for Intercultural Action, European network against nationalism, racism, fascism and in support of migrants and refugees - Amsterdam Refugee Campaign Secretariat

Postbus 413, NL-1000 AK Amsterdam, Netherlands, tel +31-6-48808808, listofdeaths@unitedagainstracism.org

This **'UNITED List of Refugee Deaths'** can be re-used, translated and re-distributed, see conditions on UnitedAgainstRefugeeDeaths.eu. On request you can obtain this list with more searchable data in xls format from UNITED.

Support this research and campaign and donate through Paypal: http://bit.ly/Donate-List

found dead	number	name, gender, age	region of origin	cause of death	source
29/05/22	1	N.N. (man)	Africa	presumed suicide, hit by freight train in Calais (FR), was lying on the track in a sleeping bag	Europe1/info/InfoMigrants
25/05/22	76	N.N.	sub-Saharan Africa, Western	drowned, crowded boat on way from Zawara (LY) sank off Sfax (TN); 1 body found, 75 missing, 24 rescued	BBC/Euronews/Rel/Reuters/IOMTunisia/A
19/05/22	14	N.N.	Tunisia	drowned, overcrowded boat sank off Louza (TN) on way to Italy; 4 bodies found, 10 missing, 44 rescued	AfricaNews/Euronews/IOMTunisia/Reuten
17/05/22	11	N.N.	Algeria	drowned, boat sank off Tipaza (DZ) on way to Balearic Islands (ES); 11 missing, 5 rescued	AfricaNews
15/05/22	14	N.N.	unknown	died of unknown cause on boat that was missing on way from Africa to the Canaries (ES); 45 rescued	Txemita
13/05/22	1	N.N. (young man)	unknown	died of unknown cause, body found during rescue off Island of Gran Canaria (ES); 14 rescued	Txemita
12/05/22	3	N.N.	Africa	drowned, bodies recovered after boat sank off coast of El Awabed in Sfax Governorate (Tunisia)	SABC
12/05/22	1	N.N. (young man)	Syria	shot by Turkish border guards near Ain Dewar (Syria) while trying to cross the Syrian/Turkish border	SOHR
11/05/22	1	Hassan (man, 27)	Sudan	suicide, found hanging in trailer in Transmarck near Calais (FR); was rejected asylum in 3 countries	NordLittoral/Witter/InfoMigrants
09/05/22	28	N.N.	unknown	drowned, inflatable dinghy on way from Western Sahara sank off island of Gran Canaria (ES); 13 rescued	TRT/MorWN/InfoMigrants
08/05/22	44	N.N.	unknown	drowned, boat capsized off Cape Boujdour (Western Sahara) on way to Spain; 16 BF, 28 mis, 12 rescued	HelenaMaleno/SpanishNewsToday/Aljaze
07/05/22	2	N.N.	unknown	bodies recovered after sailboat on way from Libya ran aground near jetty in south Italy; 100 rescued	ArabNews
03/05/22	1	N.N. (man, 20)	North Africa	homeless refugee, probably sleeping in a dumpster that was emptied and crushed by garbage truck	NAIZ
in May 22	1	Abdulmajeed Khaled Al-Ashmouri	Yemen	died of starvation & extreme cold on Belarusian-Polish border; was known youtuber in Yemen	Yemen24
in May 22	8	N.N.	Tunisia	presumed drowned, boat sank off coast of Sfax province (TN); 8 missing, all came from Monastir (TN)	BBC/EastAfrHerald
30/04/22	1	N.N. (young man)	unknown	drowned, body found in the port of Spanish enclave of Melilla (ES), tried to swim from Morocco	InfoMigrants
26/04/22	25	N.N. (7 babies; 14 women; 4men)	Sub-Saharan Africa	drowned, boat sank between Bojador(EH) and the Canaries (ES); 1 body found, 24 missing, 36 rescued	El Diario/HelenaMaleno/MurciaToday/Salv
24/04/22	30	N.N. (incl 1 baby, 1 woman)	Sub-Saharan Africa, Ivory C	drowned, 4 small boats capsized off Sfax(TN) on way to IT; 17 bodies found, 13 missing, 98 rescued	Aljazeera/Spiegel/InfoMigrants/OMTunisia
24/04/22	1	Khadeeja Al-Nemr (woman)	Lebanon	drowned, body found floating off Tripoli beach (Lebanon) after boat crashed; 39 missing, 45 rescued	Aljazeera/Guardian/Reuters/APNews/Infol
24/04/22	12	N.N.	Sub-Saharan Africa	drowned off Libya on way to Italy, fell exhausted from overcrowded rubber boat; 94 rescued	NowHeadline/SOSMed
24/04/22	2	N.N.	Southern Asia	**vehicle accident, bus overturned near Büvetli (TR) near Iranian border; smuggler arrested, 11 injured**	TurkeyAlaan/IOM
23/04/22	33	N.N (incl baby, 40 days, 1 w, 1m)	Lebanon, Syria, Palestine	drowned when patrol ship crashed into overcrowded boat near Tripoli (Lebanon); 39 missing, 45 rescued	Aljazeera/Guardian/AlArabia/Reuters/APN
23/04/22	6	N.N.	unknown	drowned, when boat sank off the Libyan coast on the way to Italy	InfoMigrants/IOMLibya
23/04/22	1	Hashem Betlashi (man, 21)	Lebanon	drowned when patrol ship crashed into overcrowded boat near Tripoli (Lebanon)	Aljazeera/Guardian/Reuters/APNews/Infol
23/04/22	1	Salam (woman, 31)	Lebanon	drowned together with sister, patrol ship crashed into boat near Tripoli (Lebanon)	Aljazeera/Guardian/Reuters/APNews/Infol
23/04/22	1	Rania (woman, 27)	Lebanon	drowned together with sister, patrol ship crashed into boat near Tripoli (Lebanon)	Aljazeera/Guardian/Reuters/APNews/Infol
23/04/22	1	Jenda Saeed (woman, 27)	Syria	Kurd, drowned on way to partner in DE, crash with patrol ship near Tripoli (Lebanon)	Rudaw/Aljazeera/Guardian/Reuters/APNe
23/04/22	1	Inas Abdel Salam (woman, 23)	Syria	Kurd, drowned on way to partner in DE, crash with patrol ship near Tripoli (Lebanon)	Rudaw/Aljazeera/Guardian/Reuters/APNe
21/04/22	1	N.N. (man, 42)	Syria	tortured to death by Turkish boarder guards near Idlib (SY), body was dropped into Syrian territory	SOHR
20/04/22	1	N.N.	unknown	drowned, boat sank off Samos (GR), body recovered in Aegan sea near Kuşadasi (TR); 31 rescued	TurkCoastG
19/04/22	4	N.N.	unknown	drowned, boat sank off Samos(GR), survivors were pushed back to Turkish territory; 4 missing, 31 rescued	TurkCoastG
17/04/22	1	N.N. (man)	Gambia or Senegal	drowned while trying to cross river Mrežnic near Donje Dubrave (HR) on way to Slovenia; 8 survived	PoliceKarlovac/IOM
17/04/22	1	N.N. (man)	Gambia or Senegal	drowned while trying to cross river Mrežnic near Svojići (HR) on way to Slovenia; 8 survived	PoliceKarlovac/IOM
16/04/22	1	N.N. (woman, 22)	Eritrea	shot in chest at close range while trying to cross Evros River to enter Greece from Turkey; 10 survived	KTG/GreekReporter/Seebruecke/EFSYN/
15/04/22	35	N.N.	Southern Asia	drowned, small wooden boat capsized off Sabratha (Libya); 6 bodies found, 29 missing	Guardian/TSF/NoticiasPT/Spiegel/AlArabi
15/04/22	1	N.N. (child 12-15)	unknown	presumed drowned, body in advanced state of decay wearing only a blouse floated off Heraklia (GR)	KTG/Seebruecke
11/04/22	18	N.N.	North Africa	drowned, boat sank off coast Surman (Libya) on way to Italy; 4 bodies found, 14 missing, 2 rescued	AlArabia/AlarmPhone/InfoMigrants/IOMLil
11/04/22	4	N.N.	Western Asia	van accident, minibus rolled over near Bahçedere village (TR), near Turkey-Iran border; 25 injured	Bianet/IOM
10/04/22	2	N.N.	North Africa	suicide, jumped overboard, could not resist agony of being days adrift at North Atlantic Ocean; 18rescued	EFE/IOM
09/04/22	25	N.N. (6 children; 6 women; 1 man)	Sub-Saharan Africa	drowned, two boat capsized on the way from Tunisia to Italy; 13 bodies found, 12 missing, 37 rescued	Al Arabiya/NationalAE/NCAf/AA/InfoMigra
09/04/22	14	N.N (incl 2 children; 2 women)	Sub-Saharan Africa	drowned, boat capsized off Sfax (Tunisia) on way to Italy; 4 bodies found, 10 missing, 19 rescued	Euromed/AlarmPhone/InfoMigrants
09/04/22	19	N.N.	unknown	drowned, dinghy sank in the Mediterranean, dozens of people struggled to survive; 34 rescued	SeaWatch/InfoMigrants
08/04/22	11	N.N. (incl 4 children; 4 women)	Sub-Saharan Africa	drowned, boat sank off coast Sfax (Tunesia) on the way to Italy; 9 bodies found, 2 missing,18 rescued	Swiss.ch/AlarmPhone/GuardeNatTN/InfoN
05/04/22	2	N.N.	Afghanistan	accident, military truck with migrants crashes on way to police station in Hungary at TR border; 10 injured	Novinite/BMBul/Nova/IOMN
03/04/22	1	N.N. (man)	Congo	died of hypothermia, despite medical assistance, along Kupa River (HR) on Croatia-Slovenia border	NoviList/Welcome/IOMCroatia
03/04/22	1	N.N. (man)	Congo	body found by police officers in the Kupa River near Vrbovsko (HR) on Croatian-Slovenian border	RTLHR/NoviList/IOMCroatia
03/04/22	1	N.N. (man)	Congo	died of hypothermia despite resuscitation by police, near Vrbovsko (HR) on Croatian-Slovenian border	RTLHR/NoviList
02/04/22	96	N.N.	Sub-Saharan Africa	drowned, boat capsized after drifting 4 days at sea trying to cross from Libya to Europe; 4 rescued	MSF/NewArab/ZEIT/InfoMigrants/ABCNe
02/04/22	2	N.N.	Sri Lanka	hit and killed by a lorry while crossing highway near Bordighera (IT) on way to France; 1 injured	InfoMigrants
31/03/22	11	N.N. (4 children, 7 women)	Western Africa	found dead in overcrowded rubber boat after spending hours drifting off coast of Libya; 126 rescued	MSF/AlarmPhone/InfoMigrants/IOM
28/03/22	1	Mohamed (young man)	Somalia	Young Somali sleeping in a paperbin died when compactor truck collected the waste	La Nazione
28/03/22	1	N.N. (man)	Cameroon	body found by police officers in the Kupa River near Vrbovsko (HR) on Croatian-Slovenian border	RTLHR/NoviList
27/03/22	2	N.N (men)	unknown	drowned, bodies washed up following a shipwreck off the Moroccan coast on way to Canary Islands	Euromed/Euractiv/Statewatch/InfoMigrant
27/03/22	25	N.N. (1 minor)	Sub-Saharan Africa	died of dehydration on 8 day trip from Mauritania to El Hiero (ES), bodies thrown into sea; 48 rescued	EFECanarias/InfoMigrants/IOM
27/03/22	1	N.N. (child)	Sub-Saharan Africa	died of dehydration on 8 day trip from Mauritania to El Hiero (ES), body found on boat; 48 rescued	EFECanarias/InfoMigrants/IOM
25/03/22	1	Yassin Osman (man, early 20ties)	Eritrea	electrocuted, jumped on train wagon headed for Calais at station of Valenciennes (FR); 3 survived	RailFreight/CMS
25/03/22	2	N.N.	unknown	found dead at bottom of inflatable boat in Mediterranean sea; only 1 body recovered, 128 rescued	FAZ/SOSMed
24/03/22	1	N.N. (man)	unknown	body in state of decay discovered in forest near Białowieża (PL) at Polish-Belarusian border	Wydarzenia
22/03/22	8	N.N. (8 men)	Algeria	drowned, boat on way from Ghazaouet (DZ) to Europe shipwrecked; 5 bodies washed ashore, 3missing	Heroes/IOM
19/03/22	48	N.N.	Tunisia, Syria	presumed drowned, boat went missing, 8 bodies washed up on the beach of Nabeul (TN); 40 missing	Rel/AfricanManager/AlarmPhone/InfoMigr
19/03/22	24	N.N.	Tunisia, Syria	presumed drowned, boat went missing at sea on way from Sfax (Tunisia) to Italy	AlarmPhone/InfoMigrants/Al Arabiya/IOM
18/03/22	12	N.N.	Tunisia, Syria	presumed drowned, boat went missing, bodies washed up on the beach of Nabeul (TN)	AlarmPhone/InfoMigrants/IOMTunisia
18/03/22	1	Ayman Al Saleh (boy, 4)	unknown	drowned, was stranded 5 days on island in Evros river at TR-GR border, fell into water during rescue	EFSYN/BVMN/InfoMigrants/AlarmPhone
13/03/22	1	N.N.	Syria	tortured and shot dead by Turkish boarder guards at Turkish-Syrian border near Darbasiyah (SY)	NewArab/IOM
12/03/22	19	N.N.	Egypt, Syria	drowned, boat capsized off Tobruk (LY) on way to Greece; 7 bodies found, 12 missing, 6 rescued	Guardian/BusiWeek/SaudiG/InfoMigrants/
12/03/22	44	N.N. (incl 2 babies; 5 women)	Western Africa	drowned, inflatable sank off Tarfaya (MA) on way to Canaries; 7 bodies found, 37 missing, 17 rescued	AlArabia/Euromed/HelenaMaleno/Scheng
12/03/22	1	Adel Mohammed Badr (man, 21)	Syria	tortured and shot dead by Turkish boarder guards at Turkish-Syrian border near Darbasiyah (SY)	NewArab/IOM
10/03/22	1	**Omar Ismail Tela (man)**	Sudan	hit by vehicle while walking along A16 motorway near to Nouvelle-Eglise (FR) on way to Britain	CMS
08/03/22	1	Cemil Karabidek (man, 52)	Turkey	froze to death trying to cross Maritsa river on Turkey-Greece border; was fleeing post-coup purge	TurkeyPurge

Figure 12 From the "UNITED List of Refugee Deaths". Reproduced by permission of "UNITED for Intercultural Action" – campaign 'Fortress Europe No More Deaths' unitedagainstrefugeedeaths.eu – listofdeaths@unitedagainstracism.org.

At first, my encounter with this list was cold both for the content of the document, and for the medium through which I found it, the internet. I did not pay attention right away to who had compiled it or to the intentions of its writers. I only saw the thousands of entries, typed in small font and tight lines, in a thick spreadsheet. It felt antiseptic, impersonal, yet precise and attentive to the often scarce details available for identification (or misidentification).[4] I wondered: Would the list of dead people have felt differently had someone in an office handed it to me? Would it have conveyed feelings other than coldness and dryness, had one of the relatives of someone listed shared it with me at a funeral? These questions came up as I continued to engage it.

The list's logical and linear form simultaneously performs the banality and the tragedy of these deaths. It pretends to be neutral, a piece of news without a narrative line, while it also reverberates untold stories. On the one hand, it is straightforward in its enumerations; it conveys the succinctness of a catalogue, and the rawness of language deserted by adjectives. However, to someone who appreciates catalogues and rawness, a list doesn't engage language with the purpose of explaining and analyzing. It relieves the reader of the burden of interpretation, leaving room to think and wander around the words that compose it. It can become evocative, affective almost—a site, or a stage, onto which images can be projected and meanings made or suspended, and then made again.

As I spent time with it, reading each line carefully, sometimes letting the repetitive rhythm of it guide my attention, I started to wonder whether the list—in all its efficiency, scarceness, matter-of-factness—could be a story. And if so, of what? And for whom? Is it as linear as it first appears? Or does it perform a free association of sorts, labyrinthine in its movements, poetic in its coldness?

Its ambivalence captured me: the listing oscillates between simplifying the reality of death at borders and producing a different affective space where other encounters become possible. The emptiness I felt when I first encountered it—the emptiness of death—was replaced by a sense of crowdedness that the list produced in me. This empty crowdedness carries unarticulated stories, devoid of complex narrative. But what kind of story? What's in a list?

Found dead: 19/05/2022
Number: 14
Name: N.N.
Gender and Age: n/a
Country of origin: Tunisia

Cause of death: drowned, overcrowded boat sank off Louza (TN) on way to Italy; 4 bodies found, 10 missing, 44 rescued
Source: Africanews/Euronews/IOMTunisia/Routers

Found dead: 24/04/2022
Number: 1
Name: Khadeeja Al-Nemr
Gender and Age: woman
Country of origin: Lebanon
Cause of death: drowned, body found floating off Tripoli beach (Lebanon)
after boat crashed; 39 missing, 45 rescued
Source: Aljazeera/Guardian/Reuters/APNews

To the policymakers, the politicians, the humanitarians, it proves the existence of a crisis. The repetitions perform the despair of a situation, endlessly repeating itself. But the same repetitions also embody one of the ways in which catastrophes are bureaucratized and routinized, made normal in order to be recognized, comprehended, managed. Yet, the list also performs the opposite of the information conveyed. One could say the urge to organize these stories in the form of a list form is conjured by the depth of the angst provoked by these thousands of deaths. What is performed is its negative, its opposite: order in the face of chaos, clarity in the place of darkness.

A List Is More than the Sum of Its Lines

This document was one of the first nontheatrical source materials that we used in the series of *Unstories* workshops at UC Davis. Over the two years of collaboration, several of us made episodes with it, often returned to it, felt affected by it, and used it in its various evocative and literal aspects. Although we never included it in our final performance events, its reverberations remained present for me throughout the process. It was the combination of the essentialist language of the list and the gravity of the stories contained, alluded to, and invoked by that very language that remained a tragic riddle and permeated much of the work I did with the group during the workshops. The following is a theatrical moment that a group of our collaborators made in fall 2018:

Episode—List Typewriter Two Lights #2[5]
(Makers: John, Maria, Bettina)

<u>Setup:</u> Two play spaces (1. Upstage Right and 2. Downstage Left), each with a clip light, both of which are turned off. Maria sits in space 2 on the floor behind an imaginary manual typewriter; a pile of paper is on the floor on her right. The clamp light is positioned above Maria's head and just behind, pointed down toward her from stage left. John stands behind the first and gazes downward. Bettina stands in space 1 with a clamp light held at head height, stage left of John, pointed directly toward the side of his face. He holds a document.

We begin.

BETTINA *(reading from the document)*: Found dead: 29/02/12. *(Brief pause)*. Number: 2. *(John turns on the light at #2 to illuminate Maria. Maria begins typing)*. Name: No Names. One young girl; one old man. *(Brief pause.)* Country of origin: unknown. *(Brief pause.)* Cause of death: young girl and her grandfather missing after boat overturned while crossing Evros River.

Maria "types" on an invisible typewriter. She tries to keep up with the pace of Bettina's reading. It is relatively easy, at first, apparently taking dictation from Bettina. When Maria reaches the end of a line, she mimes hitting the carriage return and pulls a paper from the top of the pile on her right, stamps it, stamps it again, and hands it to John. John switches off Maria's light, turns, carries the typed page to Bettina. Bettina takes the page from John. John switches on Bettina's light, turns, and stands next to her. Bettina then starts the whole process again at a slightly accelerated speed.

BETTINA *(reading from the document, faster than before)*: Found dead: 18/09/12. *(Brief pause. Maria begins typing)*. Number: 1. *(Brief pause)* Name: No Name. One young man. *(Brief pause.)* Country of origin: unknown. *(Brief pause)* Cause of death: advanced state of decomposition, found off Ceuta (E) allegedly fell overboard boat to E.

John switches off Bettina's light, crosses to Maria, who takes the page from the typewriter's carriage, stamps it, and stamps it again. She holds it up. John switches on Maria's light, takes the page, and crosses up to Bettina. John hands Bettina the page.

BETTINA *(reading from the document, slightly faster than before)*: Found dead: 13/04/11. *(Brief pause. Maria begins typing.)* Number: 1. *(Brief pause)* Name: Cinie. (28, woman) *(Brief pause)* Country of origin: Congo. *(Brief pause)* Cause of death: drowned, jumped from boat that wrecked off Pantelleria (I) on the way from Libya.

John continues to move back and forth between the two lights/players passing the sheets from one to the other, switching lights on and off. Bettina reads the same line repeatedly, with brief pauses between each column. Maria tries to type what Bettina says, although each time (there are a total of four) she increases the pace a bit. John stands while reading/typing is happening.

BETTINA *(reading from the document, slightly faster than before)*: Found dead: 25/07/10. *(Brief pause. Maria begins typing)*. Number: 1. *(Brief pause)* Name: Osman Rasul. (27, man) *(Brief pause)* Country of origin: Iraq. *(Brief pause)* Cause of death: suicide, jumped from balcony in Nottingham (GB), couldn't find solicitor for his asylum appeal.

During this final round, Maria types in the air. Her hands don't touch the floor. She hands an imaginary page to John, who transfers it to Bettina.

We end.

The list inspired this episode because it is not *just* a list.[6] When we first engaged it in the workshop space, we felt it performed and viscerally embodied, in a literal way, the anonymity of the deaths it accounted for. It functioned as a sign that stood in place of the unknown body stranded at sea, washed ashore, abandoned at the bottom of the sea, never buried, never mourned, never seen in its materiality by those who used to be close to it. When John, Maria, and Bettina presented this episode, I was captured by the pages circulating indefinitely from one performer to the other, along an invisible Möbius strip that went from the reader dictating the text, to the typist, back to another reader, who repeated what was on the typed page. The actor in charge of the lights switched them on and off at random times. His movements became faster—and less regular or predictable—as the speed of the reading and typing increased. When the episode makers described their process of creation and assemblage of texts, space, lights, objects, and other elements of the stage to produce the episode, they talked about the affects they worked with and through. They felt frustration and confusion at the endless repetitions, which they rendered by reading the same line over and over. They wanted to make the labyrinthine nature of bureaucratic processes palpable. They encountered the list as a catalogue that archived the dead in a filing cabinet, so they could be forgotten again. They saw it as a manifestation of the state archive that produced a second death. Although the writers and promoters of the list—UNITED for Intercultural Action—are committed to countering the silencing of institutional languages, and to make the sound of anonymous death be heard, the very form of the listing carries some of the antiseptic quality of a bare enumeration, as one might expect to find in a state or police archive. Repeating the list entries out loud gave them back some life. To me, the resounding of the names felt like a calling of those presences into our audience, so that the list could be performed for those there listed.

Other workshop participants who watched the *Episode—List Typewriter Two Lights #2*[7] felt that the banging sound of the double stamping conveyed the violence and abruptness of final and irreversible processes (of dying, cataloguing, listing, witnessing). Some of them also found the switching on and off the lights marked each dead person's name with the violence of the state archive, of the final obscuring of a life. In the context of this material, some felt that the lights stood for the sterile atmosphere of a state office, a police station, a morgue, or a courtroom. They started by being turned on and off in a predictable rhythm, but later followed an erratic pattern that disoriented the spectators. For some collaborators, this resembled not only the arbitrariness of bureaucratic processes and the anonymity of protocols, but also the deceiving linearity of a catalogue turned into a Kafkaesque labyrinth. As John Zibell, actor and collaborator in the workshop, put it at the end of a workshop in fall 2018: "That list is horrifyingly powerful. It performs the banality of bureaucracy which concretizes the dead in one line." Most intense was Maria Massolo's response to the list and the episode she made. She was brought back to the time of the 1976 coup d'état in Argentina, during which many people close to her disappeared and their names in the official documents were replaced by the word *desaparecido*. "The List staggered me; it brought me into a dark space. I relived the experience of my sister-in-law disappearing overnight. She never came back."

For promoters and writers of this documentation of deaths at the borders, the list is meant to evoke the very opposite of the affective qualities that we as a company first tapped into. In their website, they indicate the list is both a political statement and a form of care for the unnamed and unrecognized dead. The listing is a gesture to re-humanize the anonymous corpse by making it seen and heard through its inscription in language. It is a way to rescue the unrecognized body from the order of numbers into the register of biography, however tentatively sketched and fragmented a life can be when narrated in the space of a line. In this spirit, the list is also conceived as a moment of justice, when names and corpses are made public, and translated out of their status of mere figures. However, there is something powerful and performative about numbers alone. Although the list is supposed to reclaim the space for an individual biography at the heart of a simple figure, the mere number of listed deaths gives the list strength. One almost feels that it is numbers, repetitions, enumerations, and the monotone of each line that are loud and palpable. As Greg put it, "There's something about the fact that you just can't read the entire list, but you know it goes on in the same way for 98 pages that has that affective power." In a way, it is precisely through numbers (and the sum of the lines) that a certain "humanity" is given back to each individual incident. Both language and numbers perform something that exceeds themselves; the form of the physical list is a site that holds them so that they can exceed their literal signification.

Returning to the question of stories and un-storying, the list as a catalogue functions as information, as a sensational way of talking about tragic death as one possible outcome of border control. I am here thinking with Walter Benjamin's distinction between information and storytelling (1968). For him, information draws its power from what is nearest and sensational; it feeds itself with what is verifiable, understandable, plausible, and interpretable; it thrives with news that can receive the highest attention from its readers and be consumed quickly. Benjamin explains how the life of a piece of information lasts only the moment in which it is new. It declines and disappears soon after. It doesn't flourish the way story does—through the process of repetition that creates bonds between storytellers and listeners. For these reasons, information and storytelling are incompatible (1968: 89). For him, a story exerts its power over time and space in ways that are "miraculous," information in ways which are "plausible" (1968: 90).

I also associate the list with Benjamin's library and his collection of books. In any process of cataloguing there is a sense of order that is nothing but "a balancing act of extreme precariousness" (1968: 60). Citing Anatole France, Benjamin reminds us that the only exact knowledge that exists in a library is the date of publication and the format of books: "If there is a counterpart to the confusion of a library, it is the order of its catalogue" (60). Maybe it is the extreme sense of precariousness Benjamin evokes that leaks out of the list of the dead, and that made it possible for our workshop group to create theatrical moments that are charged and evocative. The list always has a precarious equilibrium and could at any moment tip over and get sucked into the disarray and messiness of dying and of crossing. Through the workshop, the information-like quality of the list—its orderly and sensational mode—was transformed so that an experience, not just data, could be conveyed and lived. This experience is somewhat interspersed throughout the list; it animates it in ways that are invisible, perceptible in the unsaid more than in the details of each individual line. The theatrical episode picked up the coldness of bureaucracy and the absurdity of archival processes, but it also named the unnamed, and turned the written word into sound, just like corpses were turned into language through their inscription in the list itself. The devising process turned information into a theatrical moment that doesn't (just) inform, as the list intends to, but also creates an experience in and of itself. In some ways, we un-storied the list *qua* list (in its urge to document and count) and connected with—or restored and re-storied—its potential to tell something beyond its literality. This is the value of our process, Affect Theater, and its analytical power. We tapped into the storyness of the list (in Benjamin's sense of story), its capacity to survive its author and the moment of utterance in the spectators' experience. To me, storytelling doesn't stand in opposition to information, as Benjamin seems to suggest. On the contrary, they are intertwined and woven together. Each story is made of a degree of information, but not only; and information may carry a hidden story within its rush to tell, interpret, and account for. Consider this other theatrical episode inspired by The List.

Episode—The Bucket
(Makers: Cristiana, Regina, Alvaro)

We begin

Alvaro is standing Upstage Left and holds a roll of paper towels. On the floor next to him lies a broom. Cristiana is standing Upstage Center holding a few sheets of The List. Regina is behind the curtains. Cristiana starts reading entries from The List. As she starts reading the second one, Regina enters from Upstage Right carrying a round green plastic bucket. She places it Center Stage. While Cristiana continues to read entries from The List, Regina steps into the bucket and starts a dance; she struggles to stay in balance, she falls on the ground with her feet inside the bucket, she stands up again, struggle with balance and ends up with her head in the bucket and her feet up in the air.

While Cristiana keeps on reading and Regina does her dance with the green bucket, Alvaro from Upstage Left rolls out the roll of paper towels on the floor until it reaches Downstage Left. The paper towels are written over with squiggly black lines on them, evoking the names from The List. Alvaro walks the length of the rolled-out paper towels and acts as if he is silently reading. Meanwhile Cristiana and Regina continue reading and dancing respectively. When Alvaro reaches the end of the list/paper towels, Cristiana stops reading and Regina stands still next to the bucket for a few seconds and then exits the scene. Alvaro walks towards the broom Upstage Left and sweeps the paper towels off the stage.

We end

After making this episode, Greg and I had a long conversation. Greg noticed that when he first encountered the list, he didn't want to read it and felt like the list itself was making a demand on him to acknowledge all the people mentioned. "I kind of wanted to skim it rather than give it my attention." To Greg, in the episode Regina was either a housewife or a person living a pedestrian life in an apartment with cleaning supplies (paper towel, a broom, and a bucket). This created a contrast between the gravity of the list and the kind of quotidian and domestic material being used as props. Over the course of the episode, Regina moved from having a pedestrian relationship to the objects—cleaning the house in an ordinary life—to dancing with anguished movement that ended with her placing her head in the bucket, legs up in the air. He associated this with a drowning. All the while, the list was being read in a monotone, articulating what Greg expressed as "the level of grief and sense of overwhelm about the list." Through this episode, the list became another space of expressionistic turmoil and anguish. Two worlds were made to live simultaneously in the episode, pointing to the gravity of the list being embedded and not attended to in the quotidian experience of our life. The episode performed a fundamental ambivalence. On the one hand, the list humanizes the anonymous dead, and, on the other, it evokes the violence of the archive. Greg: "these two very strong and different types of affects mix and mingle in the body as you encounter these massive archives of human suffering; you encounter the problem of the archive and the humanness of the people being archived."

There was another layer of encounter that occurred in The Bucket episode. I created it in collaboration with Regina Gutiérrez and Alvaro Rodriguez, both theater makers and performers from Colombia whose theatrical work revolves around the representation of the experience of political violence and disappearance in their home country. In the episode they responded to The List also through the personal experience of their own body of work and research. This speaks to how Affect Theater allows for different bodies of empirical material to cross-pollinate; their embodied experience of their own research encountered The List and new relations were created.

The list as an object continued to transform for us during the workshops. To me, it had turned into an increasingly ambivalent object filled with poetry and chilling coldness. Its ambivalence, as I said, caught me at first and continues to this day. The Bucket episode allowed Greg to tune in to the quick affective experience he had the first time he attempted to read it:

> When I saw that episode, it opened an insight into my own affective response that I hadn't noticed when I first encountered the list and tried to read through quickly and then moved on. [. . .] This is something you can't accomplish with

the text of a list alone. The lines and codes only present one side of the list, the archival side, the problematic side, the dehumanized side.

It is because we had the support of the elements of the stage, of the human body and voice, that we were able to tune in the different affects and facets of this document. Through devising we perform both the humanness that gets lost by the archive and the complication of our relationship to the archive itself. Once again, I am reminded of Benjamin's storyteller when he writes: "(After all, storytelling, in its sensory aspect, is by no means a job for the voice alone. Rather, in genuine storytelling the hand plays a part which supports what is expressed in a hundred ways with its gestures trained by work") (1968: 108). While Benjamin goes from voice to include the hand and gesture, in Affect Theater we add all the elements of the stage to support storytelling, going beyond the human elements that Benjamin lists.

Making these theatrical episodes allowed me and our collaborators to experience the list as a different way of telling a variety of stories. Reading it aloud created a meditative space of repetition, where new images emerged at each iteration, in an in-between of sorts. When we performed the list, it felt at times like reading an obituary, which is the celebration of one's life, or the documentation of it in a few lines attempting to glimpse its essence, like the *punctum* that Barthes writes about in relation to photos, the fleeting capture of an individual trait that conjures their uniqueness (1981). From yet a different angle, some of us felt that each repeated line, and their sum, became a tomb, a cemetery, and a story full of holes that the reader, the listener, the performer, and the spectator could fill in.[8] Others felt the list was a form of care, holding the dead, sheltering them from forgetfulness. To me, the list held a space for being affected by the experience of dying, its language and form became a kind of abode for the dead, a material site of their repose. Uncannily, the list also invoked the dead as simultaneously characters of a story, inhabitants of a cemetery in language, and spectators for whom the list has been staged.

Found dead: 22/02/2022
Number: 1
Name: N.N.
Gender and Age: n/a
Country of origin: unknown
Cause of death: body, reported dead for days; found during rescue of overloaded boat off Calabria (I); 573 rescued
Source: InfoMigrants/IOM

Stage directions for the Reader: Download the full list of deaths from here: http://uni
tedagainstrefugeedeaths.eu/about-the-campaign/about-the-united-list-of-deaths/.
Read as many lines from The List as you like, out loud. Read them more than once
(three to four times), until you enter a rhythm. Pay attention to how they resonate
when they are spoken rather than read silently. What does this reading inspire in
you? Does the reading conjure stories that go beyond the lines, and beyond the
entire list? Or, what else? Jot down some notes or images.

Part III

The Trouble with Storytelling

Representing the Real

Greg Pierotti

An Ambivalence about Narrative

Most of my career I have worked in the form of documentary theater or what is now frequently called Theater of the Real.[1] Theater is primarily a storytelling art. Story is a potent, some would say central, element of this kind of theater. Yet, over my years of working with the "real," I have developed an ambivalence about narrative and its uses, particularly in documentary theater. This ambivalence emerged during my very first efforts as a theatrical devisor working with documentary material, as a co-writer of *The Laramie Project* with Tectonic Theater Project (Kaufman 2014). One of the central questions addressed by the play is: what happened to the town and townspeople of Laramie, Wyoming, after the kidnapping and murder of Matthew Shepard and the media frenzy that arose in response to it?

On October 6, 1998, Matthew Shepard was abducted by Russell Henderson and Aaron McKinney. His body was discovered the following day by a cyclist. Shepard had been struck on the head and face by Aaron McKinney between nineteen and twenty-one times with the butt end of a .357 caliber pistol while he was tied with a rope to the bottom of a split rail fence in a field not far from a new suburban housing development on the outskirts of Laramie.[2] He was airlifted to Poudre Valley Hospital in Ft. Collins, Colorado, a hospital better equipped to deal with the severity of his head injuries. He remained there in a coma for six days until finally succumbing to his injuries on October 12, 1998. Over the course of the following year, Russel Henderson and Aaron McKinney both pleaded guilty to felony murder, second-degree murder, kidnapping, and aggravated robbery. Each perpetrator received two consecutive life sentences.

In press coverage of the story, the discovery of Matthew's body tied to a fence was often referred to by the media and by activists as a "crucifixion."[3] The first media images of the fence itself were usually oriented in such a way that they excluded the suburban housing development nearby and favored the background of a wind-swept prairie. Matthew was small of frame, white, blonde, and had a "boy next door quality" that many white Americans could identify with. These were all powerful frames that enabled a potent media narrative: an iconic homophobic hate crime committed against an innocent man, who might be your neighbor or son, in a sleepy western town. The question of whether Matthew Shepard would survive his injuries dominated the news cycle for the six days during which he lay in a coma in Ft. Collins, Colorado. When he died, many around the world grieved alongside Matthew's family, friends, and the queer community. All these images and frames were true, real. Matthew Shepard suffered a horrific homophobic attack, was dealt violent fatal injuries, and was left to die, abandoned in freezing temperatures for eighteen hours, tied to a fence in the middle of a Wyoming prairie. They also, however, made for a story that might draw more compassion from a white middle-class media consumer than the coverage of the many other violent hate crimes committed in 1998 against less accepted or media-friendly victims, a Black pier queen in New York City, for example, and who as a result escaped the kind of mainstream media attention that was directed toward Matthew Shepard's story.

It was, in fact, the media's response that brought the story to the attention of us members of Tectonic Theater Project. Our play *Gross Indecency: The Three Trials of Oscar Wilde* had been running off-Broadway for almost two years and was about to close (Kaufman 1998).[4] We had been gathering as a company to read plays and share ideas about what we might commit to as a next piece to produce, but we had not been able to agree on anything. During one of these meetings, as we were sharing our shock, grief, and outrage with each other over the breaking story, our artistic director, Moisés Kaufman, proposed that we go to Laramie as a company and see if there was a play to be written about the subject. He didn't propose that we create a play, only that we go to Laramie to see if we, as a theater company, could contribute to a conversation around current events as we had to a conversation around a historical event (the trials) in *Gross Indecency*. Very soon after his proposition, we embarked on a first research trip which was followed immediately by a Moment Work workshop.[5]

The sharing of material that we performed at the end of our first workshop at the Atlantic Theater Company in New York was a great success. This success was less about the content shared and more about the affect felt in the room. It was less than two months after the hate crime narrative had unfolded on the national stage. The impact of the media story and the power and symbolism of Matthew's murder for the gay and theater communities in New York was very palpable in the room among performers and audience alike. There were incredibly emotional monologues in the presentation—like one from the hospital chaplain who attended Matthew in his last days, and who described his first meeting with Matthew, bandaged and unconscious, in biblical terms: "Lazarus! Come out of the tomb!" The affect in the room was tremendously potent, and during the feedback a mandate arose from the audience made up of committed theater folk, producers, and theater illuminati, that this work absolutely must get made. Over the course of the next two years, we made eight research trips, each followed by an approximately two-week long workshop. The final scripted version of the play we created, however, bears little resemblance to this initial presentation.

The powerful storytelling mobilized around the Matthew Shepard's murder initially by the media, and later by our play, our ensuing HBO film based on the play, and by an NBC television movie also made about the Matthew Shepard's story, brought the questions of homophobia, hate crimes, and hate crimes legislation more into the mainstream cultural conversation where it remained for over a decade. After eleven years of constant lobbying by Matthew's parents, law enforcement officers involved in his case, and many others, including the mother of James Byrd Jr., Congress finally passed the Matthew Shepard and James Byrd Junior Hate Crimes Prevention Act, which was signed into law by Barack Obama on October 28, 2009.[6] One of the co-authors of the play and artistic director of our theater company, Moisés Kaufman, and his husband, Jeff LaHoste, were invited to the signing in the White House Rose Garden in recognition of the role that the telling of the story in *The Laramie Project* had played in the cultural and political work that went into the passing of this law eleven years after Mathew Shepard was killed.

This triumph in legislation was primarily due to the tireless work and lobbying done by Matthew's parents, Dennis and Judy Shepard, as well as to the activism of the investigating officers of the murder, Rob Debree from the Albany County Sherriff's office and Dave O'Malley from the Laramie Police Department. Over the years, I observed that the narrative of Matthew's story that we constructed in *The Laramie Project* helped to shape the public perception of what happened in Laramie in a powerful way. The notion that the way we, in Tectonic Theater Project (as well as the mainstream media), framed and represented Matthew's story was useful culturally and politically is not a cynical diminishment of the personal tragedy that Matthew Shepard and his family suffered. It is simply a recognition that the ways in which narratives are framed is significant and has consequences. Adroitly represented stories have currency in political economies. They can create legislative change and emotional healing. It is worth observing, for example, that without media attention on this easily frameable media event in the first place, our company would have probably never been compelled to do the research and write the play.

Throughlines

The play has three main throughlines that run parallel to each other. The central throughline is what happened to the town (and townspeople) of Laramie because of Matthew's murder. We get to know the everyday contours of the town, Matthew's murder takes place, the story becomes a media sensation, the town is inundated by reporters and painted as the hate crime capital of the world, the town responds to the national news (sometimes genuinely, sometimes defensively or performatively), the town examines its feelings about homosexuality, the arraignment and then the trials of the perpetrators take place, the town examines its feelings about hate crimes legislation and the death penalty, the trials are concluded. The town has closure with the story, with their national reputation, and with the members of Tectonic Theater Project whom they have gotten to know.

The second throughline is the story of Matthew himself. He moves from Denver to Laramie to study at the University of Wyoming, he is abducted at the Fireside Bar, his body is discovered, he is in a coma at Poudre Valley Hospital, the media story about him goes worldwide, he dies and is mourned around the world, the trials of his perpetrators take place, his father speaks about him at the trial of Aaron McKinney, he is buried amid homophobic protests and supportive counter-protests, friends and townspeople talk about him, find closure about his life and death, and acknowledge his legacy and impact on their lives.

The third throughline traces the journeys of members of Tectonic Theater Project themselves as they conduct research in the town. To develop this throughline, those of us who researched the play took fragments from our field journals along with personal lines from the transcripts of interviews we conducted and collaged them together to represent ourselves as characters in the field.

My own character's experience in the text of the play unfolds in a well-organized narrative arc. In Act I, upon my arrival in Laramie, I make a joke about the Wyoming State sign, pointing out that it says, "Wyoming! Like no place on earth," instead of "Wyoming! Like no place *else* on earth," which establishes me as a wise cracking—perhaps cynical and intellectually defended— "city slicker" (Kaufman 2014: 11). Shortly after my arrival I meet two of my interlocutors in Laramie: Allison Mears and Marge Murray. They are charming, kind, approachable, and funny. We connect. They wholly disarm me with their colorful language, and their homespun jokes and stories about "Olde Laramie" (which was indeed the case during that interview). Later, as described in my field notes, I go to the fence where Matthew's body was discovered, and my defenses are further dismantled. I cry and share with the audience that, as a gay man, I feel a strong kinship with Matthew. It is a moment in the play that we, as a company, felt would provide a point of connection and entry for many queer people who also had had this kind of profound response to and identification with Matthew Shepard's story. In Act II, I meet with another interlocutor, Father Roger Schmidt. Standing at the threshold of his office with my lesbian colleague, Leigh Fondakowski, I introduce the scene from field notes with my earlier wise cracking bravado: "Here we go, 7:30 am, two queers and a catholic priest." Again, the people of Laramie defy my expectations, and I am completely disarmed by this rural catholic priest's loving, almost activist embrace of the gay community. Finally, in Act III in my parting exchange with the people of Laramie, Marge Murray, who in act I explain, somewhat condescendingly, "taught me a thing or two," now says goodbye to me with the words, "Now, you take care. I love ya, honey!"[7] The cynicism has dissolved, and the heart connection is made (Kaufman 2014).

Everything represented in the play as "my character's arc" was drawn from my journal entries and interviews and did indeed happen. I wept at the fence. I came to have a meaningful, loving relationship with Marge Murray. Father Roger was a font of kindness and an encouragement to me whenever my spirit flagged during the two years that we spent developing the play. Yet, my arc as depicted in the play does not feel to me reflective of my whole experience in the field over my years of developing the piece. My on-stage story was a dramaturgical construction designed using pieces of empirical material collected in the field and reflecting fragments of some of the experiences I had had in Laramie. This construction implied that through my encounters in Laramie, I had made a coherent progressive journey, that I had been changed—improved—through my experience, from an intellectually defended man to a more emotionally honest and connected one. I was indeed changed through many encounters in Laramie into that kind of man. But I was also changed at other times into a frightened man, a confused man, an angry man, an embarrassed man, a man jealous of the good work his colleagues were doing on a given day, a man having a compassionate response to an interlocutor's suffering while simultaneously noting with excitement that what was being shared was "good material" and feeling ashamed of that response as well. My affective states were a jumble of chaos and perpetual change every day during my fieldwork. In fact, rather than taking shape in a coherent dramatic arc, my real experience in the field might be better described by Virginia Woolf's words in her essay on modern fiction:

> Look within and life, it seems, is very far from being "like this." Examine for a moment an ordinary mind on an ordinary day. The mind receives a myriad impression—trivial, fantastic, evanescent, or engraved with the sharpness of steel. From all sides they come, an incessant shower of innumerable atoms; and as they fall, as they shape themselves into the life of Monday or Tuesday, the accent falls differently from of old; the moment of importance came not here but there. (Woolf 1984: 160)

I am very proud of what I consider to be the good work that *The Laramie Project* accomplished in the real world. In retrospect, there is very little I would change about the final text we produced. At the same time, conducting the research and developing the play, was a complicated experience. While many important truths about Matthew's story, and about homophobia in America, were expressed in the work that we finally produced, I felt my own direct experience in the field— of my environments, my interlocutors, their stories, and of myself—was often not fully or accurately represented. These inaccuracies and omissions—I cannot call them misrepresentations—were not disingenuous. They were the results of the practical steps we took, with my agreement, to ensure the clear storytelling that we hoped would add up to a cogent and unified experience for the audience and succeed in the commercial market. My concern was not that representing my "personal truth" was particularly important for the audience to understand the "larger truth" of the story. Rather, because I had my personal experience as a referent against which I could compare the representation of my character's narrative in the play, I could plainly see that what was being dramatized as my experience, while not untrue, only barely resembled the raw, confusing, and complex experience that I had had in the field.[8] I observed this too as I compared my experience of my colleagues in the field against their characters' arcs in the play.

Life doesn't happen in clear, communicative narrative arcs, even if those kinds of stories do real work in the real world. Life happens as a series of complex, often confusing, affective encounters, which we sometimes organize into narrative arcs, and so it was, I felt, with the stories of the company members in *The Laramie Project*. And if this was the case for me and for my colleagues, might it not also be the case with the larger and more resonant stories of Matthew Shepard and the townspeople of Laramie who became our central characters? This process of simplification and clarification was always at work in the dramaturgy of *The Laramie Project*. It also underscored my concern that those who lack the capacity to construct a narrative of their experience in legible and digestible ways, or do not have someone interested in helping them make that kind of translation, may never gain the same kinds of access to a platform and to power that more skillful narrators might attain.

While we chose as a company to share my writing about my identification with Matthew as a young gay man as I wept at the fence for example, we also chose as a company to not share that my weeping arose too out of a sudden flash of sadness I felt at the fence for the impoverished youths and wasted lives of Russell Henderson and Aaron McKinney, Matthew's attackers. It would have been jarring in the midst of the moment of encounter with the fence that we were carefully leading the audience to. It would also not have been "fair" to my character to have him share those thoughts in that moment without taking more stage time than we could afford in order to fairly contextualize my compassion for the perpetrators so it would not be read as excusing their crimes or minimizing the atrocity of the violence that they perpetrated against Matthew Shepard, which was never once an impulse of mine. To serve the story, we opted for a clean cut and emotional (and truthful) narrative over the affect and complexity of my complete experience in the moment.

As we moved closer to our world premiere,[9] another concern arose for me about our narrative practices. There was a shift in our decision-making around what new research we needed to pursue. We became less concerned with representing what we experienced in the field, and more concerned with conventional dramaturgy, in the service of creating clear, efficient narrative arcs. In fact, we even developed a dramaturgical language in the service of this. We labeled some characters punctual and others arcing. Punctual characters appeared one time and the value of their appearance in the play was derived entirely from the content they delivered rather than in any kind of plot or character progression. For example, the character/interlocutor Murdoch Cooper says, "Some people are saying that [Matt] made a pass at them. You don't pick up regular people . . . I'm not excusing their actions, but it made me feel better because it was partially Matthew Shepard's fault and partially the guys who did it

. . . you know, maybe it's fifty-fifty" (Kaufman 2014: 56). This was his one line in the play. We weren't interested in Murdoch's story, we only wanted him to share this idea which, in our view, was the most compelling articulation of an idea we had heard expressed frequently by several interlocutors.

On the other hand, the character/interlocutor officer Reggie Fluty performs many important narrative functions in the play. She is the first responding officer to encounter Matthew's body after he is discovered at the fence. She has compelling personal experience too. She soon learns that as a result of her contact with Matthew at the fence, because her latex gloves kept ripping, she was exposed to HIV. She endures a grueling course of AZT as a prophylactic against HIV infection. During a later research trip, we also discovered that she was the daughter of my interlocutor, Marge Murray, who figures prominently in my character's arc as described above. Reggie Fluty is clearly an arcing character because she has strong relationships and plot points related to all three of the play's throughlines—the town, Matthew Shepard, and the theater company.

As we refined the script, our way of dealing with arcing characters became formulaic. Most arcing characters had to have a beginning, middle, and end. Our formula was tremendously useful dramaturgically. It helped to unfold a very coherent set of stories over the course of this long play. It could also be reductive by instances. Did Reggie have a beginning, middle, and an end? Did she have a moment in each of the three acts? If a particular character only had two moments—as was the case initially for Reggie Fluty who had strong material in Act I and Act II—we would return to our transcripts to find content that "felt like an ending moment" and could be added to an existing moment in Act III, or we would create a brand new moment in Act III to fulfill the three moment journey that our dramaturgy required. If the material could not be found in the already collected research, as had also initially been the case for Reggie, we would return to the field for another interview where we would intentionally point our questioning toward acquiring content that felt like Act III material. In Reggie's case, that meant re-interviewing both Reggie and her mom, Marge Marray to have them both talk about when she got the news from the doctors that she "knew I was negative for good" after her AZT treatment (Kaufman 2014: 84). Again, this made for a coherent script that moved in a clear way from a set of beginning or establishing moments in Act I, through the middle or developing moments of Act II, and on to the concluding or resolving moments of Act III. Nothing was ever untrue, and in fact, in Reggie's case, it was great storytelling. A joyful positive resolution for two characters we have come to love and respect over the course of the play. But the construct was also artificial and omitted the affective mess of the field for the tidy narrative arcs that organized material in a manageable and dramatically compelling way.

Frames

Most problematic of all for me were the ways in which we grappled with contextualizing ourselves—the company members—as figures in the play. Many in the company felt that we should not be represented as merely observers encountering interlocutors in the field, but that we should also be seen to be active story editors, who were constantly making decisions about what to share with the audience about the story. During the almost two-year period working on *The Laramie Project*, we held a series of workshops where we would pose to ourselves dramatic challenges and then attempt to stage, explore, and solve them theatrically.[10] During one such workshop at the Classica Stage Company in New York, we challenged ourselves to create theatrical moments exploring the formal ways we might represent ourselves both as characters on a journey and as figures who were constructing and representing the residents/characters of the town of Laramie, Wyoming to our audience. One company member, Maude Mitchell, presented a moment in response to this provocation, which created a crisis in the company and deepened my ambivalence about narrative representation.

Her moment introduced the character Rebecca Hiliker, a University of Wyoming Theater Professor whom most of the company had met several times. On our first trip to Laramie, we encountered her at a barbecue that she and her husband hosted for our theater company. At that party she was drinking red wine from a big wineglass. She often wore cowboy boots. There was a lot more to Rebecca, of course, but these details were part of our shared experience of this friend of our theater company. Before the moment began, Mitchell placed a rehearsal block on a raised platform with a chair beside it. On the rehearsal block she placed a thick stack of papers, an empty wineglass, a bottle of red wine, a rag, and a tin of shoe polish. On the floor in front of the block she placed a pair of women's cowboy boots. Mitchell sat in the chair in her stocking feet.

She said, "I begin." She poured herself a glass of red wine. She picked up a piece of paper from the top of the stack and seemed to read to herself for a while. She turned the page over and lay it down. Picking up another page, she read a while more. She took a sip of wine. She picked up a third page. It seemed that something on the page caught her interest, she read aloud from the page, in her own voice with no trace of character acting, "There's so much space between people and towns here. So much time for reflection." She looked up at the audience as if to say, "striking text, right?" She turned this page over and laid it down. She put down her wine glass. She picked up a cowboy boot and the rag and began to polish the boot, as she continued to read to herself, turning pages. This went on for a while. Then she read another line aloud in her own voice. "You know, I really love my students because they are free thinkers. And you may not like what they have to say, and you may not like their opinions, because they can be very redneck. But they are honest and they are truthful." She gave another significant look into the audience. She continued in this manner, dispassionately, acting just like herself, polishing the boots, drinking wine, and occasionally reading a line she seemed to appreciate from the pages, or, at other times, seeming to be about to read something and then changing her mind and setting the page aside. After about ten minutes, having finished perhaps a half a glass of wine, polished one boot, and read ten or twelve more lines from the stack of papers (that seemed to represent a transcript of an interview with Rebecca), Mitchell said, "I end."

The moment struck a chord with everyone in the room. As an actor, she performed some of the gestures of the figure, Rebecca. She also performed her observation of the character. She performed the character's recorded words. She also performed the act of editing lines together, and of editing other lines entirely out of the character's text. The moment initiated many other moments during that workshop that called attention to the act of constructing representations: actors listening to headphones and practicing mimicking tape recordings, actors narrating descriptions of characters and then "stepping into the role" to speak some of their lines, actors making costume changes while "transforming" physically from actor into character. But almost immediately during the analysis of this moment, conflicts around the "rightness" of this approach for our play began to arise.

Moisés Kaufman, the lead playwright in the group, objected to what I and the other members of the core writers' group, Leigh Fondakowski and Stephen Belber, loved about the moment. The heart of the conflict, all agreed, was that the moment decentered a real-seeming character in the midst of a dramatic narrative and centered instead the theatrical representation of the actor curating and editing that character. For the rest of the writing group (and for Mitchell who created the moment) this felt closer to the "truth" of our experience as a company of storytellers back from the field and grappling with our fieldwork. Mitchell was not representing Rebecca, rather she was pointing to observations we had made of Rebecca; she was pointing to Rebecca's ideas and words. For the spectators, the moment created a tension between (and perhaps a sense of suspicion about) the content Mitchell allowed to be shared and the content that she chose to obscure. We were allowed to hear only about twelve lines from what looked like a stack of several hundred pages of text. Mitchell played only herself, although she surrounded herself on stage with some of the signifiers we associated with Rebecca. Her relationship to the elements that represented Rebecca was relaxed to the point of being dispassionate—she was sharing the space with Rebecca's words and stuff, but she was more observing it than being affected by it. Most importantly, she placed her decision-making process at the center of the event. She showed us that, while seemingly dispassionate, she was completely in charge of what was shared and what was not. There was nothing sinister in her performance of this control over the selection process. It was just an actress sharing the bits of texts and objects from Rebecca's world that had caught her particular interest, but the acts of selection and curation were central and clear.

For most in the workshop, "the Maude moment" (as it came to be known) grappled with an important truth about our process as theater makers charged with representing real events. It felt weighty, possessed of an ethical gravitas. We were not from Laramie, none of us knew Matthew Shepard, we had accessed only a few parts of the story shared only by the people who were willing to talk to a group of liberal theater makers from New York. We had not even spoken to Matthew's family at this point.[11] Kaufman too appreciated the moment's power, but he began to rework it right away. In his versions, he pushed Mitchell toward a more representational performance and focused on the poetry of the lines of text she had selected rather than on the pile of paper and the reading and selection process she had highlighted. In Kaufman's rework, the stack of papers was removed, the lines were memorized. These revisions made it apparent to the rest of the company that Kaufman was not interested in using such a form as part of the final production.

During the rest of the workshop, a struggle ensued over how to represent the process of representation. As collaborators do, we had fights. Feelings were hurt. People got offended. Moments about representation were reworked. Their critical edges were softened. It all felt deeply personal. Shortly after this workshop Maude Mitchell left the play development process and then left Tectonic Theater Project entirely.[12] In the production we premiered a year later, we made some minor gestures that called attention to the act of representation. We carried tape recorders at the beginning of the play, though they disappeared entirely within the first fifteen minutes; we narrated our personal experience as company members, as I've described above; we changed into our character's costumes in full view of the audience; company members interrupted monologues to announce the names and titles of the character who was speaking ("Rulon Stacy—CEO Poudre Valley Hospital"), but it was the dramatic event—the story of Matthew Shepard and of the residents of Laramie—that ultimately took center stage, and any framing or problematizing of the act of representation was eclipsed by the extremely dramatic events of those main stories. The theatrical frame we settled on might have been read by an audience like this: Here is a group of actors (without a lot of agenda) who went to Laramie, learned about Matthew's and the town's stories, and now are back to directly report that story to us by acting out what they have learned.

The trouble is that representing narrative as an observer's direct experience may make stories *seem* more real. This appearance of sharing unadorned direct experience may in fact give the narrators' subjectivities the appearance of objective storytelling. "Well, it was their experience, it must be so," the audience may be left to assume. The process of how we were representing the real, and certainly the notion that that process of representation might be problematic and, to at least a small degree unreliable, never really took shape in a significant way in our play.

For example, at the beginning of the play, before I represented (my edit of) my interview with Detective Sergeant Hing, company member Stephen Belber gestured to me and introduced me as "Company Member, Greg Pierotti," at which point I explained, "my first interview was with Detective Sergeant Hing of the Laramie Police Department. At the start of the interview, he was sitting behind his desk, sitting something like this" (Figure 13). While I spoke the line, as I uttered the name "Detective Sergeant Hing," I held up a police windbreaker and put it on," then with the words "sitting something like this," I carefully sat at a desk "like this." I then bowed my head, there was a light change, and after the new light cue settled, I looked up at the audience with a different facial gesture and in a Western inflected Midwestern accent I said Sergeant Hing's first text, "Well, I was born and raised here" (Kaufman 2014: 3).

While we were developing the play, I was frustrated with these sorts of moves. I felt that the ethical way to represent our research was to prominently feature the trouble made by the act of editing and selecting material in the process of representing the real. After all, I reasoned, we were not just the dramatic representatives of our interlocutors; we were their curators as well. For me, the inclusion of ourselves, toting our tape recorders and our journals full of field notes, was not a sufficient gesture to point to this problem—as the Maude

Figure 13 From left standing: James Ascher, Stephen Belber, Amanda Gronich. Seated ("Sitting something like this"): Greg Pierotti. The Laramie Project by Moisés Kaufman and the Members of Tectonic Theater Project, Berkeley Repertory Theater, May 17, 2001. Photo by Betsy Adams, reproduced with permission.

moment had been. Perhaps for some in our audience, this subtle framing was a sufficient reminder of our privileged position as editors—not just researchers and reporters. But I worried that it made us appear to many in the audience as more reliable—and empathic—not less.

Years later, with the experience of hindsight, I see it differently. It may have been more authentic to create a play closer to the one I and others in the company initially envisioned, a play which represented the affective jumble of experience in the field, a play that highlighted the subjective nature and moral complexity of our editing process. I have come to appreciate that representations of the flow of jumbled affective experience, or of the suspect position of the researcher in the sharing of experience from the field, while they are still my preference, will just never be as theatrically engaging for most audiences as a clear and progressive narrative arc. Had we emphasized our subjective editorial process to the degree that I had wanted to, we would have distracted spectators from the power of Matthew's story.

By telling what I considered at the time to be an incomplete truth, we shared a story that became important to thousands of young people and their communities in what has come to be one of the most produced plays in the last twenty years. I continue to get emails from teachers producing the play in their high school or college asking me to speak to the students in their cast. Student actors have described to me how they came out to their communities because of working on the play. I have seen audience members come out for the first time during public talk backs after a performance of the show. Straight students have related difficult conversations about homophobia and allyship they have had with their conservative families. The play continues to be transformative for many who encounter it. It still creates controversy and elicits protest, allowing communities to grapple publicly with their ideas around LGBTQI+ issues and homophobia.[13] When I consider all these experiences, I am glad that we kept our storytelling simple and increased the play's reach and marketability.[14] Whatever ethical concern I once had over not sufficiently troubling our documentary form, or not adequately representing the complexity of affect in the field, is overshadowed by what I see as the good that the play and Matthew Shepard's story have done in the world. While we could have made a valuable and interesting piece of theater that was more reflective of our "real" experience in the field, it would certainly not have had the popular impact that it did, and so would not have performed the real work that it did, and continues to do, in the real world.

Brecht: Troubling the Aristotle Problem

Another struggle that I have always had with narrative is the unexamined assumption among theater people that the impulse to share stories is inherently altruistic and humane. It certainly can be. But telling stories just as often can create confusion, division, and distraction. Narrative can stupefy or dissemble as easily as it can unify or inspire. In Affect Theater, we grapple with the double-edged nature of narrative in novel ways. And, while impacted by all sorts of great theorists and thinkers in theater and anthropology, we are, like many in the contemporary theater, influenced by Aristotle and helped by Bertolt Brecht.

As for Aristotle's influence, audiences have been trained to expect certain formal shapes of stories that have been around for a very long time in Western theater, film, TV, and now new media and gaming. In the creation of works for the great play competitions of ancient Greece, Aeschylus was the first master tragedian followed shortly after by Sophocles. Based on these two writers' greatest works Aristotle wrote his rule book, *The Poetics* (1961), about how a good play should be made.[15] For Aristotle, tragic story representations (he considered tragedy the superior form of theatrical storytelling) are meant to create a catharsis, whereby, through identification with the character, negative emotions—terror and pity—are released or purged from the spectator (Aristotle 1961: 78–9). His frame has become the gold standard in dramatic storytelling, followed and embellished by many dramaturgs and theorists along the way.

Gotthold Ephraim Lessing, an eighteenth-century German dramaturge, expanded upon Aristotle to establish the current Western understanding of how a good theatrical story should function. For Lessing, tragedy not only brought to the surface terror and pity, but it also strengthened positive human emotions and affects. Lessing emphasized that while drama should surface and purge pity and terror, it should also create and strengthen compassion and empathy (2019: 19–20).

In 1979, Syd Field's seminal screenwriting textbook *Screenplay: The Foundations of Screen Writing* provides a basic definition of storytelling structure from which, according to Field, a screenwriter ought never to deviate. Field extrapolates this from his reading of Aristotle's treatment of plot (one of the six elements of tragedy in *The Poetics*). He explains that a story written for the screen must be divided into a three-act structure that includes elements drawn from Aristotle's plot template.[16] For Field, these elements are: Act I—exposition, inciting incident; Act II—rising action—plot point one, midpoint, plot point two; and Act III—climax, falling action, and resolution. He is explicit about how and when these elements must unfold progressively on the pages of the screenplay, assigning them page numbers—the midpoint for example should happen on page 60 (2005). Drawing on Aristotle and Lessing, Field codified this into a system that still influences Hollywood, one of the biggest storytelling industries in the world today. Film and TV show formats and lengths have changed with the rise of video streaming and the glut of content that came along with it. With those changes, other Hollywood storytelling practices and standards have come and gone, but this way of structuring character driven stories into "acts" that contain all or most of these plot points at designated page numbers in the development of an evening's episode is part of any screenwriting pedagogy one might now encounter. This type of storytelling is industry standard and learning and playing this structure game makes big money in big story markets.

Following characters' arcs as we identify and empathize is central to Field's spin on Aristotle. In Lessing's extrapolation of Aristotle's dramaturgy and in Field's more contemporary adaptation of both Aristotle and Lessing, the purpose of theatrical narrative is to bring the human system into clarified order through catharsis achieved through the identification with a character going through an arcing dramatic crisis. That structure is organized around a series of mounting crises rising to an ultimate critical climax. In all these Aristotelian models, we want to lose ourselves in identification with story and through that identification experience and relieve ourselves of negative feeling.

Bertolt Brecht challenged this model. He set about trying to rectify what he viewed as a problematic approach to narrative construction in the theater. Empathy, the audience's urge to identify with characters was a central challenge for Brecht. He recognized that empathy is a normal human response that audiences will naturally and inevitably experience. Brecht worried that when an audience, through closely identifying with the character, is swept up in story, and their empathy is roused, they lose their capacity to question both the dramatic figure's actions and the historical contexts or circumstances that allow them to emerge. He was concerned that when theater relieved the audience of feeling, they were let off the hook. Where Aristotle is concerned with uncovering and purging feeling, Brecht is concerned with interrupting the release of feeling to provoke critical thought that might lead to political action outside the theater. Precisely because empathy is inevitable, Brecht created theatrical tools to disrupt it (Barnett 2014).

For Brecht, the solution to empathy is in performing or representing difference. He offers tools to writers, directors, and performers to help them accomplish this performance of difference that he encouraged.[17] One of the key differences that Brecht seeks to highlight is the difference between the actor and the figure they represent. This is a critical element of Brechtian performance. In his writings on theater, Brecht made a distinction between character and figure. A character is a representation of a fixed personality, a continuous changeless person with inherent qualities. A figure, in Brechtian drama, is the presentation of a discontinuous changing series of actions conditioned by context presented to an audience by an actor. To draw this distinction, Brecht encouraged actors to represent two people in performance: themselves and the figure. The actor should not become one with or disappear into the role. The ideal was for an audience to never lose the sense that they were watching an actor showing them the figure (Barnett 2014: 61–4).

Once that dual performance vocabulary was established, then the actor could engage two more of Brecht's tools, *Verfremdungseffekt*, often translated as "alienation effect," and what he called "historicization." *Verfremdungseffekt*, simply put, is a manner of using performance styles and theatrical forms to point to things that we may ordinarily take for granted in daily life and make them appear strange or new (different) thus providing an opportunity to the audience to question or reassess. "Historicization" is a way of writing and performing work for the theater that acknowledges that actions taken in the world are not absolute or natural, rather they are historicized—that is, understood and contextualized through place, epoch, social position, social structures, cultural norms, and so on (Barnett 2014: 64–74).

An example of how these two tools might work together can be found in the celebrated example of Helene Weigel's prop purse in the Berliner Ensemble's production of Brecht's play *Mother Courage*. Weigel wore an oversized purse around her neck throughout the production, and she called attention to the object in her performance with a conspicuous gesture. Whenever, during the play, Mother Courage (the figure) made a business transaction, Weigel (the actress) would complete the exchange by holding the purse up to the gaze of the audience and snapping it shut on her earnings. The actress seemed to comment on the figure with the snapping shut of the purse. This kind of performative gesture is what Brecht called *Gestus*, another tool Brecht developed to create *Verfremdungseffekt* and "historicization." He asked actors to develop gestural vocabularies that would disrupt a typical empathetic response to plot and draw attention instead to the context of the action being played in the moment using difference to point the audience away from empathetic identification and toward political analysis and critical thought.

For example, in Scene Two of the play, Mother Courage loses a son to the war because she is bargaining to make a sale to an army sergeant with so much passion that she fails to notice a recruiting officer making off with her boy behind her back. We may want to criticize Mother Courage for allowing her mercantile relationship to the war to make her neglectful, but at this point Helene Weigel— the actress—holds up her coin purse for the audience's view and conspicuously drops her just earned coins into it and snaps it shut—*Gestus*. With the snapping shut of the purse, the figure—Mother Courage—wakes from her bargaining trance, realizes her loss and is devastated. At the same time, with the snapping shut of the purse, the actress—Helene Weigel—has used *Gestus* to call the audience's attention to the play's critique of war, how "in wartime, big profits are not made by little people. That war, which is a continuation of business by other means, makes human virtues fatal" (Brecht 2015: 187–8). Through *Gestus* the actress comments on both the figure of Mother Courage's virtue—her instinct to profit from the war to feed and protect her family—and on the way the war has turned it fatal—the loss of the very son she aims to protect. Simultaneously, with the *Gestus* of snapping shut her purse around some coins, the actress, Helene Weigel performs the figure of Mother Courage's simultaneous victimization by and participation in the business of war.

In an Aristotelian representation, these same two events—the bargaining with the Sergeant and the loss of the son—might unfold in a realistic style and separately, creating a character journey that rouses empathy and release in the audience. A suffering wartime mother, played by the actor with great pathos, struggles to earn money to feed her family. She earns a few meager coins, joyfully returning home only to find that her cherished son has been stolen away by a military recruiter. She imagines his inevitable death, grieves, and curses the war that has ruined her family. Brecht and Weigel do a very different kind of representational work. They practice *Verfrumdungseffekt* and "historicization" to give their audience, neither simply a sentimental and desperate mother nor a conniving merchant profiting from the war machine. Instead, they represent a changing, socially constructed, human figure stuck with the facts on the ground of capitalism and war that are, in part of, her own making.

Weigel and Brecht distance us from our habitual empathetic responses. They short-circuit the habitual Aristotelian tendency to purge and release our feelings of pity and fear about the tragedy of war and ask us to see it instead as a historically constructed process in which we participate. We are pointed toward analysis and action rather than toward emotion and release. Brecht argues that by not providing easy resolution or catharsis for the audience but instead leaving them troubled and unrelieved of the emotional turmoil caused by the problem— in this case the problem of war—the spectator is more likely to return to their role as a citizen outside the theater inclined to seek relief from the discomfort caused by their analysis through political action in the real world.

Antecedents: Brecht and Tectonic Theater Project

Brecht's theory and dramaturgy permeates contemporary theater, and Tectonic Theater Project was deeply influenced by him. "The Street Scene" is probably Brecht's writing that most informed the dramaturgy and play creation we practiced in the company (Brecht 1964). The essay is a wonderful articulation of why and how Brecht's theories and practices described above might be mobilized in the theater. He explains that a play is like a "street scene" where someone who has witnessed a car accident, at some later time, describes the scene to a crowd gathered on a street corner. There is no pretense that this is the actual accident; he does not have to "be realistic" in his portrayals. He might say, "the woman leapt from the car and screamed," and then he might alter his voice in such a way that he "points to" this character in the street. But he also might choose gestures and ways of expressing what the woman said that highlight his performer's perspective on the woman's role in the story, as Weigel did in her performance of *Mother Courage*. He may perform his perspective or point of view or political agenda. Brecht describes the narrator's relationship to his audience as he demonstrates how the accident took place. "The bystanders may not have observed what happened, or they may simply not agree with him, may 'see things a different way'; the point is that the demonstrator acts the behavior of driver or victim or both in such a way that the bystanders are able to form an opinion about the accident" (Brecht 1964: 121). When we present a play based on the real or on empirical research, as we consider our relationship to both the story we are telling and to the audience to whom we are telling it, Brecht's street scene can act as a useful metaphor or model.

In Tectonic, most of our work based on the real was made with this street scene perspective in mind, and we extrapolated this into a practical dramaturgy where we made a distinction between what we called the dramatic and the theatrical events. Ideally these events happened together in a piece. In Tectonic's dramaturgy, the dramatic event is what might be called the conventional or literary dramaturgy in a piece (in "The Street Scene" the dramatic event would be the car accident being described). It is the story we are asked by the storyteller to imagine. Characters are developed, conflicts arise, and story progresses driven by the desires and needs of the characters. Character stories arc—they have an inciting incident or crisis (beginning), a climax (middle), and a resolution (end). The theatrical event, on the other hand, concerns itself more with what an audience actually sees and hears happening and with the rules of the storytelling (in "The Street Scene" the theatrical event would be the actual scene on the street corner where a narrator re-enacts the story with no attempt to conceal that this isn't really happening or that he does so to emphasize his particular interpretation of events). Where the dramatic event might be considered more literary, the theatrical event might be considered more directorial (Kaufman and Pitts 2018: 22–3). The theatrical event is the logic of how the story gets told and is created through the manipulation of the elements of the stage in the specific theatrical world we are building. The theatrical event can also be understood as the frame around the dramatic event—the more conventional or literary story.

This framing of a dramatic event inside a theatrical event can have a powerful effect on the ways in which an audience understands a story and the creators' relationships to that story and to the empirical material. Ultimately, the conflict that arose while devising *The Laramie Project* over the Maude Moment was over what our theatrical event would be. Many in the group had wanted to frame the work to lean more heavily on the Brechtian model, pointing out our biases and our control over how the dramatic event unfolded. We ultimately opted for a less disruptive theatrical event to frame our story. We did point to the fact that we were indeed present in the field, but primarily we focused on the dramatic event and in the end our theatrical frame presented us as a well-intentioned and relatively trustworthy group of theater makers sharing the details we had uncovered in a relatively unbiased manner as we conducted research in the field. While I have come to believe, over time, that this was a good move, my initial inclination is still to want to represent the trouble in the relationship between the researcher/storyteller to the story being told. Affect Theater makes plenty of room for this kind of experiment.

Affect, Narrative, Analysis

In Affect Theater we also draw on Brecht's ideas of *Verfremdungseffekt* and "historicization." The geographical and historical contexts of our interlocutors are something we recognize in our research in the field and then find ways to represent in our productions. The ways that migrants were understood and received in Italy at one point in history, as dramatized in *Unstories*'s "Episode 4—Fishing Boat," are different from how they are understood and received now, as is dramatized in *Unstories*'s "Episode 10—Neighborhood People" (Chapter 2). This attunement to historical context in both writing and field work makes us more sensitive to other ways in which context may work within a given Affect Theater sequence. Just as more broadly history and place condition behavior and thinking, dramaturgy—the way we sequence episodes within a performance— conditions how an audience receives and responds to the episodes that follow. Positioning a moment like "Episode 3—Participation Podium" that challenges the reliability of the practice of participant observation early in *Unstories*, we create a different kind of context for the reception the audience may have of later moments that present empirical material gathered through that very process. In "Episode 5—Magli Ocean Video," the pathos we feel for Magli, a young man drowned during an attempted crossing of the Mediterranean, may complicate and be complicated by our response to the charismatic Paola and Silvio (in "Episode 10—Neighborhood People"), who we meet a few episodes later, and who question the rights of immigrants to take the jobs they feel they have waited for and earned by playing by the rules all their lives.

In Affect Theater, we also find Tectonic's conceptualizations of dramatic and theatrical events quite useful. I have never managed to shake off my ambivalence about the practices of narrative construction and the truth claims attached to them in Theater of the Real. This ambivalence drives my explorations in Affect Theater. In both *Unstories* and *The Laramie Project* I worked with empirical research gathered in the field. *The Laramie Project* achieved great narrative power and some cultural influence by using a crisis narrative as its central dramatic event and decentering—perhaps slightly obscuring—the theatrical event, the members of Tectonic as the constructors of that narrative. In *Unstories*, we decenter crisis narratives as dramatic events. While we do include some crisis narratives in our storytelling, we devote a great deal of stage time to narrating stories that fall outside of the crisis frame (what we call "unstories"). We are conditioned by Aristotle to understand crisis as central to a proper theatrical experience, but in *Unstories* we choose to center affect and perform the uneventful. There are no arcing characters to follow over the course of the whole event. Our dramaturgies are primarily associative. Rather than following character arcs, over the course of the play we follow the gradual filling of a row of fishbowls with paper boats (Figure 14).

One theatrical event or frame we offer ("Episode 3—Participation Podium") calls into question some of the very research practices that we also rely on. In

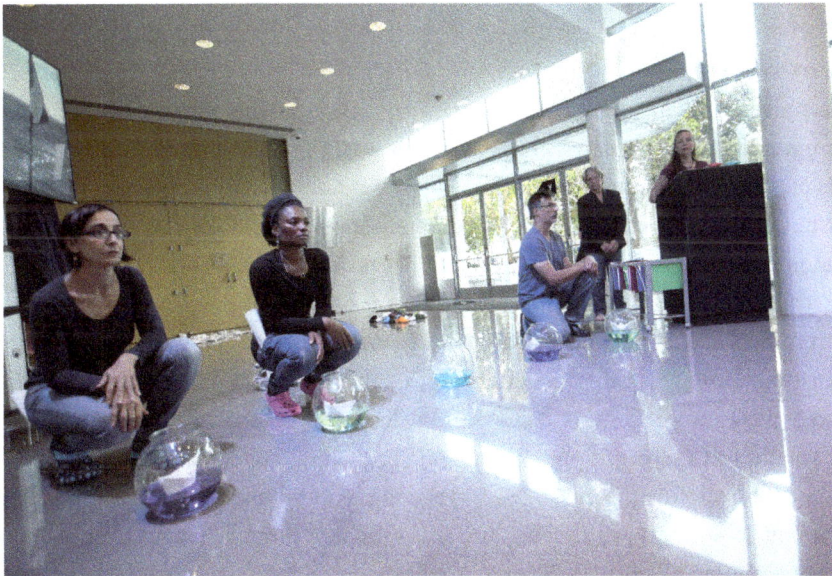

Figure 14 From left: Cristiana Giordano, Ugo Edu, John Zibell, Maria Massolo, and Sarah Hart in *Unstories*, written by Cristiana Giordano and Greg Pierotti, directed by Greg Pierotti. Yerba Buena Center for the Arts, San Francisco, September 23, 2017. Photo by Tommy Lau. Reproduced with the permission of Yerba Buena Center for the Arts. San Francisco, CA, 2017.

"Episode 1—GPS Head," we present ourselves as a company of performers and anthropologists encountering a body of research and grappling with how to re-present it to an audience. This lack of crisis narrative and emphasis on the subjective position of the makers likely places us outside the realm of cultural influence that a play like *The Laramie Project* wields.

To me, telling stories is valuable, but it is a byproduct of Affect Theater not its purpose. The main point is to explore what happens during our analyses in the workshop and the ways they may change our relationship to the shared empirical material. As we outline in Chapter 1, analysis comes at many points in the process. We analyze our transcripts and field notes to unearth the materials (light, sound, costume, spatial relationships, objects, etc.) that we might use in composition. We analyze our own frames and assumptions about our research when we try to separate structural analyses (what we actually saw and heard in an episode), from interpretative analyses (the stories, meanings, symbolisms, collisions, and contradictions we attribute to the structural arrangements that make up an episode). We analyze our own affective responses to our collaborators and to our empirical material and we analyze how that affect impacts our experience as we watch an episode performed. Sometimes through analysis we see that our affective response is based on the phenomenological aspects of an episode ("when the light suddenly turned on, I was surprised"); sometimes we find it is tied to the semiotic or interpretative aspects ("when you turned your back to the man in the hat, I felt both angry and guilty about the way our culture treats immigrants"). Our analysis impacts our practice of dramaturgy, ("the narrative is picking up too much speed when episode B immediately follows episode A. If I put episode C between them, its different mood and affect can interrupt that momentum"). In the end, and often most productively, through analyses with an audience after a public performance, we open ourselves up to what comes from our spectators who bring completely fresh eyes to the series of episodes that we present. It is this analytical process that reveals to us the kinds of stories we tell about our world and sites, and the kinds of affects we are prone to. Our habitual ways of meaning-making and storytelling are revealed to us. We can then return to the practice of episode creation and dramaturgy to disrupt some of our habitual ways of seeing and make what is familiar strange; see it anew (Giordano and Pierotti 2020).

Noticing our affective response to other people's analyses is also important. An illogical felt sense that someone is drawing the wrong perspective from what we were trying to do with an episode may unearth our own blind spots about what we are hoping people may think and feel about our sites or interlocutors.

Or it may send us back to the drawing board to reconstitute our episodes differently to "get it right." Or, best of all, we may experience delight when our intent is misunderstood, and we prefer the "erroneous" analysis to the stale or unexamined thinking that motivated our original attempt. This kind of surprise can encourage us to develop our thinking in a completely new direction in our writing or through continued episode composition. It is important to remember that we are not making theater. We are making Affect Theater. This is what makes the analytical process among practitioners and with the audience so critical and lively. We don't have the luxury to claim that the audience "doesn't get" what we are going for. They are as expert in their meaning-making and affective responses as we are in ours. This relationship with the audience is as much about the audience teaching us something new about our own empirical material as it is about us teaching the audience. These unsought revelations, though sometimes embarrassing, are great gifts.

Affect Theater often exists outside frames of utility and production. It is about play as much as production. In the theater, you write or devise a play, you design it, you tweak it and polish it, and you produce it. You get it "out there." In Affect Theater we don't always do that. We play. But even play sounds more constructive than what I wish to describe. Affect Theater's type of play does indeed create many moments of fun and freedom. It can also create moments of discord, uncertainty, and disagreement about what the next good move might be. Creating this kind of trouble is in and of itself a successful move. The power of the work is in the associative. The words "free association" sound nice: positive, healthy. But if association is truly free, all sorts of unpleasantness can arise, too. Some of the less nice stuff that can come up are confusion, frustration, irritation, strong stakes, a sense of ownership of one's research; feelings that arise around meanings that seem uncomfortably vague; feelings about meanings that don't get quickly and clearly articulated into positions that feel like correct interpretations of our research; feelings that don't immediately dispel our discomfort; feelings of betrayal that arise from the representing of another's experience, feeling ethically compromised; the anxiety that we may be seen as uncaring or insensitive to the concerns of others who are victims of harm, violence, or oppression; the fear of being associated with the oppressor or the oppressing institutions and cultures that we are in fact beneficiaries of.

We can open and allow all these collisions to occur—collisions between our habitual ways of understanding, feeling, communicating, wanting to be understood, and the raw feedback coming back to us—in the moment of episode analysis. That vulnerability allows new knowledges to be produced. We can even make episodes about our resistances to all of it. We create epistemological impacts through our work with our empirical material without necessarily having to make theoretical claims about it. All this can come up and be added into the raw materials with which we play and compose.

If in Affect Theater we aren't really in the business of creating narrative, are we instead in the business of creating affect? Not that entirely either. Everything is on the table. A particular episode or a sequence may create a story or fragments of different stories, it may generate in the spectator a series of complimentary or contradictory affects. Most likely, it will be experienced in the body/mind of the spectator as jockeying between poles of affect and narrative. Because we are so habituated to using the theater—and ethnographic writing—as a mode of storytelling, we may privilege affect in our work sometimes, making a bigger space to attend to it as it arises in ourselves and in our audiences. As Brecht observed, disrupting narrative progressions, and the empathy that tends to accompany story, creates new affects and analyses. When carefully attended to, affect is something we all experience quite palpably, but that we may have a harder time comprehending or articulating. Because of affect's dual qualities—it is both potent and elusive—we find it a useful analytic. It helps us approach the creative space that Favret-Saada theorizes where we create a relationship of not-knowing with our research before trying to share, much less interpret, our field sites. Affect's potency allows our sites to impact us anew, repeatedly and deeply. Affect's elusiveness denies us a position of power from which to make indisputable truth claims. The "productions" of Affect Theater may be actual theater performances that live on a stage, essays that live in the pages of a book, or new ways of understanding that live in our minds and bodies. Whatever sorts of productions Affect Theater enables, its goal is not simply to make our productions clear and get them out there. It is to create and articulate the encounters that happen between things. Affect Theater at its most generative lives somewhere in between the chaos of the field and the clarity of the stories we tell about it; in between "getting caught" and "getting caught anew"; in between ourselves and our worlds.

Association #5

Reverberations from Collaborators

The Clothesline

By Carol Garcia

An anthropologist arrives at the home of her informant accompanied by her father, a co-researcher provided by kinship. This co-researcher facilitates connection and familiarity between the anthropologist and the informant, as he and his father once labored similarly to the man who has agreed to an interview. As the anthropologist and her father walk toward a brightly painted orange home, the informant stands by the fence ready to greet the pair that has expressed interest in asking him a few questions. The anthropologist and her father are walked through the house and into the yard, where the interview takes place under the shade of an open shed. All three—the informant and the two people with questions—sit on plastic chairs. The expanse of the backyard, filled with pots lined against a wooden fence and two running little dogs, feels larger than it looks. Roosters can be heard calling each other in the distance.

As the interview transpires, the informant's wife hangs clothing to dry on a clothesline. None of the questions are directed at her. But, every now and then, the designated informant has trouble remembering a year or the sequence of events that he is being asked about by the anthropologist and her father. When the designated informant forgets, his wife interjects and answers the questions without ceasing to pin clothes on the line. She does not turn to look at the trio, but the trio turns to look at her when she speaks.

Episode—the Clothesline
(Maker: Carol)

Elements of the stage: two chairs, headlights, clothesline, basket, clothing articles, pins
Ethnographic material: interview transcription, field notes
Two chairs up stage left. The chairs are facing each other slightly. Further upstage of the two chairs, there is a clothesline that extends from one end of the room to

the other. The room is dark except for two clamp lights that illuminate the area of the stage with the clothing line. The chairs can be seen only faintly. They are not lit directly by the clamp lights, which are positioned downstage and facing upstage towards the clothing line.

We begin

A woman with a basket in arms enters and hangs articles of clothing on the line. Occasionally, she glances quickly at the chairs and says the following two lines, in Spanish.

"No, no, that was in 1952." (No, no, eso fue en 1952.)

The woman takes a few steps down the stage as she hangs more clothing, and then resumes:

"You first came in 1950, I joined you in 1955." (Tú viniste primero en 1950 y después yo vine en 1955.)

We end

Background and Material for Episodes

In the fall of 2015, I was working on an undergraduate honors thesis at the University of California, Davis. For this project, I interviewed men who had participated in an agricultural contract labor agreement between the United States and Mexico, known as the "bracero program." Working as temporary agricultural laborers under this program initiated for most men a journey of migration, of living between two countries, for the rest of their lives.

Thus, the men's stories were the stuff of adventure, hard physical work, risk, friendship, hope and, oftentimes, a deep sorrow. There was much in the men's narration of their time as braceros that exuded declaratory emotion and an acute eagerness to share about their lives. There was also much in my field notes and interview transcriptions that exceeded what I had initially gone to ask about, namely, the bracero program. In the process of conducting the interviews, there was much that moved me.

At that time, I participated in a graduate seminar on Anthropology and Theater with Cristiana Giordano and Greg Pierotti. In this seminar, I was introduced to the practice of Affect Theater, which gave me a language to think through what had stirred me and how it might stir others.

I recorded and manually transcribed recordings of the interviews I conducted during the summer of 2015. I also took field notes as I searched for people to interview, visiting a Catholic Church in Woodland, CA and attending a play about braceros in Salinas, CA. In the seminar taught by Giordano and Pierotti in fall

2015, we were instructed to create "theatrical episodes" by placing ethnographic material in conversation with elements of the stage (light, props, architecture, time, etc.). These theatrical moments were bound by two enunciations: "We begin" and "We end." When moments were shared during class, we did not provide any background information on the research material being presented. In this process, we were encouraged to de-center the text we were working with. The practice of Affect Theater provided a new language—through objects, space, time, and movement—to work with aspects of the interview encounter that had caught my attention but that seemed rather ordinary and did not seem to tell me anything about what I thought my "research topic" was.

The process of culling material for episodes from notes and transcripts felt akin to stripping excess, placing certain aspects of the interview encounter into relief. The episode outlined above was based on a specific interview encounter in which an informant's wife was present. I was drawn by how she participated in the discussion, responding to questions her husband had a hard time answering, while appearing disinterested, almost bored, not stopping the day's work. The episode itself says close to nothing about the bracero program, but the theatrical devising practice offered a language to explore what the affective communicative quality of this woman's participation might mean. As mentioned earlier, the research material and/or context for the moments were not shared beforehand with the other seminar participants. In response to the clothing line episode, they shared that the clothing items hung on the clothing line were "like pieces of stories, parts of stories" and that hanging them was a way to "keep track" of the stories. Another participant expressed that the episode felt "like the interview was being filmed."[1]

The Practice of Care between "We Begin" and "We End"

On another occasion, as I departed a different informant's home after a two-hour-long visit, my informant stood by the frame of his door and implored, with a kind but stern finger pointed in the air, that he wanted others to know about our nice conversation and how good of a host he had been. This informant was keenly aware that I would be talking about what had transpired in his living room and wanted to ensure that I spoke well of my visit to his home. As a researcher indebted to my informants, Affect Theater practice presented itself as an apt exercise to fulfill, in some small part, this informant's request. The space between "We begin" and "We end" allowed me to communicate that ordinary interactions and observations matter and to communicate *how* they might matter. The interactions I am referring to are, for example, being offered the fruit that the men spent their lives harvesting and savoring it as we spoke, being greeted by another man outside his trailer home while he read a book as he patiently waited for me. When he saw me, he said: "You came on foot? Why so much sacrifice?" I had taken two buses from Davis to Woodland and walked the rest of the way. I did not know what to say. I was stirred. Another man, at the end of our conversation, took out his thick, black wallet to search for his friend's phone number, also a former bracero, taking out one small piece of paper after another until he found the paper that had his friend's number on the back. A man of advanced age, he dialed the phone number slowly and with much care. These moments from the field retain a photographic quality in my mind. They presented themselves as meaningful, if only because they were kind gestures. In the absence of photographs to capture what these interactions made me feel, Affect Theater allowed a refashioning of these instances, to feel again and make others feel.

New Tools: Goading the Ethnographer's "Affective Knowing" through Collage-Making

By Morganne Blais-McPherson

"Who thought," I asked myself as I clumsily clicked through various Adobe Illustrator icons, "that I'd be mimicking my interlocutors' mood boards in an attempt to perform some sort of alchemy on my dissertation project?"

Yet there I was, dancing between bits of fieldwork notes, newspaper clippings, and archived photos, swishing gritty arcs across the digital canvas. I had just returned to California after a three-month stay in Prato, an industrial fashion capital of Italy. That summer, I had spent my days in a fashion studio, observing consultants as they convinced their clients to take on the fraught project of branding their companies while keeping their collections responsive to global trends. My evenings were of a decidedly different tone. Around me, communist militants met and flyered the surrounding communities, often lambasting the fashion corporations and its enablers for causing *degrado* (degradation) in their city and country. These comrades often drew attention to a perceived hypocrisy within *Made in Italy* fashion between the ideas of luxury and Italian craftsmanship espoused by the brand, and the sweatshops of underpaid immigrant workers that manufacture *Made in Italy* garments. Only a socialist revolution led by the Party, they asserted, could put an end to this *degrado*.

And yet, incommensurate as these two spheres may seem, I came to sense that these militants were grappling with similar tensions as the fashion consultants were during the branding process. There was something about the communists' attempts to galvanize their base, all the while presenting themselves as uniquely disciplined leaders, that was reminiscent of the fashion consultants' attempts to design collections that were appealing to a wide market, all the while keeping them "on brand." But what were they? And could an on-the-ground exploration of these tensions, perhaps at the heart of branding and party-building, tell an interesting story about capitalism in contemporary Italy?

To better grasp these implicit connections, I created a mood board. My mood board, a technical term I borrow from my interlocutors working in the fashion industry to refer to a visual collage of text and images meant to evoke a feeling and/or idea for a project, was not much to look at. In fact, it was hideous. But reflecting on my elements—colors, fonts, shapes, photos, text, special effects—helped me put into words associations that had not yet been made explicit. Over time, some bits became clustered around "discipline," others, "design," and others yet, "branding" and "degrado." With the help of graphics software and months of seemingly disjointed multi-sited fieldwork, local concepts were made to proliferate dozens of imagistic, sensorial, and linguistic associations that held together just enough to inspire a new, entirely unforeseen dissertation project.

For example, the mood board's backdrop included a selfie I took from a mirror that had been hung on a colorful wooden slab. This temporary wall divided passersby such as myself from the construction site on Via Vincenzo Capelli, a Milanese street connecting important fashion area Corso Como from the skyscrapers of "new Milan." The street's "restyling," whose primary aim was to facilitate pedestrian access to the shops and put an end to the street as a place of passage, had been financed by Renzo Rosso, whose investment firm, Red Circle, owned seven of the street's shop windows (Lio 2019). At the time, I was not aware of this urban so-called rebirth project, its reliance on private investments, nor the actors involved. I had simply been intrigued by this mirror that projected the image of oneself surrounded by brand names like Moschino and Louboutin, a reflection that to me was jarringly juxtaposed with what the mirror hid: rubble and blue-collar workers.

This tension between luxury and the ordinary, capital and rubble, public and private, brandedness and facelessness, consumers and workers, came to inform my reading of other emic concepts displayed in the mood board.

I will use *degrado* and its clustered images as an example.

Image 1) Florence's *duomo*;

Image 2) an article clipping of trash in an industrial fashion zone with the heading "struggle against *degrado*";

Image 3) rapper Bello Figo (formerly Gucci Boy) who dons the persona of refugee and holds a sign demanding free "WiFFi";

Image 4) a "real" Gucci purse with "Guccy" embroidered on it;

The word "fragility" tied this cluster of images together with another cluster that I titled (to) brand. The branding cluster of my mood board contained:

Image 1) an embroidered sweater with the word "intervento";[2]

Image 2) an image of members of the Committee for Unemployed and Precarious Pratese[3] marching with the banner "Work, House, and Health for All."

How do people inhabit the tensions inherent in the (fragile) project of branding, for example, the fact that subjects identified through the lens of *degrado* can take up the language of luxury Italian brands? What kind of resistances exist among immigrant workers employed in phenomena deemed to be *degrado*— here, the illegal or illicit working conditions in the luxury fashion industry? Or that those same refugees would distance themselves from the party member and his vision to search for organizational solutions to work, housing, and healthcare access issues in other forms?

Once this mood board had been completed, I "exploded" each concept and design element, detailing in written form newfound associations for each piece of empirical evidence included. From this list, I drew out broad anthropological topics, nesting under the four emic conceptual headings (e.g., to *degrado*: citizenship, state abandonment, morality, infrastructure, precarity and unemployment, the sensible, narratives of decay). By the end of the exercise, I had made headway on research questions to frame a grant proposal.

I developed this writing practice through my participation in Giordano's and Pierotti's *Unstories* workshops. The series of workshops during 2017–18 gave me the professional tools and courage to draw on and prod the "affective knowing" (Giordano and Pierotti 2020) that I had developed through my multi-sited fieldwork. For example, in Affect Theater, theatrical episodes come to encompass a dense set of associations between stage elements, empirical material, and the participants. Similarly, my mood board was made of partial connections (Strathern 2004), bringing together the concepts used by my interlocutors, field texts, and visual elements that had come to affectively inform one another. These episodes—and mood boards—can not only evoke feelings but can also serve as generative images for more analytical concept work. Alchemy indeed.

This writing process is an admittedly slow one. And learning these techniques was even slower. At first, I did not understand what we were doing in *Unstories*. I did not really understand what we were doing in *Unstories* six months into the experiment. Truthfully, I think I only understood what we were doing weeks after our last performance in June 2018.

In conclusion, the meaning of the year-long exercise might best be described through another association, which unraveled from Strathernian-infused memories of a ball of red yarn, bits and pieces of which are still scattered across my apartment. The yarn was brought into the workshop by a participant. I liked how this red yarn evoked a cheap, sad replacement for a little girl's bow. I liked how this red yarn was soothing to curious fingers, yet chaotic upon the same touch.

I remember the moments I produced with it in the workshops. Like others at UC Davis Della Davidson Studio that year, I picked it up multiple times to make episodes, drawn to its vibrant color and its physical malleability as it transformed in many participants' episodes from round ball, to web, to small clump, to large circle. Its redness and length allowed it to be used to tie together performers while accounts of tomato cultivation in the South of Italy were read, linking their rhythmic movements into machine-like heartbeats of which I was the maestro. Its ability to be tangled and to entangle performed the ways in which people get trapped in weblike bureaucracies. This and that. The intersection of sadness and care, order and chaos, militarized borders, and the promises of holes in the fence, futures made possible by bureaucracies and the people caught in their webs, the exploitation of immigrant tomato farmers and the rhythms of solidarity that it can give rise to. That's what a ball of red yarn became in *Unstories*. And as the partial connections condensed in the red yarn emerged, so did a productive writing technique.

As I witnessed dramaturgical elements enriched over time with growing conceptual associations, I was inspired to replicate this technique at a smaller scale, having found comfort in the low-stakes, progressive build-up from the cluttered mess of empirical evidence I had accumulated over the years. I went to my archives, no longer feeling the pressure to produce essayistic prose from material straight away, and slowly began creating my mood board. And just like the dramaturgical elements, my clusters of images and design elements became dense with associations that were able to powerfully tie local concepts.

Getting Unstuck

By Rima Praspaliauskiene

I saw the first *Unstories* performance at UC Davis in May 2017. I remember being excited to see how ethnography and theater could be woven together. Back then, I had yet to learn how Affect Theater workshops were designed and what making episodes meant in practice. Before joining the workshop series the following year for the second iteration of *Unstories* (2018), I was nervous about my possible contribution to the process. I had no training in either theater or performance studies and practices.

When I joined the workshops, I was working on my book *Enveloped Lives: Caring and Relating in Lithuanian Health Care* (2022). This is an ethnography of practices of health and care in post-socialist Lithuania, where through the figure of the "envelope" in medical settings, I explore the relationship between gifts, money, and health. That year, on an average weekday, I struggled to rewrite parts of my chapters. It wasn't easy for me to let go of the paragraphs that seemed neat and logical. On the weekends, the Affect Theater workshops would bring a different dynamic into my life. They allowed me to engage with ethnographic text and group work in a more spontaneous and embodied way. When I started participating in the workshop series, I had not anticipated that the process of Affect Theater would affect my relationship with writing more broadly. For instance, I was struggling with my second chapter about chocolate, money, and storytelling in health care encounters in Lithuania. I liked many parts of it, but it wasn't coming along. Should I discard the entire chapter and start from scratch? I couldn't do that. I felt trapped. Unlike the work we did in the workshops, I was attached to the outcome of my writing, but my vision of the chapter wasn't working. I had to distance myself, shift my perspective, and find freshness.

As the workshops continued, I started to see the page as a stage, a clear space that I wanted to fill with episodes to create a more associative space on the page itself. Moments that we created with Affect Theater were minimalist and associative. I saw how much one could do with simple props, such as paper towels, tarp, old fabric, or yarn. The workshops taught me to pay more attention to what was happening on each page of my chapter. I saw my scene-page cluttered with citations and long sentences. I remember having the urge to clean my text, start anew, and rethink. Yet, my first attempts were not that successful. My pages still felt crowded and clumsy. My anthropologist friends gave me generous suggestions—to add or subtract references, choose another wording, and give more context. And so I would add explanations. During the year-long Affect Theater workshops, I started to get rid of many paragraphs in that chapter and re-evaluated the whole book manuscript. Finally, I let the chocolate and storytelling chapter go and completely re-thought the purpose of that writing, which I later turned into several interludes that punctuated the overall narrative arc of the book.

What happened to me in the workshops was that I stopped thinking about productivity. I loved playing with what we had. Surprisingly, this led to unexpected turns and openings. For instance, we were asked to bring an object to the workshop. The day I attended the first workshop session, I remember taking a long time to pick one. I picked a hat and an old tablecloth. I was overthinking the purpose of the objects. The following Saturday morning, I was in my garage, and my eye caught a bicycle wheel with a broken link. I picked it up and brought it to the group without thinking much. I was amazed at how the broken wheel ended up being used by all the participants in numerous scenes exploring and opening up all we could create with it. In the studio where the workshops took place, the bike wheel turned into a versatile musical instrument, a dance partner, an expression of movement, and a décor element, and finally ended up in the performance itself as a valuable possession in a character's life.

Besides playing with objects, collective reading of field notes and making associations allowed me to see texts differently. We would all sit on the floor, and each of us would read a passage, a sentence, or a word from the shared empirical material. I was amazed at how this simple act of reading out loud and listening to other participants' selections made field notes so animated. When I heard a word or a sentence, I noticed how my mind would wander effortlessly and create associations. There was a difference between how I silently read the sentences by myself and the words we read as a group. I caught new nuances. Seemingly pointless phrases, documented in the field notes—such as "What happened? Nothing. Nothing, you pretend that this type of reality does not exist"—when repeated over and again, it created a particular atmosphere that drew me in. This collective practice of reading highlighted seemingly endless possibilities of engaging with the text beyond the text itself by bringing in sound and movement. I felt at ease joining other participants who noticed different nuances in the text. Reacting to some descriptions of scenes, words, and rhythm, I had to step out of the text and rely on my intuition.

The whole process of reading, commenting, and creating moments was playful. Perhaps because we did so many of them, I learned not to be attached to the episodes that I and others made to whether they worked or not. Episodes generated other episodes. I speak English with an Eastern European accent. Once, I uttered a phrase selected from the field notes, which was misheard because of my accent. "I roam a lot" was heard as "I read a lot." "What did she say?" Cristiana asked. That simple moment of miscommunication led us into a reflection on listening. It later generated episodes and sequences. This particular misunderstanding gave me more confidence. I also write in accented English, however hard I try not to. I stopped obsessing about the appropriateness of English and started noticing a more creative use of language. It seems elementary and perhaps even banal, but being aware that different accents are seeping in and creating new meanings allows me to be more assertive in my writing.

In my current creative nonfiction projects, I am experimenting with Lithuanian words.

Precisely focusing on the present moment, being there and playing with an object, not seeing, and not attempting to map out future moments helped me relax at my desk and look for new entries into my text. During the year of the workshop, I felt inspired to experiment with text. Besides breaking apart the chapter on chocolate and storytelling, I was urged to start writing something from scratch. It was refreshing to see each page as a stage. I opened a blank word document and copy pasted the photo of a bas-relief of Lenin's head that I had found in the closet of my apartment in Vilnius the previous summer and began to write associations and memories that it evoked. I had no expectations. I didn't start from an outline or an argument.

Very soon, the pages grew, filling up with episodes about my last trip to Lithuania and the finding of the bas-relief. Then it spilled into writing about the Lenin pin that I had to wear as an Octobrist, my grandmother, and a longer history of transformations after the end of the Soviet occupation. It compelled me to go back to the journal I kept during that trip to Vilnius. On several Fridays that summer of 2018, I spent an hour or so freewriting. Eventually, this associative freewriting became an essay titled "Three Lenins," which I later submitted for a creative nonfiction contest organized by the Society of Humanistic Anthropology. I got a prize for it!

Now, when I am stuck with my writing, I read my notes or browse photos and start freewriting by association.

Otro Lugar

By Lisa Stevenson

From June 11 to 15, 2016, Cristiana Giordano, Eduardo Kohn, and I collaborated with seventeen Colombian forced migrants to create an experimental theater piece that reflected the experiences that led them to flee Colombia. Using images culled from my ethnographic interviews, we spent five days at a Zen retreat center in Quito (Ecuador) creating a work entitled *Otro Lugar* (*Another Place*). Led by Cristiana Giordano, we used a combination of theater techniques drawing on the rich Latin American tradition of Theater of the Oppressed (Boal 2002) as well as what Cristiana and Greg Pierotti now call Affect Theater. Central to our process was the technique they call "episode composition."

I want to argue, or maybe just to swear, that something important happened during the work we did together.[4] But in the register of this essay, let me say that the process of creating and performing the piece allowed the Colombians to communicate (infect others with) their fear worlds: it opened up the possibility that they would be heard by an audience (the theater audience) whose role was *not* that of testing the veracity of their facts (did you or did you not give the guerilla food, did you or did you not leave your home of the 24th of May in the middle of the night?[5]) but was instead to "see" what had happened to them.

One of the most powerful "episodes" in the theater piece emerged from the memory-image that one participant recounted to me of keeping their boots at the side of the bed—the image of being always ready to flee. This scene opens with a bedsheet draped over a wooden box. A pillow and a pair of *lycra* (leggings) rest on the box. A woman enters and quietly places a pair of rubber boots on the floor beside the box (Figure 15). After a pause, where a fragment of the original text from our interview is read, a man enters, slowly folds the lycra, then walks around the box, picks up the boots and exits. That's it. That's all that happens in the scene. But for the Colombians, the boots at the side of the bed are a gripping image both of the civil war (the guerillas, the paramilitaries, the army and the peasants all wore such boots) and of their constant state of hyper-alertness. Living in the countryside of Colombia, they never knew when the armed forces would enter their town: they never knew

Figure 15 Quito, Ecuador, 2016. Photo by Lisa Stevenson, reproduced with permission.

when they would hear an unexpected sound in the night (the revving of a motorcycle, the sound of men's boots hitting the ground) and would have to escape as fast as they could to the hills behind their houses. So, they kept their boots beside the bed and slept in their lycra.

But I want to reflect on a fascinating disagreement we the anthropologists—Cristiana, Eduardo, and I—had with the Colombians we were working with. The crucial thing to remember is that faced with the repeated disbelief of Ecuadorean State agents, the Colombians felt that their theater project became a way to "speak" so that Ecuadoreans could actually "hear" them. In fact, after one presentation of the play, an official of the Ecuadorean Department of External Affairs asked us to present it again to his functionaries. "They don't understand what these people have really gone through," he told us, "But this could help."

With that in mind I will say that the disagreement revolved around the pair of lycra. Eduardo, Cristiana, and I were convinced that the scene demanded a minimalist staging—we wanted to see a simple wooden box with a pillow resting on top and a pair of boots placed carefully at what would be the "foot" of the bed. But the Colombians were adamant too: they wanted to add a pair of lycra hanging off the box. Their argument for the lycra was clear and yet seemed to us beside the point. "The Ecuadoreans do not believe us when we tell them what happened. When they see this, they will believe us." Why would a pair of lycra make the story more real? Why would a pair of lycra prove a point that they had, over and over again in interviews with the UNHCR and NGOs in Ecuador, failed to prove?

While our different aesthetic experiences and tastes may account for some of our disagreement, I think there is more to it than that. In the end, this is what I would call the desire for the materiality of the world—a desire that surges up in a moment when you keep being told that you are misrepresenting, lying, or crucially, not suffering enough to warrant help. The lycra on the table are physically present. No one can deny them their materiality: their shiny, albeit limp presence on the box. Somehow it seemed as if, for the Colombians, there was a circuit from the "there-ness" or the presence of the lycra to the factuality and "truth" of their story. It was important somehow to keep that circuit intact.

The lycra, as you already know, remained. The Colombians had their way. And in truth, whether because of, or despite the lycra, the scene with the boots became the most important scene in the play. This was partly due to Alvaro who had the role of removing the props from the stage. We had envisioned his role as that of a stagehand, but it became much more than that. Alvaro, a man who looks about fifty, but may be much younger, has a kind of graveness that always made me want to slow down and speak a little more exactly. He himself speaks very little, and when he does, he often pauses before speaking. He is solidly built with a lined face, and he wears his hair short, military style. In Colombia he worked as a security guard.

As I said before, all Alvaro does in the scene is enter from offstage, slowly fold the lycra, pick up the pillow and then walk around the box, pick up the boots and exit. But the still despair his body exuded and the reverence with which he folded the lycra, and collected the pillow and boots disturbed any sense that this was *just* another pair of lycra, just another pair of boots, that this was just a play, that this was just a "moment." It stopped us all short.

Afterward, when asked about his role in the play and whether he could explain the particular power it had for all of us, Alvaro said that every time he picked up the lycra and the pillow and the boots, he remembered the time he had had to collect up the body of his dead brother from his sister-in-law's house. He uses the word "*recoger*" to describe collecting the body, the same word you would use for tidying up a pillow, lycra, and a pair of boots. The power that came from his performance, where the lycra, the pillow and the boots become the body of his dead "*hermano de sangre*"—was there, whether (or not) we knew what he was remembering as he enacted it. Something was communicated to us without words.

This is important, I think, when we try to understand what is communicated through images, whether expressed through theater, film, or our anthropological writing. Lycra is never just lycra. And its limp presence, its materiality, may be very important. Affect Theater, and especially the technique of "episode composition," allowed for something beyond words—even beyond facts—to emerge.

Tools for Teaching and Practice

Cristiana Giordano and Greg Pierotti

What follows is a pedagogical progression for various classroom formats and disciplines, as well as exercises, workshop prompts, and support materials. If you want to organize an Affect Theater workshop in your classroom, or center a workshop around your empirical research to develop a performance (or any other sort of written work), here are the basic steps of the process. There is no perfect way to do this, but following these guidelines is a simple way to start.

We recommend that you supply a single body of research on a focused topic the first time you teach or practice with Affect Theater. We have also taught workshops where each participant works on their own specific research material. This is a more complex way of working. Sharing the same empirical material, like we did for *Unstories* and *b more*, makes for a simpler and more manageable process.

The Workshop

Preparation for the Workshop

1. Gather a group of interested collaborators who are working with empirical and ethnographic material (eight to ten is a good number).
2. Give the participants some guiding initial instructions (see email template below).
3. Put the research material that either you or participants plan to work with into shareable files. This may include interview transcripts, field notes, images, and so on.
4. Ask each participant to select some text from the material that speaks to them. This can be as short as a line and no longer than a page. Participants should highlight striking words, images, or phrases.

5. Participants may bring in elements of the stage related to the body of research: costumes, objects, sound cues, light sources, and so on.
6. Remind everyone to dress comfortably for movement and bring water.
7. Start each day with a short physical warm-up.

Episode Composition

1. Make episodes exploring each element of the stage that participants have brought (see below for an extensive list of possible elements of the stage). Don't begin with text.
2. Start your episode making with the elements of gesture, architecture, costumes, spatial relationship, and props. Later explore light, sound, and text.[1]
3. Break into small groups. Let each group choose one element to explore.
4. Give groups three minutes to explore the theatrical potential of their element.
5. Give groups another three minutes to compose a short episode sharing their discoveries (be firm about time limits). These initial episodes may be very short, from thirty seconds to three minutes.
6. Present episodes to each other, framing them with "We begin"—"We end" (these explorations don't have to be good or "successful").
7. Engage in feedback for each episode that generates interest (see below).
8. At the beginning, you may want to offer feedback to everyone to build confidence. Eventually, you can skip feedback for episodes that don't grab attention. The most important thing is to keep generating them.
9. Make a list of the possible uses of text in episodes: that is, dialogue, monologue, voice-over, direct address, written on posters or costumes, and so on (see the following list). How you choose to render text in an episode changes its affective qualities.
10. Layer text into existing episodes.
11. Make new episodes starting with text as the primary element.
12. Make as many episodes as possible, using all the elements of the stage simultaneously. It is still clarifying to decide what your primary and secondary elements are.
13. You can also encourage participants to plan episodes outside of the workshop to bring in and try. In preparation, they may write up what they want to see happen, that is, the number of people, the actions they take, text (if any), cues (a cue is when precisely something happens in an

episode with lights, sound, objects, etc.), stage directions (where people move on the stage), and audience orientation.

Feedback

1. Only spectators—not presenters—give feedback on episodes.
2. Spectators start by sharing anything that they loved about the episode for any reason.
3. Structural analysis: they describe exactly what they saw and heard between "We begin" and "We end."
4. Interpretative analysis: they describe the stories/logics that they made up based on what they saw and heard.
5. Spectators articulate the connection between what they made up and what they saw and heard.
6. Episode makers may (or may not) revise episodes based on spectators' feedback.
7. Title any episodes that generate a lot of interest and feedback among participants, so that the group can then document and revisit them later.

Documentation

1. Once you have titled an episode, the makers of the episode are in charge of writing out the description in a shared document.
2. By the end of a weekend long workshop, you should have at least 20–25 episodes that are documented in this way.
3. If you want to document episodes with photos and short videos, that is an option; you can upload in a shared file so all the participants can access it.[2]

Dramaturgy

1. To begin to organize your documented episodes, make a list of the stories, characters, elements of the stage, text, and themes that recur in documented episodes.
2. Select three or four episodes with shared elements and practice making sequences.
3. Develop transitional episodes in your sequences to connect the episodes you selected in step #2.
4. Treat transitional episodes as important aspects of your performance (not something to quickly get through between the "important" parts).

5. Use transitional episodes as an opportunity to include new empirical material or develop the poetics of an element of the stage that interests you.
6. As you develop sequences, you may begin to put them in relationship to one another to create both narrative and non-narrative progressions.
7. Try layering sequences—performing them simultaneously.
8. Try making longer arcs—connecting the short sequences you have made into a longer structure.
9. As your revisions and transitional episodes begin to impact the work, remove episodes that no longer feel relevant; add new documented episodes to your list.

At the end of a workshop (or a series of workshops), you may find it useful to share the sequences you have created in an informal presentation to an invited audience. We suggest you conduct the same feedback process that you practiced among workshop participants. Remember to allow the audience to share their thoughts without the presenters (your group) explaining their intentions. This always brings new insight and information about the empirical material, affects, and narratives that are mobilized. We also find it useful to explain the nature of the presentation before beginning. This is not a polished or produced play, but a series of thought pieces performed, often with scripts in hand, by non-actors, for the purpose of thinking together and generating dialogue. Of course, this does not preclude the production of a polished piece, should that interest you. Or, the drafting of an article, book, short story, and so on based on your documentation. Whatever your inclination about next steps may be, this process often clarifies places in your empirical material that may need further exploration.

Return to the field

1. Based on what you have learned, collect new empirical materials (hopefully, what you now need from the field is not what you had anticipated).
2. Repeat: continue this iterative process between fieldwork and workshop for as long as it is useful.

Resources

Here are a number of tools and suggestions that may support your practice of Affect Theater in the workshop space.

<u>Introductory Email</u>

This is a template for an email we send before meeting a new group of participants to give them the lay of the land that we cover in the workshop.

Dear workshop participants,

We are looking forward to meeting you all and working together!

1. Please dress comfortably and for movement as we will start our days with a short and easy physical warm up. We suggest you bring water for the day.

2. Please bring some text (1 page max) from your research material: it can be from interview transcripts, field notes, newspaper articles, etc. It has to contain some language. If you don't have any research, bring in any text that intrigues you: this can be a poem, a passage from a novel, a theoretical text, or even a cookbook recipe.

3. Please highlight, write out, or type up a few sentences from any of the text that you have chosen to bring to the workshop. This needn't be too labor intensive. Maybe you already remember a striking image or phrase from something you have read. Just one or two lines that are compelling to you for whatever reason is sufficient.

4. Bring a few costume/clothing pieces—these can be anything. It would be nice if we had some pedestrian items as well as some more theatrical or frivolous things. If you have one or two of each sort, great. Otherwise, just bring a couple of pieces of clothing that interest you for whatever reason: color, shape, weight, texture, pattern, function.

5. Please bring some objects/props to explore. Again, a wide spectrum from pedestrian to extraordinary is great. Bear in mind the audience experience. If your object is quite tiny, it may not read. We would encourage you to bring something small if it interests you, but if it's teensy weensy maybe bring a couple of other options as well!

6. We may work with some sound. If you would like to bring links on your smartphone to sound samples, please do. Check out the website Freesound. https://freesound.org/

7. Bring in one light source (non-flammable). Your phones and computers are light sources, but you can also bring a flashlight, a pin light, etc.

You can bring absolutely anything from any of these categories. It is generative to bring in things directly related to your empirical research. We won't use everything, but the more choices we have to work with the better.

The final caveat about your objects: we share these things as workshop participants and we explore them with some vigor. Obviously, we will work with the intention of being respectful of each other's belongings, but we would caution you from bringing anything super fragile, unless you are interested in exploring the theatricality of the way it smashes into a million pieces! So, dramatically compelling though they may be, we would probably leave our great grandmother's fabergé eggs at home.

Warmly,

Greg and Cristiana

Warm-up Exercises

We find it helpful to practice some warm-up exercises at the beginning of our workshop days. This serves to slow down our thinking, gets us reconnected to our bodies, and tunes us into the shared affect of our collaborators and the environment around us. We sometimes lead the warm-ups ourselves and sometimes pull from the shared experience of participants and invite them to lead a warm-up they know. Any warm-up exercises from a number of different disciplines can be useful as long as they help us raise our awareness and get connected to our bodies, each other, and the space we are in. We often use the exercises in the books of Mary Overlie, Anne Bogart and Tina Landau, and Augusto Boal. We may use practices drawn from yoga, tai chi, or other traditional modes of engaging embodied awareness. If you have experience working with any kind of physical warm-ups, experiment with those methods. Here are some titles you can turn to for support or inspiration. There are many others. Explore what works for you.

Boal, A. 2002 (2nd edition). *Games for Actors and Non-Actors.* London: Routledge.

Bogart, A. and Tina Landau. 2005. *The Viewpoints Book: A Practical Guide to Viewpoints and Composition Paperback.* New York: Theatre Communications Group.

Hayashi, A. 2021. *Social Presencing Theater.* Cambridge: PI Press.

Overlie, M. 2016. *Standing in Space: The Six Viewpoints Theory and Practice.* Billings, MT: Fallon Press.

Spolin, V. 1963. *Improvisation for the Theater: A Handbook of Teaching and Directing Techniques.* Evanston: Northwestern University Press.

Worley, L. 2001. *Coming From Nothing: The Sacred Art of Acting.* Boulder: Turquoise Dragon Publisher.

List of Elements of the Stage

Before beginning to make episodes, we find it helpful to brainstorm with the group and develop a list of elements of the stage that we can use in our compositions. Here is an example of an extended list created by participants in a workshop. Remember certain basic elements will always appear (see the ones underlined); others will be specific to the group you are working with, such as lip-synching, animals, or puppets from the following list.

Movement
Video
Light/darkness
Spatial relationships (levels, distance, direction, and stage positions)
Wigs/makeup
The elements (earth, water, fire, air)
Time (rhythm, duration, tempo)
Text
Costume
Bodies
Set
Puppets
Props
Special effects
Color
Choreography
Audience
Audience placement
Music
Sound/silence
Gesture
Activity
Animals
Smell
Media (projections, recordings, etc.)
Accents
Musical instruments
Lip-Synching
Curtains

List of Ways You Can Deliver Text in a Performance

Before introducing text into episode making, we find it useful to list different ways text may be used. Here is another sample list generated by workshop participants.

Dialogue
Monologue
Voice-over
Direct address
Written (on posters or costumes)
Projected
Sung
Chanted (choral)
Lip-Synch
Citation
Announcements
Written in program
Soliloquy
Poetry
Disordered speech (separated from meaning)
Recorded
As journalistic reporting
As legalese

Prompts and Reminders for Creating Episodes

As you follow these prompts, keep in mind that you can make episodes on the spot, working collaboratively and improvisationally; or individuals can think up episodes beforehand, write them down, and direct them in the workshop.

- Create individual episodes with each of these primary elements: costume, prop/objects, spatial relationship, gesture, architecture (this may include set pieces like tables, chairs, and rehearsal blocks), light, and sound. Keep these simple and focused on exploring the qualities of the element itself, not on storytelling.
- Create more complex episodes using several elements at once. Make a decision about which element is the primary focus of the moment.
- Layer a single random line of text into one of these episodes (remember the various uses of text: dialogue, monologue, voice-over, direct address, etc.).
- Layer a line of text more intentionally into one of these episodes.
- Choose a theme or piece of language from the shared research and ask everyone to make moments about that, individually or in groups.
- Choose a specific element of the stage and ask everyone to make moments about that, individually or in groups.
- Revise another person's episodes.
- Revise one of your own episodes.

Episodes can be long and complex. They can also be short and simple, including all or just a few of the suggestions above.

Keep in mind these are experiments. An episode may be ready to perform exactly as presented, but more often than not it will provide information about other episodes or versions that you may want to try. It doesn't have to be good or "successful."

Questions to Guide the Dramaturgical Process and Organize Your Episodes into a Larger Piece of Work

Once you have a number of documented episodes you can begin to consider how to structure them. You can use the following questions to help you organize a performance. Remember, you can also go through the same process to develop an article, book, or other creations based on your empirical research. These prompts can help you create an organizing principle or central question for a longer piece.

- What are you writing or composing about?
- What in particular excites you about the episodes you have created so far?
- What are the texts you particularly appreciate?
- What are the theatrical forms you appreciate?
- Are there particular characters that are emerging as important (interlocutors, authors of source materials, other types of people)?
- What themes, content and theatrical forms are emerging?
- What conversations do you want to have with an audience through this piece?
- Are there aspects of your research that you haven't developed yet? Do you need to return to the field to gather more material or to interview certain people further?
- What are the greatest challenges to the piece?
- Based on all your answers, articulate questions that can organize your episodes into a final work.

Here below, we share our responses to these prompts which helped us develop the version of the performance *Unstories*, which makes up Chapter 2. Some of these responses were not addressed nor employed in the final performance, but it is important to answer these questions fully as you develop an organizing principle because they help to generate and clarify ideas. It is also important to have a complete list of everything that excites you before making final decisions about what ultimately gets included in your final presentation, whether that is a play, an essay, or something else.

What are you writing or composing about?

- "Refugee crisis" in Italy
- What does not make it into the register of the "refugee crisis"
- Methods (Favret-Saada, "getting caught," research, and ethnography)

What in particular excites you about the episodes you have created so far?

- Contrasts between crisis and non-crisis moments
- State categories of refugees
- Crocs
- Projections of drawings, WhatsApp conversations, photos, and videos
- Unrelated texts speaking to each other
- Episodes about translation
- Regina and Ugo as dancers and researchers
- The square of natural light in the studio space and what can happen inside or outside of it
- The upstage orange curtains
- Using clip lights
- The rolling filing cabinet
- The helpers' table

What are the texts you particularly appreciate?

- Amadou: "People like us don't have stories"
- Translation texts
- Roitman's work on crisis and anti-crisis
- Ahmed's story
- Favret-Saada's article "On Participation"
- Interview with social worker Viviana
- Interview with immigration lawyer Donatella
- Interview with neighborhood people Paola and Silvia
- *Denuncia* documents[3]
- Field notes
- *Bighellonare* interview[4]
- Homiex's WhatsApp conversation
- UNITED List of Refugee Deaths
- Media texts

What are the theatrical forms you appreciate?

- Fishbowls
- Crocs

- Stacks of paper standing for research (interview transcripts, field notes, archival documents, medical files, etc.)
- Speaking at a podium
- Homiex's photos of his artwork
- The blue bureaucrat's jacket
- Regina carrying a projector and projecting a video of the ocean on the back wall
- The podium
- The helpers' table
- Regina's dance with headlamps
- Media Voices

Are there particular characters that are emerging as important (interlocutors, authors of source material, other types of people)?

Interlocutors:

- Ahmed
- Homiex
- Mary
- Paola and Silvia
- The Legal Doctor
- Antonino
- Magli
- Ramzi

Authors of source material:

- Favret-Saada
- Janet Roitman
- Media Voices
- Antonino

Other types of people:

- Observer
- Lawyers
- Bureaucrats/helpers
- Woman Denouncer (from *Denuncia*)
- *Bighellonanti*
- Performer/company member (as anthropologist)
- Performer/company member (as dancer)

What themes, content and theatrical forms are emerging?

- The lack of non-sensational stories about the issue of borders and movement in the news and academic production
- How do you perform the ordinariness of movement and migration?
- The journey of the body of the migrant both in crisis and anti-crisis moments
- Cross-pollination of theater and anthropology
- The disconnect between the research on and the lived experience of border crossing (Ante's fishbowl episode)
- Legal categories and the work of state recognition (Crocs episodes)
- "Getting caught"—the work of affect in research and writing (Participation Podium episode, Media Voices episode)
- If anti-crisis is non-narrative, and crisis is an easy to follow story, how do you fairly represent both on stage or page?

What conversation do you want to have with an audience through this piece?

- Can we think of movement as ordinary rather than sensational?
- Can we be okay not knowing our position around questions of borders and migration?
- How can we frame stories in all their complexity without a rush to take a side or assign blame?
- How does the situation in Europe relate to the one in the United States and other parts of the world?
- We don't want the audience to leave thinking that they now understand the migrant experience

Are there aspects of your research that you haven't developed yet? Do you need to return to the field to gather more material or to interview certain people further?

- The Legal Doctor and background laws around the identification of minor foreigners
- Background information about visas for minor foreigners
- Homiex and his relationship to his artwork
- Homiex's graphic novel contribution
- Photos of housing projects referred to by Silvia and Paola
- Interviews about what *bighellonare* means
- Luca (humanitarian doctor)
- Legal documents (UN reports, Dublin Agreement, Immigration Laws, Documents on agricultural workers, etc.)

<u>What are the greatest challenges to the piece?</u>

- The lack of a central dramatic event
- Not enough cohesive stories and too much metaphorical, theoretical, or abstract material
- The breadth to this conversation is excluded by the language of the state
- The privileged position of the observing anthropologist
- Limited technical capacity in the performance space
- Scarcity of funding

<u>Are there specific dramatic events that stand out in your mind?</u>

- Ahmed/Magli's story
- Antonino's story
- Neighborhood people episode
- The Legal Doctor episode
- Mary's story of *denuncia*

<u>Based on all your answers, articulate questions that can organize your episodes into a final work.</u>

- What falls through the cracks of official stories about borders and migration?
- What are the forces/opinions/positions mobilized around the "refugee crisis" in the Mediterranean and Europe?

Additional Readings

These are some readings that we have found useful in our explorations of theatrical devising and experimental research practices.

Aronson, A. 2005. *Looking Into The Abyss: Essays On Scenography*. Ann Arbor: University of Michigan Press.

Barba, E. 2010. *On Directing and Dramaturgy. Burning the House*. London and New York: Routledge.

Favret-Saada, J. 1990. "About Participation." *Culture, Medicine, and Psychiatry*, 14: 189–199.

Kaufman, M. and Barbara Pitts et al. 2018. *Moment Work: Tectonic Theater Project's Process of Devising Theater*. New York: Vintage Books.

Kondo, D. 2018. *World-making. Race, Performance, and the Work of Creativity*. Durham and London: Duke University Press.

Martin, C. 2013. *Theater of the Real*. New York: Palgrave Macmillan.

McLean, S. 2017. *Fictionalizing Anthropology. Encounters and Fabulations at the Edges of the Human*. Minneapolis: University of Minnesota Press.

Overlie, M. 2006. "The Six Viewpoints." In Bartow, Arthur (editor). *Training of the American Actor*. New York: Theater Communications Group. Pp. 187–222.

Pandian, A. and Stuart McLean (editors). 2017. *Crumpled Paper Boat*. Durham and London: Duke University Press.

Radosavljević, D. 2013. *The Contemporary Ensemble: Interviews with Theatre-Makers*. Abingdon and New York: Routledge.

Smith, A. D. 1994. *Twilight in LA, 1992*. New York: Anchor Books.

Epilogue

Cristiana Giordano and Greg Pierotti

The best collaborative processes are fluid. In this book we share a precise practice, but our intent is not to convey a discipline that must be strictly learnt and applied. We hope that our approach to creation, research, and analysis will be seen as an invitation to play. Practitioners (of theater, anthropology, and the arts and social sciences broadly) may incorporate Affect Theater into their own creative and ethnographic practice. In other words, readers may take what they like, leave what doesn't work, and change what needs to be changed.

In this book we chose to write about the *Unstories* performances we created at the University of California, Davis, but over the years we have used versions of this work in other contexts and with other groups. In New York, Greg blended the emerging principles of Affect Theater with Arawana Hayashi's Social Presencing Theater (2021) to create a play based on the experiences of neurodiverse clients at Job Path, an innovative social justice agency that fosters "lives of distinction" for people with developmental disabilities, their families, and support workers. In this instance, the clients themselves were the primary drivers of the creative process and devised a short performance representing their frustrations, challenges, and successes navigating New York's public health care systems and other bureaucracies. On August 7, 2010, nearly eighty people from seven New York City agencies witnessed the performance, which was followed by a conversation (and analysis) between agencies and clients. The intent of the project was to impact the ways that these department and agency heads approached client relations within this community to create policy change.

In 2016, Cristiana led a series of theater workshops with a group of African youth in Sicily, Italy, who had just arrived after living through abusive situations and forms of enslavement while crossing Africa and the Mediterranean. In this case, they explored experience through the composition of nonverbal episodes where they explored the memories of violence that resisted narration. The episodes were a series of bodily reenactments that were followed by conversations about movement and borders.

That same year, Cristiana collaborated on another theater workshop with Lisa Stevenson, Eduardo Kohn, and a group of Colombian refugees in Ecuador. We combined Affect Theater with Theater of the Oppressed (Boal 2002) to explore the circumstances that led this group to flee Colombia. Using Lisa's conversations with them as a jumping off point, we devised a short performance, *Otro Lugar* (Another Place). In Quito, the group of refugees performed the pieces (described in detail in Stevenson's contribution to this book) for the Ministry of Economic and Social Inclusion, the United Nations High Commissioner for Refugees, and the Ministry for External Affairs and Migration. The process of creating and performing opened up a space for the Colombians to feel heard by different institutional audiences on their own terms, rather than on the terms of the state which typically demands victim stories where facts, dates, circumstances need to be verifiable to qualify for asylum.

We hope that readers will find Affect Theater useful in projects fueled by a diversity of motivations. As described above, the process may be used to allow spaces for communities to be heard on their own terms, to create new relations, to transform public policy, to bring social justice issues to light, or, as in the case of *Unstories*, to share ethnographic research in a more visceral way with communities different from those encountered in the field. Or, simply, it can be used to make a play, documentary or otherwise.

This practice has both a structure to support rigorous explorations of empirical material and the flexibility to adapt to new sites, groups, methods, and research questions. Our wish is that the reader may experience Affect Theater not as a method to master but rather as an opportunity to play, get caught anew in research, and engage worlds with curiosity.

Contributors

Cristiana Giordano is Associate Professor at the University of California, Davis, in the Department of Anthropology. Her research addresses the politics of borders and migration in Europe through the lens of medical anthropology and a critique of psychiatric, legal, and moral categories of recognition of foreign others. Her current research investigates new ways of rendering ethnographic material into artistic forms. She is the author of *Migrants in Translation. Caring and the Logics of Difference in Contemporary Italy* (2014), winner the Victor Turner Book Prize for ethnographic writing (2016), and the Boyer Prize in Psychoanalytic Anthropology (2017).

Greg Pierotti is Assistant Professor of Theater Studies at the University of Arizona. He is an actor, director, dramaturge, and playwright. He is the co-creator of *The Laramie Project, Laramie: 10 Years Later,* and *The People's Temple,* and a co-writer of the HBO film *The Laramie Project.* His plays have been performed worldwide and translated into more than a dozen languages. He has received a Bay Area Theater Critics Award, a Will Glickman Award, a Humanitas Prize, and has been nominated for New York Drama Desk, Alpert, and Emmy awards. His academic research focuses on theatrical devising, and narrative and dramaturgical practices in experimental theater and the theater of the real.

Morganne Blais-McPherson is a Ph.D candidate at the University of California, Davis, in the Department of Anthropology. She conducted research in Prato, Italy, on sustainability in the *Made in Italy* fashion industry. Her dissertation focuses on sustainability certifications and supply chain traceability; immigrant workers and industrial relations; and social movement theory.

Tristyn Caneso is a freelance designer and illustrator based in the Bay Area, California. She holds a BA in Design from the University of California, Davis. She is interested in the interrelationship between design and illustration and in the marriage of form and function.

Carol Garcia is a Ph.D student at the University of California, Davis, in the Department of Anthropology. She holds an MA in Social Sciences from the University of Chicago. Her current research interests include human-animal relations and environmental anthropology.

Homiex is a young artist from Nigeria who lives in Italy. He is a cartoonist, painter, and tattoo artist.

Naichè Luzzana is an Italian painter, sculptor, and art restorer @nadikillart.

Rima Praspaliauskiene, Ph.D, is an anthropologist and a teacher based in Oakland, California, and a visiting scholar at the Institute for the Study of Societal Issues at the University of California, Berkeley. Her research interests focus on medical anthropology and memory in Lithuania. She is the author of *Enveloped Lives: Giving and Caring in Lithuanian Health Care* (2022) and *Nereikalingi ir Pavojingi: Marginalines Visuomenes Grupes XVIII-XIX amziuje* (*Discarded and Dangerous: Marginalized People in the 18-19th Centuries Lithuania,* Vilnius 2001).

Lisa Stevenson is Associate Professor at McGill University in the Department of Anthropology. Her research focuses on violence, subjectivity, experimental film, and the power of the image. Her book *Life beside Itself: Imagining Care in the Canadian Arctic* (2014) won the 2015 Victor Turner Book Prize and the 2020 Staley Prize. Her short film, *Into Unknown Parts*, debuted at the Margaret Mead Film Festival (2017). Her recent work among Colombian refugees in Ecuador engages experimental theater techniques to find new imagistic ways of thinking and representing the violence of everyday life.

Notes

Preface

1 Theatrical devising is a practice that has gained in popularity since the mid-1960s. Currently, a great deal of experimental theater, and more mainstream theater, is created through theatrical-devising practices. While devising methodologies vary wildly from company to company, two general definitions are useful for our discussion. First of all, in most companies, whether through improvisations or structured practices, the whole company tends to be involved in the creation of the entire performance—everyone contributing to a greater or lesser degree to the text, staging, movement, and design of the final performance. As such, the usual categorization of theater artists (designer, director, writer, performer, etc.) is broken down and responsibilities shared and/or redistributed. By empirical material we mean all the non-theatrical texts that we gather from our fieldwork research, such as field notes, interview transcripts, legal documents, medical reports, news coverage, video footage, images, artwork, or even a WhatsApp chat.

2 The Viewpoints of Mary Overlie (2016), and Anne Bogart and Tina Landau (2005) posit six or nine viewpoints as compositional vocabularies; we, however, consider each element of the stage a compositional vocabulary.

3 While training in The Viewpoints can feel prescribed and controlled (especially in Bogart's and Landau's conception), it is Overlie's notion of "finding Horizontal" and what she calls "The Matrix" that we find particularly liberating in our own compositional practice. As Overlie describes it, "The Matrix is constructed of a subtle intersection of the six languages, and the actor enters it by being able to change whichever language he or she is speaking mid-action or from moment to moment. It is a little like skiing down a field of moguls: shifting from a space language to a shape language to a time language within the process of picking up a cup or saying, 'I love you'" (2006: 194). While The Viewpoints training can feel rigid and controlled at times, its intention is to prepare the artist to locate Horizontal and enter "the Matrix." It is this freedom from hierarchies and the fluidity that follows that we find most potent in Overlie's work.

4 As Barba describes it: "Theatre Anthropology is the study of the performer's pre-expressive scenic behavior which constitutes the basis of different genres, roles

and personal or collective traditions. . . . [It] is not concerned with the application of the paradigms of cultural anthropology to theatre and dance. It is not the study of the performative phenomena in those cultures which are traditionally studied by anthropologists, nor should Theatre Anthropology be confused with the anthropology of performance." Barba's notion that there are universal patterns found in performers and acting has understandably received some critique in anthropology. We acknowledge the critique and recognize that the ways in which embodied performance is practiced and expressed is contextually specific. For more information on ISTA, the International School of Theatre Anthropology, see: http:// old.odinteatret.dk/research/ista/theatre-anthropology.aspx.

5   As part of this experimentation, since the late 1980s, various collectives of researchers and art practitioners have formed with the shared interest in experimenting with different methodologies, cross-disciplinary collaborations, and moving beyond the traditional ethnographic output and the centrality of the academic text. Some of these are: the Granada Centre for Visual Anthropology, the Centre for Imaginative Ethnography (CIE), the Future Anthropologies Network (FAN), and #Colleex-Collaboratory for Ethnographic Experimentation. Our work fits with a number of collaborative projects they have been developing around ethnographic performance, experimental theater and writing. We have been part of the #Colleex network; our essay entitled "How to Get Caught in the Ethnographic Material" was published in a volume that collected the work of many other #Colleex members, edited by Tomás Sánchez Criado and Adolfo Estalella: *An Ethnographic Inventory. Field Devices for Anthropological Inquiries,* Routledge (2023). #Colleex is a collective that gathers anthropologists experimenting within different fields of anthropology as well as with artists, architects, cultural producers, designers, or other professionals interested in creative experimentation around form and ethnographic fieldwork.

6   The history of the challenges in developing Hurston's play "Mule Bone" (Hughes and Hurston 1991 [1931]) is an interesting depiction of the kind of tensions that often arise between affect and narrative in ethnographic works of Theater of the Real. The play was a collaboration between Zora Neal Hurston and Langston Hughes. From the beginning, the process was fraught with conflict on personal and dramaturgical levels. The play is based on Hurston's fieldwork in the American South and set in Eatonville, Florida (where Hurston grew up). Hurston (the anthropologist) frequently pressed for more representations of minor stories and wanted to devote large amounts of stage time to the presentation of non-dramatic behavior she had observed in the field—uneventful banter, local children's games, the slow unfolding of a card game—all its rules debated and described. Hughes (the poet and writer) regularly pushed for more eventful and dramatic conflict— the partisan battles between Baptist and the Methodist communities of the town,

struggles within a love triangle, a violent crime, and the trial that ensued. This tension between an interest in the uneventful and affective on one hand, and the urge for theatrically compelling storytelling on the other, often also arises in our work. This can provide a generative tension. It can also be painful and problematic. In the case of Hurston and Hughes, it proved prohibitive. The play was never completed.

7   Katherine Dunham's influential work had three distinct aspects of particular interest to us. First, she did extensive fieldwork, observing and studying a variety of dance movements from the African Diaspora (Dunham 1936). Then, based on her field observations and documentations, she created dances that introduced entirely new movement vocabularies to the American dance world (Barzel 1947). Finally, she developed a complete practical technique that she could teach to dancers to physically prepare them to dance in these new African and Caribbean movement idioms (Carter 2003).

8   Emily Mann is a notable precursor to the work of Anna Deveare Smith, and some of those following in Smith's tradition would be Marc Wolfe, Tectonic Theater Project, Erik Jensen and Jessica Blank, Sarah Jones, Tetsuro Shigematsu, and Cliff Cardinal.

9   While we have described here some performance makers working at the borders of theater and ethnography, there is a larger history of Theater of the Real. Examples include The Living Newspapers in Bolshevik Russia, Eastern Europe, and Germany by artists like Boris Yuzhanin, Mikhail Sokolovsky, Erwin Piscator as well as by Hallie Flannagan, the producer of the Federal Theater Project in the United States. Later examples of political documentary theater focused on social justice issues can be found in the work of Bread and Puppet Theater, Teatro Campesino, The San Francisco Mime troupe in the United States and Augusto Boal's Theatre of the Oppressed in Brazil. Additionally, diverse forms of Theatre of the Real continued to expand in an array of postdramatic works, such as the interview- and research-based productions by Ping Chong, Elfriede Jelinek, Milo Rau, Caryl Churchill, Alecky Blythe, and Adam Cork, to name but a few.

10 This metric of crisis is also produced by the ratio of requests for asylum and the actual number of refugee statuses granted. According to the Association for the Juridical Study of Migration, in 2016 the number of applicants was 123,370, with a rejection rate of 60.6 percent. Only 5.3 percent of the applicants received refugee status. The remaining obtained subsidiary or humanitarian statuses, which are temporary, and require renewal every two years. In 2018, the same source reported 53,596 applicants, with a rejection rate of 59 percent. In 2021, 56,388 people applied for refugee status and 29,790 requests were rejected. For updated statistics, see http://www.asylumineurope.org/reports/country/italy/statistics.

Chapter 1

1 In psychoanalytic treatment, "transference" is the term used to describe how the relationship between the analyst and the analysand is translated by and through the lens of the analysand's past relational experience. In the therapeutic setting, old memories and experiences are reenacted and emotions are projected onto the analyst. Through the process of unconscious reenactment, the patient assigns the analyst specific roles that resemble relationships in the patient's life. The setting thus becomes a theater of the unconscious where the patient can act out past traumatic experiences and, with the analyst's support, work through past traumas by revisiting the relationship that caused it. In doing fieldwork research, like in the experience of transference, we are positioned by others, by discourse, and by power in subject positions that we don't necessarily will. This allows us to be caught in the set of relations and affects that make up any given research site. Like in transference, this experience produces a form of affective knowledge.

2 Several of the founding members of Tectonic Theater Project were students of Overlie at New York University's Experimental Theater Wing at Tisch School of the Arts.

3 Liberal democracies use specific legal categories, such as "refugee," "victim of human trafficking," "economic migrant," and "asylum seeker." The state enacts a violent translation, not seeing the migrant as an individual with rights and privileges, but rather as an autobiographical narrative that must fit the categories of recognition made available by the state. Cristiana's ethnography unveils the ambivalent mechanisms of exclusion/inclusion embedded in these categories of recognition in contemporary Italy (Giordano 2014). To acknowledge this classificatory process, we place the words typically applied to people who cross borders in quotation marks.

4 Upon a foreigner's arrival at ports of entry in Italy, NGOs and state agencies distribute new plastic shoes and discard old dirty ones for sanitation purposes. This is one way in which the body of the foreigner is both taken care of and marked by the state, which holds the ultimate power to include and/or exclude newcomers.

5 *b more* examines race in America by looking at a moment in Baltimore's history through a variety of theatrical lenses and using verbatim text drawn from interviews with its residents across a broad spectrum of class and race. Setting these voices into relationship with one another in various interpretations and retellings of Freddie Gray's death and the subsequent community actions and court proceedings that responded to it, the play creates a complex conversation—without offering a conclusion—about the impact of race and structural racism in a variety of forums: public space, city planning, police practices, jurisprudence, health services, community activism, and so on. The play brings into focus how the field of race relations is inextricably woven into the fabric of American culture.

6 Janet Roitman (2014) argues that crisis has become a narrative device that allows for certain questions to be posed and others to be silenced. As researchers, our interest lies in attending to that which doesn't get framed as a "crisis" and thus may go unnoticed. In the context of our research on migration to Italy, to pay attention to those experiences that are not captured by the category of "crisis" implies attending to bodies that are not rescued at sea or that are not recognized as legal by the nation-state, but that nonetheless create lives at the margins of the crisis and the state.

7 Redlining was a US government economic policy and practice, initiated through the Homeowner's Refinancing Act of 1933, in which neighborhoods were zoned according to property value and race, which led to the ghettoization of minorities in most major American cities.

8 Funding for the 2017 performance of *Unstories* was granted by the UC Davis Humanities Institute, the Mellon Initiative in Comparative Border Studies at the University of California, Davis, and San Francisco's Yerba Buena Center for the Arts.

9 Interview conducted by Greg Pierotti and Ugo Edu in November 2015.

10 When people in the Bocage understood a series of incidents that happened to Favret-Saada (1980) as the sign of a spell cast upon her, she was "caught" in the witchcraft logic, which allowed her to experience rather than intellectually understand what bewitching and un-witching felt like as subject positions.

11 Our engagement with objects and other elements of the stage resonates with some conversations in theater, performance studies, and philosophy on new forms of materialism. Inspired by post-humanist theories, many thinkers and practitioners foreground the agency of environments, objects, animals, and forces to decenter the human and challenge the taken for granted human exceptionalism of western forms of life (Barad 2003, Latour 2005). This scholarship aims at discovering new forms of collaboration between human and nonhuman elements and ways of co-laboring. We think with scholars such as Schweitzer and Zerdy (2014) who propose an object-centric methodology which acknowledges and engages physical materials not as inert human possessions but as agents "with particular frequencies, energies, and potentials to affect human and nonhuman worlds" (2014: 2). Gillespie draws our attention to how "in theater and performance scholarship, objects have not received their proper due as both animate and animating participants in the practice and performance of collective social worlds onstage" (2014:149). If we recognize objects "as life-forms that function in both material and immaterial ways" humans and objects "become co-creators with infinite capacities for performance" (2014: 150). Jones understands new materialism and thing theory as approaches "that allow for a focus on how action intersects with materials to produce new spaces of meaning" (2015: 21).

While we are inspired by these researchers and engaged in decentering text as
well as the human figure to allow other elements of the stage to guide our devising
and analysis of the empirical, we are interested in the generative relations *between*
human researchers/creators and *all* the elements at our disposal in the workshop.
For us, decentering text and the body does not imply permanently centering any
other of the elements of the stage. Instead, we allow ourselves to be curious about
the possible relations and power dynamics occurring between the human body
and the other "bodies" of the elements of the stage. In Affect Theater we do not
completely de-privilege text to foreground other things. After decentering text,
we do bring narrative and text back in, in a potent way that often means centering
human stories. Text is another living "material" that has an impact on the other
living materials on stage. Just like objects, light and the human body have their own
materiality, there are "text bodies" and "narrative bodies" that inhabit the workshop
and interact with other bodies. Overall, we are interested in the affective force of the
elements of the stage, rather than engaging them as collaborators with their own
agency. Further, while many new materialists seem to privilege things or "stuff," for
us the list of material participants in our workshop is more expansive and includes
light, sound, space, image, gesture, time, atmosphere, affect, as well as things or
objects such as props, costumes, architecture, and set pieces. For us, action and
agency intersect with text and stories, and all the other materials encountered in
our empirical research and in the workshop. At times, text and story can also be
the actor or agent in our work. While we avoid creating hierarchies that privilege
story over affect or the human over the nonhuman, we are equally concerned with
avoiding other hierarchies where the body takes precedence over text, or objects
over the human; we are interested in the alternating hierarchies and alchemies
produced by the myriad relationships that occur among all of them. When we
create theatrical episodes, we create relations between all the elements through
affective associations on the stage, and between the stage and the audience.

In fact, as researchers we like the theoretical and practical terrain that exists
in the "in between." We explore the tensions and spaces that exist in between new
materialists' object/agents and humanist storytellers, in between dramatic meaning
constructors and postmodern de-constructors, in between the visible stage event
and the invisible interpretive event, in between the dramaturgy of story and the
dramaturgy of "stuff." With Affect Theater we seek to uncover the generative
tensions between all these polarities and hope to unearth new knowledge about our
sites and our thinking in the in between.

12   Documentation is a crucial aspect of our process and could be considered both
research and composition. We pass over many of the episodes presented, but
we make sure to document in writing every episode that the group has a strong
affective response to.

13 "GPS Head Inside/Outside" is a good example of how documentation of an episode is done. We also keep an index of episode titles so we can refer to them and rearrange them easily in the dramaturgical phase. This index may be compiled on white boards, butcher paper, in a simple Word document, or in a shared document like Google Docs, whatever the group finds most efficient or generative.

14 In this collaborative practice, once an episode is made it belongs to the group and anyone can follow any impulse they have about it in their own episode making. This means they might extend the image into an episode of their own or even completely revise the original episode in whatever way they wish.

15 An example of how this sort of "theoretical leakage" occurs with audiences as well as among collaborators took place during talkbacks for *b more*, when Greg was sometimes criticized for telling the story of a Black man from his position as a white outsider. One response he would give is that there is a larger field of race relations in America, and though he was certainly an outsider to the experience of blackness in this culture, no American is an outsider to that larger field of race relations. We are all positioned right in the middle of it, whether we know it or not. Since so much of the trouble in the conversation about racism is located in white people, and since so many in the white community seek to evade the trouble by simply staying silent out of guilt or a feeling of being unequal to the task, then even if he was wrongly positioned to tell the story, even if his attitudes about race were not fully and properly evolved, perhaps he was still able to open a valuable conversation about race.

16 While the play does not address this, the impact of urban planning and public transportation is easily recognizable as well in the lack of equal access to public transportation in the south. It is estimated that close to 90 percent of Black women in the south were employed as domestic workers prior to the civil rights movement. The planning of access and scheduling of public transportation routes for so many Black workers to and from the white neighborhoods they served and relied upon was clearly a powerful means of social control. Of course, this same reliance eventually became one of the greatest tools leveraged by the Black community during the civil rights movement.

17 We are inspired by the work of Marilyn Strathern, who has written extensively on the concept of relation to reflect upon the ways in which anthropological knowledge emerges in fieldwork and writing ethnographies. Her argument allows us to reflect on the process of episode making as well. Strathern argues that things and people don't exist in isolation; they don't preexist the relations of which they are part. Rather, they are brought into existence by sets of relations with other things and other people in their worlds. Therefore, relations are not only connections between things and/or people, but people and things are in and of themselves relations. Understood in this light, "The relation [appears] as a model of

complex phenomena . . . which has the power to bring dissimilar orders of levels of knowledge together while conserving their difference" (Strathern 2004: 19).

18 Interview conducted on May 21, 2017, in Davis, California.

19 We understand this kind of relation as akin to Kathleen Stewart's concept of "ordinary affect," as "a surging, a rubbing, a connection of some kind that has an impact. It's transpersonal or prepersonal—not about one person's feelings becoming another's but about bodies literally affecting one another and generating intensities: human bodies, discursive bodies, bodies of thought, bodies of water" (2007: 128).

Association #1

1 In theatrical practice, stage directions are written from the actor's perspective as they stand facing the audience, so "Stage Right" in fact refers to the area of the stage that would be on the spectators' left. We have maintained this convention. When the reader sees SR or "Stage Right" in the text of *Unstories*, it refers to the left-hand side of the stage viewed from the reader's or spectator's perspective as is reflected in the map pictured.

Association #2

1 In the process of translating a complex performance experience into a performative text we faced the challenge of conveying some of the traces of our original performance (including our collaborators' and our own bodies, the spaces where we created and performed, the drawings, the initial script) into new material forms to be experienced in the reader's body and imagination. We share this generative dilemma with other thinkers who engage new materialist theories in performance (Jones 2015, Schwietzer and Zerdy 2014), or in other forms of "co-production, curation, choreography, and display" (Schneider 2015). We ask: How else might we include material traces of performing bodies, and expand our idea of what an actual interactive body is, when we also work with text, script, the physical page, and design, in writing a book?

Chapter 3

1 Since 1994, the Italian humanitarian NGO Emergency has been offering free medical care in war-torn countries such as Afghanistan, the Central African

Republic, Iraq, Sierra Leone, and Sudan. Fostering a "human rights-based medicine," Emergency has opened hospitals, first-aid posts, pediatric clinics, centers for the rehabilitation of victims of anti-personnel mines and other war traumas, outpatient clinics, and polyclinics. In 2006, Emergency started several projects in Italy. Under the umbrella of *Programma Italia* (Program Italy), thirteen projects of social and medical support were opened in nine Italian regions. These projects are comprised of mobile and outpatient clinics at ports, in or near shantytowns, and in urban neighborhoods. They serve a population of unserved and underserved foreigners and Italians alike. The main purpose of *Programma Italia* is to provide primary care to vulnerable populations and to facilitate the relation between marginalized users and the Italian health care system. The two projects I refer to in this chapter were partly funded by the Italian state: the interventions at the ports in Sicily received support from the Ministry of Interior, and the one in the agricultural areas in the south from the Region of Puglia. Due to changing politics of reception and the change in the Italian government leadership in March 2018, Emergency's service at the ports of entry was temporarily suspended. See also https://en .emergency.it/what-we-do/italy/.

2 See the online version of the publication that resulted from this collaboration: https://dovelerbatrema.emergency.it/pdf/EMERGENCY-Dove-l-erba-trema.pdf.

3 Cultural mediators work in institutional settings such as hospitals, schools, immigration offices, shelters, camps, courtrooms. They translate not only between the mother tongues of clients and Italian, but also between the worlds and cultural backgrounds of those involved in the encounter. For an in-depth account of the work of cultural mediators in psychiatric and ethno-psychiatric contexts in Italy, see Giordano (2014).

4 A variety of helping government agencies and nongovernmental organizations can always be found at these sites such as: the Local Health Care Agency (ASL), the Immigration Office, Protezione Civile; international agencies such as UNHCR, Save the Children, Terres des Hommes, UNICEF, IOM, the Red Cross; local NGOs; police forces: Carabinieri, Coast Guard, Frontex, municipal police; TV and radio channels; and newspapers.

5 For information on EU border control and directives, see the European Parliament website at https://www.europarl.europa.eu/factsheets/en/sheet/153/management-of -the-external-borders, and the European Council website at https://www.consilium .europa.eu/en/policies/eu-migration-policy/.

6 Until the summer of 2018, Italy remained one of the easiest entry points into the continent because of its geopolitical position and difficult cooperation with other EU member states. In March 2018, the shift in political leadership and the coming into power of a right-wing populist coalition with Matteo Salvini (Northern League) as Ministry of Interior led to the closure of Italian ports of entry, and to the

passing of a Security Decree (approved by the Italian government on November 28, 2018) that, among other things, sanctioned the closure of several reception centers for asylum seekers and other categories of applicants, and an overall hardline politics of border control.

7 For more information on the 2022 IOM World Migration Report, see: https://publications.iom.int/books/world-migration-report-2022.

8 The IOM 2022 World Migration Report states: "Despite the COVID-19 pandemic, there was an increase in arrivals on both the Central and Western Mediterranean routes in 2020. Arrivals in Europe on both routes saw an 86 percent increase, from more than 41,000 to nearly 77,000. Along the Central Mediterranean routes to Italy, Tunisians comprised the largest number of arrivals. The harrowing journeys across both routes resulted in many deaths, and in 2020 alone, more than 1,500 migrants from West and North Africa heading to Spain, Malta and Italy were reported as dead or missing at sea" (p. 73). For more on the impacts of Covid-19, see Chapter 5 "The Great Disrupter: Covid-19's Impact on Migration, Mobility and Migrants Globally" (pp. 151-171). For updated reports on border controls during the Covid-19 pandemic and the Russia-Ukraine conflict, see the European Union Migration and Home Affairs website: https://ec.europa.eu/home-affairs/what-we-do/policies/borders-and-visas/schengen/reintroduction-border-control_en.

9 According to the IOM 2020 World Migration Report, "More than 2,000 migrants died in the Mediterranean in 2018, with the Central Mediterranean route by far the deadliest route for irregular migrants in 2018" (over 1,300 deaths) (World Migration Report 2020: 94–5).

10 According to the IOM 2022 World Migration Report, in 2016 approximately 364,000 people arrived in Europe by sea, while in 2017 the number decreased to around 172,000 and in 2018 to 117,000. In 2016 and 2017, people mostly used the so called "Central Mediterranean route" (from Libya to Italy), while in 2018 maritime arrivals took the "Western Mediterranean route" (from Morocco to Spain). Close to 59,000 people arrived in Spain and 23,000 in Italy (2022: 67).

11 Since the 1980s, there has been a proliferation of anthropological literature on humanitarianism and its ethical, political, and moral underpinnings. To cite only a few ethnographic reflections addressing the conundrums of humanitarian interventions and offering an overview of the debates, see Redfield (2006), Fassin (2007), Pandolfi (2008), Ticktin (2011), Cabot (2014), Dunn (2018).

12 In the essay on "The Moses of Michelangelo," Freud cites the work of Morelli and his method, and notes: "It seems to me that his method of inquiry is closely related to the technique of psychoanalysis. It, too, is accustomed to divine secret and concealed things from despised or unnoticed features, from the rubbish-heap, as it were, of our observations" (Freud 1914: 222).

13 For media coverage on these events, see:
   https://www.thedailybeast.com/italian-migrants-sew-mouths-shut-in-protest
   https://www.mirror.co.uk/news/uk-news/desperate-migrants-sew-mouths-together
   -7480333
   https://www.dailymail.co.uk/news/article-1201126/Calais-migrants-mutilate
   -fingertips-hide-true-identity.html.

14 Carlo Ginzburg argues that the *processo indiziario*, typical of the human sciences,
   is effective precisely because "[t]iny details provide the key to a deeper reality,
   inaccessible by other methods" (Ginzburg 1980: 11).

15 Although language-games have usually been interpreted as different conventions
   (or cultures), Italian philosopher Silvana Borutti argues (1993) that in Wittgenstein's
   work, language-games don't form different epistemes of the world, but ontologically
   different forms of life.

16 The etymology of the term "crisis" comes from the ancient Greek *krino*, which
   means to separate, to choose, to decide, and to cut. Intrinsic to the term is the
   requirement of a final judgment, a definite decision. Historically, crisis has had
   an important role in the domains of law, theology, theater, and medicine, but by
   the fifth and fourth centuries BCE, its medical meaning prevailed. In the medical
   grammar, crisis meant a turning point of a disease—not the disease itself—or a
   critical phase that called for a radical decision because life and death were at stake.
   It pointed to the sudden change of events, an unexpected situation that, for its
   gravity, called for judgment, action, and intervention (Koselleck 2002). However, if
   crisis once signified a decisive moment, it is now broadly used to signify a condition
   of ongoing struggle and enduring turmoil (Roitman 2014).

17 Michael Taussig has proposed a posture for anthropological listening that resonates
   with Bataille's idea of "mastery of nonmastery" (2006). Following Nietzsche's
   invitation to think carefully about "the fact that when we explain the unknown we
   reduce it too quickly to the known, . . . we strip the unknown of all that is strange,"
   Taussig reminds us of "how strange is the known," and how estrangement is "the
   gift of ethnography no less than of literature" (Taussig 2006: viii).

18 In my practice of ethnographic devising, I am often reminded of this quote by
   psychoanalyst Jean-Bertrand Pontalis: "To write is not in the first instance to
   express or to communicate nor even to recount; even less, as too many scholarly
   critics of today repeat like parrots, 'to produce a text'. It is to seek to give shape to
   the shapeless, some basis to the transitory, a life—but how fragile a life—to the
   lifeless. What both author and reader then hope to arrive at is not, as in the case
   of scientific writing, a conclusive truth or even a unique fragment of truth, but the
   illusion of an endless beginning" (1993: xix).

19 See fall 2015 Savage Minds Writers' Workshop series at https://savageminds.org
   /2015/10/19/anthropology-as-theoretical-storytelling/

20 See "Episode 9—Mary (Monosyllabic)" in Chapter 2 for the rendition of *denuncia* in the performance *Unstories* (2017).

21 Private conversation with Lisa Stevenson.

22 There is a double deterritorialization that occurs in dreaming: that of consciousness, which receives the interference of the unconscious, and that of the unconscious, which is displaced through dream work into the form of the dream we see while sleeping. In this process, both consciousness and the unconscious are estranged from themselves.

23 Indulge me for a little longer in my digression through Freud to come back to associative thought and the process of Affect Theater. The content of the unconscious is displaced (deterritorialized) in the dream similarly to how it gets incarnated in the symptom. Unlike Ginzburg, who identifies the symptom only as a clue, an evidence that helps reveal an underlying pathology, I prefer to think of it as a minor language in which the unconscious speaks obliquely. In the symptom, the unconscious presents itself in its partial absence. In fact, the symptom is never literal, never in a straight forward relation to the unconscious, and it forms through processes of omission, displacement, and erasure. In *The Psychopathology of Everyday Life*, Freud describes the symptom as something that forms halfway between the interior life of the individual and exterior conditions: "It is probable indeed that a suppressed element always strives to assert itself elsewhere, but is successful in this only when suitable conditions meet it half way. At other times the suppression succeeds without any functional disturbance, or, as we can justly say, without any symptom" (1965: 15). For Freud, the dream falls within the category of the symptom, and as such it becomes a commentary on the present, like a parable that tells without describing (Freud 1899: 340).

24 As Eugenio Barba put it: "We make this mistake [equating corporeality with the body] which creates a division between mind/body/soul." All direct citations in this section are from my fieldnotes from the workshops with Odin Teatret actors and Eugenio Barba in Albino (Italy), in October 2018.

25 I am grateful to Setrag Manoukian for a conversation we had around this issue during the conference in memory of Ugo Fabietti, a mentor we shared, that took place at the Milano-Bicocca University (Italy) on October 24–25, 2018.

26 As Carole McGranahan (2015) writes, "We miss that the stories are the point," that there shouldn't be a gap between the telling and its content, that the story is about being at the center of the place where things happen and worlds exist. This also resonates with these passages by Kathleen Stewart (1996: 34): "Picture how the authority to narrate comes of having been somehow marked by events, in mind if not in body, and how the listeners, too, place themselves in the scene of story and follow along in its track so that they too can be somehow marked with its impression. Picture the dense sociality of mutual impact. . . . Imagine how narrator

and audience find themselves in the space of a doubled, haunting epistemology that comes of speaking from within the object spoken of. How they find themselves both subject and object of story, both inside and outside storied events, simultaneously seduced and watchful, firmly placed in the immanence of remembered scenes and unfolding events yet always cognizant of the culturally marked skill of 'makin' somethin' of thangs.'"

27 For an interview with Faye Harrison see: https://savageminds.org/2016/05/02/ decolonizing-anthropology-a-conversation-with-faye-v-harrison-part-i/.

Chapter 4

1 Ramzi's art functions as "an imaginative counter-politics" that plays with the unexamined fluidity of walls and borders to show the often contradictory ways "in which people, animals and things move and are kept in place" (Multiple Mobilities Research Cluster 2017: 25). The Multiple Mobilities Research Cluster argues: "An imaginative counter-politics seeks to move beyond the taken-for-granted conception of borders as clear one-dimensional lines, as 'open' or 'closed,' and move beyond border politics as driven by clearly differentiated and singular political forces. . . . This is an approach that attends to traces, disfigurements and ambiguities to illuminate a complex field of multiple political agencies. It expands the frame, enabling us to see the landscapes and political ecologies in which walls are situated as well as the assemblages in which they participate. . . . They encompass corridors, regions and nodes that exceed the spaces next to the border" (2017: 25).

2 On boats turned into art, see media coverage on Venice Biennale 2019 and other art venues: https://www.veneziatoday.it/attualita/barca-migranti-morti-biennale -venezia-2019.html and https://www.law.ox.ac.uk/research-subject-groups/centre -criminology/centreborder-criminologies/blog/2019/06/name-art.

3 Writing about concentrationary cinema and its resuscitation of the remnant, Debarati Sanyal discusses the post-Holocaust artistic use of objects and cites camp survivor Jean Cayrol when he says that this kind of art aims to "restore life, so that a shoe lost in a garbage can may be part of our legacy. The concentrationary taught me to leave nothing aside. Man lives on in his remains" (2017: 11).

4 For another example of installations made in Churches throughout Europe, see Yalouri 2019: 225–8. War artist Arabella Dorman made an installation entitled "The Flight," where she suspended a refugee boat from the ceiling of St James's Church in Piccadilly, London (UK). Working on the question of empathy, the artist clarified that her intent was not to "give voice to others" but to evoke a sense of anguish in those who stood in the Church. Yalouri observes that Dorman's work is not a representation of the crisis, but an attempt at challenging the very ideology

that feeds the crisis narrative: "I . . . see her work as an intervention in the heart of a European capital meant to ironically comment on and unsettle humanitarian proclaims and values of 'an allegedly caring Christian world', rather than as an appeal to the Christian humanitarian feelings of the Church's congregation" (Yalouri 2019: 228).

5   I am referring to Karen Barad's theory of new materialism (2003) and its relation to Bruno Latour's Art-Network-Theory (2005) and the decentering of the human as the privileged meaning-making agent in the world.

6   Ramzi turns broken objects into what Miriam Ticktin has called "tools of mobilization against border walls—the kind of politically inclined artefacts that expose walls as exclusionary technologies" (2017: 26).

7   Bollas writes: "In the course of a day, a week, or a lifetime we are engaged in successive selection of objects, each of which suits us at the moment, 'provides' us with a certain kind of experience, and, as our choice, may serve to articulate our idiom, recall some earlier historical situation, or foreclose true self articulation. . . . We do not know why we choose objects, but certainly one reason is because of their 'experience potential', as each object provides 'textures of self experience'" (2009: 55).

8   Speaking of form, Christopher Bollas writes: "A poem is enacted expression. 'Poems communicate before they are understood and the structure operates on, or inside, the reader even as the words infiltrate the consciousness,' writes Edward Hirsch. 'The form is the shape of the poem's understanding, its way of being in the world, and it is the form that structures our experience'" (2009: 12).

9   The Italian words *frantumi* and *frantumaglia* share the same root and could be synonymous, if it wasn't for the fact that the latter is a term from the Napoletean dialect that Elena Ferrante uses in an expanded way.

10 The debris Ramzi collects at the beach are a kind of border themselves, between the sea and the land, life and death, there and here. They resemble the liminal that Victor Turner (1967) and Stuart McLean (2017) think with, where a suspension of the linearity of narration and experience allows for the "dissolution of familiar forms and the emergence of interstitial, metamorphic beings" (McLean 2017: 113).

11 For media coverage of the event see https://www.ansa.it/europa/notizie/rubriche /voceeurodeputati/2015/04/29/naufragio-soru-rischio-nuovo-olocausto-nel -mediterraneo_01809ab3-abfb-4106-97f5-331d9d0347ac.html.

Association #3

1   The names of places and people have been changed to guarantee anonymity.

2   This collaboration resulted in the following publication: https://dovelerbatrema .emergency.it/pdf/EMERGENCY-Dove-l-erba-trema.pdf

3 Engineering, medicine, and science provided the paradigms of this fascist approach to governance. In fact, Mussolini used to refer to himself as a "clinician" (Ben-Ghiat 2001, 5).

Chapter 5

1 According to the Geneva Convention Relating to the Status of Refugees (1951), a refugee is defined as: "A person who owing to a well-founded fear of being persecuted for reasons of race, religion, nationality, membership of a particular social group or political opinion, is outside the country of his nationality and is unable or, owing to such fear, is unwilling to avail himself of the protection of that country; or who, not having a nationality and being outside the country of his former habitual residence as a result of such events, is unable or, owing to such fear, is unwilling to return to it." The Convention expands on Article 14 of the 1948 Universal Declaration of Human Rights. See full text: https://web.archive.org/web/20120607013438/http://www2.ohchr.org/english/law/refugees.htm.

2 For another example of an evocative art installation around the crossing and deaths in the Mediterranean, see Danish sculptor and video artist Nikolaj Larsen's *End of Dreams* in the Italian port town of Pizzo Calabro (Calabria): https://www.nbsl.info/end-of-dreams-portraits and Rhiannon Welch's article "Time Out of Joint: Larsen's *End of Dreams* and Italy's "Colonial Unconscious" (2016).

3 I am aware that in Western traditions, the artist is often portrayed as someone who doesn't know how to speak about his or her art. Instead, I choose to hear Homiex's stuttered responses as a stand—unconscious or conscious—that speaks to dominant discourses around movement and borders in ways that powerfully exceed the mere figure of the aloof artist. Art is a process that allows him to refuse the straightforward processes of recognition that reduce experience to legal categories.

4 In my own associations, the space in which Homiex's explorations take place through colors, shapes, and shades resonates with Donald Winnicott's ideas of transitional objects and phenomena. As a child psychologist, Winnicott was particularly interested in the ways in which infants approached the world beyond the mother by exploring specific objects such as the teddy bear, a special pillow, a piece of cloth, etc. He understood these objects as "transitional" because they marked a first attempt on the part of the child to detach from the mother and learn to experience the environment on its own. Transitional objects are an "intermediate area of experiencing, to which inner reality and external life both contribute" (Winnicott 1971: 2). They are not part of the infant's body and yet are not fully recognized as belonging to an external reality other than the mother, either. They are staged by the child in an in-between that is simultaneously separate from and connected to

the world of the mother. They belong to the domain of illusion and represent a necessary initiation to experience. They provide a resting place to the individual who is engaged in "the perpetual human task of keeping inner and outer reality separate and yet interrelated" (1971: 14). Experiencing this in-between-ness allows for a radical deferral of the world of signification and meaning to create something anew. The mother is not the literal mother but is experienced through transitional objects and spaces. Winnicott was concerned with the issue of creativity well beyond the question of art because it is through a creative impulse that the child both learns about the world and makes it its own. Creativity is the ability to explore potentialities that extend and expand the time of playing in the middle, in the space created by the partial dis-identification from the world of the mother, and the creation of a world otherwise; in this transitional space one exists in pure potentiality, not actualized or identified *yet* in any category or identity. Winnicott thus introduces the possibility— corporeal, affective, simultaneously verbal and nonverbal—of an affective space that allows experiencing (without containing) that which exceeds any grammar.

5 As Audra Simpson has argued in the context of Canada and its history of settler colonialism, indigenous groups' refusal of the gifts of recognition is "a possibility for doing things differently, for thinking beyond the recognition paradigm" (2017: 12), as a practice that defies "reduction and ethnographic containment" (2017: 4). In Simpson's work, refusal is grounded in indigenous groups' conscious "turning away" from the state's gifts to keep their own sovereignty alive (a world that exists nested within a dominant one and refuses to be subsumed by it). In Homiex's case, refusal manifests through his not necessarily conscious process of exploration of alternative subject positions through art (this process may or may not lead to the emergence of a new grammar-world).

6 I am particularly indebted to an anonymous reviewer who raised important questions about whether it is possible to live beside a world or not, and what a world is. In this final section, I follow some of their suggestions.

7 In psychodynamic parlance, the transitional space is pre-linguistic and pre-symbolic; it is a nonverbal space of experience and emotions—outside interpretation—that is held and contained by the safe presence of the world-mother. The child can explore if it feels held and secure by the existence of a perimeter wherein the exploration occurs.

Association #4

1 We are grateful to UNITED for allowing us to use "UNITED List of Refugee Deaths." For access to the full list, see: http://unitedagainstrefugeedeaths.eu/about-the -campaign/about-the-united-list-of-deaths/.

2   The expression "Fortress Europe" is often used to refer to the restrictive immigration policies and border control implemented by various European nation-states.

3   See Media Release at: http://unitedagainstrefugeedeaths.eu/about-the-campaign/20 -june-international-refugee-day/media-release-20-june-2020/.

4   The List resonates with other lists such as the "slave manifests" of the transatlantic slave trade. These lists included the gender, age, name, place of origin, and physical characteristics of each enslaved person. They were used to keep track of the numbers of people transported in the ships and sold on the markets in the Americas. Christina Sharpe (2016) writes of the slave manifests as documents of the violence and dehumanization of people, commodified through slavery and the archive. The List and the slave manifests are clearly different kind of objects of power, the former intended for humanitarian purposes and the latter for the opposite. But they both keep track of large numbers of people forced to move because of systems of oppression, violence, and capitalist expansion. I am grateful to Rhiannon N. Welch and Debarati Sanyal for our conversations around the resonances between the current migration patterns and the history and legacies of slavery.

5   This documentation was authored by the makers of the episode and included in the shared Google doc in which we all wrote the episode descriptions at the end of each workshop.

6   The List was used in several artistic installations. At the 2018 Liverpool Biennale, Turkish artist Banu Cennetoğlu created an installation entitled "The List" using the document created by UNITED. She pasted it outdoors on tall billboards on Great George Street, in Liverpool's Chinatown. See article: https://www.artribune.com/ arti-visive/arte-contemporanea/2018/08/biennale-liverpool-opera-migranti-artista -turca-banu-cennetoglu/. In December 2018, the city of Modena, Italy, organized the "Marathon of humanity." This was a collective reading during which the population of Modena gathered in Piazza Grande between 8 am on December 22 and 1 pm on December 23, to read out loud each name listed up to that moment. See article: https://ilmanifesto.it/una-maratona-con-34-mila-nomi-di-migranti-morti/. Artist and performer Fabio Saccomani used The List for an installation in the pedestrian part of the Pigneto neighborhood in Rome. See article: https://www.nev.it/nev/2019 /12/24/un-isola-per-i-morti-nel-mediterraneo/. For images of other installations that drew inspiration from The List, see: http://unitedagainstrefugeedeaths.eu/ homepage/photo-gallery-actions-with-the-list/.

7   In our documentation process we write out the description of each episode we make in a workshop. Sometime the same episode is picked up by different participants who wish to rework it by adding new text or replacing elements of the stage. The new version is labeled with the original title and the #2, #3, and so on indicating its new iteration.

8   In her book, *Naufraghi senza volto. Dare un nome alle vittime del Mediterraneo* (2018), Cristina Cattaneo chronicles her work as a forensic scientist and criminologist identifying victims of the crossing of the Mediterranean. She reflects on how every individual case is a different story that accumulates inside her, like the layers of sediments. Bodies become more eloquent as corpses than when alive, bearing witness to the violence and despair of the present moment. I am grateful to Debarati Sanyal for pointing out to me how Cattaneo's experience evokes something akin to the process of working on the list through Affect Theater, where, in her words, "the interplay of story, name, and affective palimpsest" is articulated through theatrical episodes and the ways in which workshop participants relate to the archive inscribed in the list.

Chapter 6

1   Carol Martin defines "Theatre of the Real" as: the "wide range of theatre practices and styles that recycle reality, whether that reality is personal, social, political, or historical" (2013: 5). In her book, Martin points out that "theatre of the real can make a generative and critical intervention in people's prejudices and the limitations of public understanding. Theatre of the real can also oversimplify, inflame prejudices, and support one-sided perspectives" (2013: 120).

2   These details were shared with me directly by investigating officer Detective Sergeant Rob Debree of the Laramie County Sheriff's Department in an interview conducted in Laramie, Wyoming, in late September of 2008. The facts of the attack are fully detailed in the transcripts of the Aaron McKinney trial of 1999.

3   See Vanity Fair's March 1999 feature article, "The Crucifixion of Matthew Shepard," which is one mainstream example of this kind of symbolic narrativizing.

4   This play by Moisés Kaufman interrogates the series of three trials that ultimately led to Wilde's imprisonment for the crime of Gross Indecency (the legal term in Victorian England for sex between men).

5   Moment Work is a theatrical devising practice developed by Tectonic Theater Project and an important antecedent of Affect Theater. Its most similar aspect is the development of moments (in Affect Theater we call these episodes) framed by the words "we begin" and "we end." After a workshop, a series of moments is strung together to present in an informal sharing for feedback. After a series of such workshops, a more formalized progression of moments may be presented as a more polished theatrical production.

6   The other man named by the act is James Byrd Junior, a Black man who was murdered by three men who were documented members of racist and white

supremacist groups in the same year that Matthew Shepard was murdered. The Matthew Shepard and James Byrd Junior hate crimes prevention act provides additional penalties as well as federal support to local law enforcement to prosecute crimes identified as hate crimes and expands the federally protected status of groups of people to include the actual or perceived religion, national origin, gender, sexual orientation, gender identity, or disability of any person.

7   This last exchange between Marge and me was since cut from the print version published in 2014 which we cite in this book, but it is still in the original acting-version of the play licensed by Dramatist Play Services when the play first premiered.

8   In "About Participation," Favret-Saada expresses her concern about the researcher who in the writing process gets uncaught, rather than "getting caught again." She makes an elegant articulation of the tension that I felt between my own actual affective experience in the field (being caught) and the later organization of that experience into a representation of a tidy narrative arc (from an uncaught position) (192).

9   The world premiere of *The Laramie Project* took place at the Ricketson Theater at The Denver Center for the Performing Arts (the professional resident theater company closest to Laramie) on February 6, 2000.

10   This lengthy development process was made possible by a generous Rockefeller Grant. Developing work for the commercial theater in this way is time consuming and expensive. Affect Theater requires time to develop as well, but because it has different goals apart from professional production, the funding of the work is less prohibitive.

11   Before the world premiere the Shepard family, though they chose to not come to see the play, did give us their blessing to do the work, and since that time have become supporters of the play and friends of Tectonic Theater Project.

12   Mitchell left the project because she was offered the part of Nora in Mabou Mines' groundbreaking production of *A Doll's House*, but I always felt that her rift with our project began at this moment. By the time she was offered the role of Nora, she was ready to move on.

13   During the writing of this chapter in February, 2023 the play was banned from public school curriculum in Lansing, Kansas. The play, along with several other texts, was removed in response to the bizarre and erroneous allegation that it teaches critical race theory.

14   In the ten years between 2010 and 2020 there were 2,273 licensed productions of the play.

15   In *The Poetics*, Aristotle also occasionally points to the third of the great tragedians, the experimenter Euripides as an example of how to NOT follow the rules of good playwrighting.

16   The key structural elements of Field's dramaturgy are attributed by him to Aristotle but are in fact drawn from ideas about plot extrapolated from Aristotle's poetics by

the novelist Gustave Freytag in the late 1800s. Freytag created a structural model for plot with most of the elements in Field's model which is called Freytag's Pyramid.

17 Brecht offered different practices and theoretical frames according to the position of the reader. In fact, his great theoretical brainstorming project, *Buying Brass*, is written as a performance, a scripted conversation between five characters: the actor (interested in his public reception), the actress (interested in the public's education), the dramaturg (interested in creating bridges between various parties), the philosopher (interested in creating a theater that is useful to the public), and the stagehand (who represents Brecht's ideal audience—the Marxist worker, dissatisfied with his lot in the capitalist system) (Brecht 2015).

Association #5

1 Course notes, 10/26/15.

2 In "commercial" fashion, as my interlocutors explained, it is to make a small change to a bland garment that is typically sold by the supplier to other brands; it is also to make a speech that takes a position in a meeting, for example, an assembly.

3 A committee of refugees, some of whom work in garment or textile factories, led by an Italian communist party member.

4 In *I Swear I Saw This* (2011), Taussig describes a scene that so captures the everyday insanity of our social world that it is simultaneously believable and unbelievable. In the face of such emergencies that have become the rule, the only response seems to be to swear, which is both a curse and a form of witness.

5 I would argue that if the piece was successful, it was successful precisely because of the simplicity and power of its images. But what does it mean for a theater piece to be successful? I might say, in this particular instance, that it was successful because it was able to communicate to the audience, to allow the audience to participate in, the fear-world the Colombians lived in.

Chapter 7

1 In our experience, light, sound, and text create more complexities in episodes. They exert more influence over the audience's experience of the episodes and, therefore, require more compositional skills.

2 In our experience, recording episodes only in writing leaves room for the imagination to continue creating new iterations of the episodes without the makers feeling bound to recreate what has been documented on video or in images. Creating video may also make for less clear written descriptions so when you translate the work into writing you will have an extra step you must develop.

3   *Denuncia* is the document that foreign women who qualifies as victims of human trafficking in Italy file at the police station to denounce their exploiters and apply for a visa. More generally, in Italian a *denuncia* is the act of filing charges against someone to denounce a wrongdoing.

4   In the Preface, we explain the meaning of *bighellonare*, a way of walking that evokes relaxed wandering around, roaming the streets aimlessly and with a lazy attitude, often used by the media to describe the ways in which African migrant men in Italy walk in the streets.

References

Agamben, G. (1998), *Homo Sacer: Sovereign Power and Bare Life*, Stanford: Stanford University Press.

Agamben, G. (1999), *Potentialities: Collected Essays in Philosophy*, Stanford: Stanford University Press.

Aristotle (1961), *Aristotle's Poetics*, New York: Hill and Wang.

Aronson, A. (2005), *Looking into the Abyss: Essays on Scenography*, Ann Arbor: University of Michigan Press.

Augé, M. (1992), *Non-lieux: Introduction à une anthropologie de la surmodernité*, Paris: Editions Seuil.

Barad, K. (2003), "Posthumanist Performativity: Toward an Understanding of How Matter Comes to Matter," *Signs: Journal of Women in Culture and Society* 28(30): 801–31.

Barba, E. (1986), *Beyond the Floating Islands*, New York: PAJ Publications.

Barba, E. (2010), *On Directing and Dramaturgy: Burning the House*, trans. J. Barba, London: Routledge.

Barba, E. and N. Savarese (2005), *A Dictionary of Theater Anthropology: The Secret Art of the Performer*, trans. R. Fowler, London: Routledge.

Barnett, D. (2014), *Brecht in Practice: Theatre, Theory and Performance*, London: Bloomsbury.

Barry, K. (2019), "Art and Materiality in the Global Refugee Crisis: Ai Weiwei's Artworks and the Emerging Aesthetics of Mobilities," *Mobilities* 14(2): 204–17.

Barthes, R. (1981), *Camera Lucida: Reflections on Photography*, New York: Hill and Wang.

Barzel, A. (dir.) (1947), *Film of Katherine Dunham Company, "Shango, 1947, video clip #27"*, Washington, DC: Library of Congress, Digital Collections. https://www.loc.gov/collections/katherine-dunham/about-this-collection/?loclr=blogflt.

Ben-Ghiat, R. (2001), *Fascist Modernities: Italy, 1922–1945*, Berkeley: University of California Press.

Benjamin, W. (1968), "The Storyteller," in W. Benjamin and H. Arendt (eds.), *Illuminations*, 83–109, New York: Schocken Books.

Bennett, J. (2010), *Vibrant Matter. A Political Ecology of Things*, Durham: Duke University Press.

Berger, J. (2007), *Berger on Drawing*, ed. J. Savage, London: Occasional Press.

Beverungen, A. and S. Dunne (2007), "'I'd Prefer Not To.' Bartleby and the Excesses of Interpretation," *Culture and Organization* 13: 171–83.

Biddle, J. L. and T. Lea (2018), "Hyperrealism and Other Indigenous Forms of 'Faking It with the Truth,'" *Visual Anthropology Review* 34(1): 5–14.

Binswanger, L. (1993), *Dream and Existence*, Atlantic Highlands: Humanities Press International.

Boal, A. (2002), *Games for Actors and Non-Actors*, 2nd ed., London: Routledge.

Bogart, A. and T. Landau (2005), *The Viewpoints Book: A Practical Guide to Viewpoints and Composition Paperback*, New York: Theatre Communications Group.

Bollas, C. (2009), *The Evocative Objects World*, London and New York: Routledge.

Borutti, S. (1993), *Per un'etica del discorso antropologico*, Milano: Guerini e Associati.

Brecht, B. (1964), "The Street Scene," in J. Willett (ed. and trans.), *Brecht on Theatre*, 121–9, New York: Hill and Wang.

Brecht, B. (2015), "Courage Model 1949," in T. Kuhn, S. Giles, and M. Silberman (eds.), *Brecht on Performance: Messingkauf and Modelbooks*, 181–222, London: Bloomsbury.

Brown, R. (2005), "Moisés Kaufman: The Copulation of Form and Content," *Theater Topics* 15(1): 51–67.

Buck, P. D. (2016), *In/Equality: An Alternative Anthropology*, 4th ed., Palo Cedro: CAT Publishing.

Cabot, H. (2014), *On the Doorstep of Europe: Asylum and Citizenship in Greece*, Philadelphia: University of Pennsylvania Press.

Calvino, I. (1974), *Invisible Cities*, New York: Harcourt.

Carter, T. (dir.) (2003), *Film of Dunham Technique*, "Yonvalou, 2003, video clip #62", "Rocking Horse, 2003, video clip #60", "Congo Paillette, 2003, video clip #63", Washington, DC: Library of Congress, Digital Collections. https://www.loc.gov/collections/katherine-dunham/about-this-collection/?loclr=blogflt

Cassirer, E. (1946), *Language and Myth*, New York: Dover Publications.

Cattaneo, C. (2018), *Naufraghi senza volto. Dare un nome alle vittime del Mediterraneo*, Milano: Raffaello Cortina Editore.

Chakrabarty, D. (2000), *Provincializing Europe. Postcolonial Thought and Historical Difference*, Princeton: Princeton University Press.

Chin, E. (2014), "Dunham Technique: Anthropological Politics of Dancing through Ethnography," in E. Chin (ed.), *Katherine Dunham: Recovering an Anthropological Legacy, Choreographing Ethnographic Futures*, 79–100, Santa Fe: School for Advanced Research Press.

Collins, S. G., M. Durington, and H. Gill (2017), "Multimodality: An Invitation," *American Anthropologist* 119(1): 142–6.

Conquergood, D. (2013), *Cultural Struggles: Performance, Ethnography, Praxis*, Ann Arbor: University of Michigan Press.

Csordas, T. (ed.) (1994), *Embodiment and Experience: The Existential Ground of Culture and Self*, Cambridge: Cambridge University Press.

Das, V. and D. Poole (eds.) (2004), *Anthropology in the Margins of the State*, Santa Fe: School of American Research Press.

Dattatreyan, E. G. and I. Marrero-Guillam (2019), "Introduction: Multimodal Anthropology and the Politics of Invention," *American Anthropologist* 121(1): 220–8.

Davis, E. A. (2015), "'We've Toiled without End': Publicity, Crisis and the Suicide 'Epidemic' in Greece," *Comparative Studies in Society and History* 57: 1007–36.

de Certeau, M. (1992), *The Mystic Fable*, Chicago: University of Chicago Press.

de la Cadena, M. and M. Blaser (2018), *A World of Many Worlds*, Durham: Duke University Press.

Deleuze, G. (1988), *Spinoza. Practical Philosophy*, San Francisco: City Lights.

Deleuze, G. (1998), *Essays Critical and Clinical*, London: Verso.

Deleuze, G. and F. Guattari (1986), *Kafka: Toward a Minor Literature*, Minneapolis: University of Minnesota Press.

Deleuze, J. and G. Guattari (1983), "What Is a Minor Literature?," *Mississippi Review* 11(3): 13–33.

Demos, T. J. (2009), "The Right to Opacity: On the Otolith Group's Nervus Rerum," *OCTOBER Magazine* 129: 113–28.

Denzin, N. K. (2003), *Performance Ethnography: Critical Pedagogy and the Politics of Culture*, Thousand Oaks: Sage.

Derrida, J. (1967), *L'écriture et la différence*, Paris: Éditions du Seuil.

Desjarlais, R. and J. Troop (2011), "Phenomenological Approaches in Anthropology," *Annual Review of Anthropology* 40: 87–102.

Dunham, K. (1936), *Fieldwork Films*, "Urban Social Dance, Jamaica and Martinique Fieldwork, 1936, video clip #22", "Traditional Dance, Haiti Fieldwork, 1936, video clip #15", Washington, DC: Library of Congress, Digital Collections. https://www.loc.gov /collections/katherine-dunham/about-this-collection/?loclr=blogflt.

Dunn, E. (2018), *No Path Home: Humanitarian Camps and the Grief of Displacement*, Ithaca: Cornell University Press.

Echeverri Zuluaga, J. (2015), "Errance and Elsewheres among Africans Waiting to Restart their Journeys in Dakar, Senegal," *Cultural Anthropology* 30: 589–610.

Elhaik, T. and G. Marcus (2019), "Curatorial Designs," in R. Sansi (ed.), *The Anthropologist as Curator*, 17–34, London: Bloomsbury Publishing.

Elliott, D. and D. Culhane (eds.) (2016), *A Different Kind of Ethnography*, Toronto: University of Toronto Press.

Estalella, A. and T. Sánchez Criado (eds.) (2018), *Experimental Collaborations: Ethnography through Fieldwork Device*, New York: Berghahn Books.

Fabian, J. (1990), *Power and Performance: Ethnographic Explorations through Proverbial Wisdom and Theatre in Shaba, Zaire*, Madison: University of Wisconsin Press.

Fabietti, U. (2012), "Errancy in Ethnography and Theory: On the Meaning and Role of "Discovery" in Anthropological Research," in H. Hazan and E. Hertzog (eds.), *Serendipity in Anthropological Research: The Nomadic Turn*, 15–30, London: Routledge.

Farquhar, J. and M. Lock (eds.) (2007), *Beyond the Body Proper: Reading the Anthropology of Material Life*, Durham: Duke University Press.

Fassin, D. (2007), "Humanitarianism as a Politics of Life," *Public Culture* 19(3): 499–520.

Favret-Saada, J. (1980), *Deadly Words. Witchcraft in the Bocage*, Cambridge: Cambridge University Press.

Favret-Saada, J. (1990), "About Participation," *Culture, Medicine, and Psychiatry* 14: 189–99.

Fernando, M. and C. Giordano (2016), "Introduction: Refugees and the Crisis of Europe," *Hot Spots*, June 28, Cultural Anthropology website.

Ferrante, E. (2016), *La frantumaglia*, Roma: Edizioni e/o.

Ferri, S., and Ferri, S. (2015), "Elena Ferrante, Art of Fiction," *The Paris Review*, 212. https://www.theparisreview.org/interviews/6370/elena-ferrante-art-of-fiction-no -228-elena-ferrante.

Field, S. (2005), *Screenplay: The Foundations of Screenwriting*, New York: Delta Trade Paperbacks.

Fondakowski, L. (2018), "Writing into Form: Creating *The People's Temple*," in M. Kaufman and B. Pitts et al. (eds.), *Moment Work: Tectonic Theater Project's Process of Devising Theater*, 275–82, New York: Vintage Books.

Foucault, M. (1991), "Governmentality," in G. Burchell, C. Gordon, and P. Miller (eds.), *The Foucault Effect: Studies in Governmentality*, 87–94, Chicago: University of Chicago Press.

Foucault, M. (1993), "Dream, Imagination and Existence: An Introduction to Ludwig Binswanger's 'Dream and Existence'," in K. Hoeller (ed.), *Dream and Existence*, 29–78, Atlantic Highlands: Humanities Press International.

Foucault, M. (1994), *The Order of Things. An Archeology of the Human Sciences*, New York: Vintage Books.

Freud, S. (1899), *The Interpretation of Dreams*, New York: The MacMillan Company.

Freud, S. (1914), "The Moses of Michelangelo," in *Collected Works*, Standard Edition, vol. XIII, 211–36.

Freud, S. (1965), *The Psychopathology of Everyday Life*, New York and London: W.W. Norton & Company.

Gillespie, B. (2014), "Que(e)rying Theatrical Objects," in M. Schweitzer and J. Zerdy (eds.), *Performing Objects and Theatrical Things*, 149–60, London: Palgrave Macmillan.

Ginzburg, C. (1980), "Morelli, Freud and Sherlock Holmes: Clues and Scientific Method," *History Workshop* 9: 5–36.

Giordano, C. (2014), *Migrants in Translation: Caring and the Logics of Difference in Contemporary Italy*, Berkeley: University of California Press.

Giordano, C. (2015), "Lying the Truth: Practices of Confession and Recognition," *Current Anthropology* 56: 211–21.

Giordano, C. (2016), "Catastrophes. In Refugees and the Crisis of Europe," *Hot Spots*, June, Cultural Anthropology website. https://culanth.org/fieldsights/911-refugees -and-the-crisis-of-europe (accessed June 28, 2016).

Giordano, C. and G. Pierotti (2020), "Getting Caught: A Collaboration On- and Off Stage Between Theater and Anthropology," *The Drama Review* 64(1): 88–106.

Giordano, C. and G. Pierotti (2023), "How to Get Caught in the Ethnographic Material," in T. Sánchez Criado and A. Estalella (eds.), *An Ethnographic Inventory. Field Devices for Anthropological Inquiries*, 112–21, New York: Routledge.

Goffman, E. (1959), *The Presentation of Self in Everyday Life*, New York: Anchor Books.

Gregg, M. and G. J. Seigworth (2010), "An Inventory of Shimmers," in M. Gregg and G. J. Seigworth (eds.), *The Affect Theory Reader*, 1–28, Durham and London: Duke University Press.

Hayashi, A. (2021), *Social Presencing Theater*, Cambridge: PI Press.

Hardt, M. and A. Negri (2000), *Empire*, Cambridge, MA: Harvard University Press.

Harrison, F. V., ed (1997), *Decolonizing Anthropology. Moving Further Toward an Anthropology for Liberation. Association of Black Anthropologists*, Arlington: American Anthropological Association.

Hartblay, C. (2020), *I Was Never Alone or Oporniki: An Ethnographic Play on Disability in Russia*, Toronto: University of Toronto Press.

Horsti, K. (2019), "Curating Objects from the European Border Zone: The 'Lampedusa Boat,'" in K. Horsti (ed.), *The Politics of Public Memories of Forced Migration and Bordering in Europe*, 53–70, London: Palgrave Macmillan.

Hughes, L. and Z. N. Hurston, edited with introductions by G. H. Bass and H. L. Gates (eds.) (1991 [1931]), *The Mule-Bone: A Comedy of Negro Life in Three Acts*, New York: HarperCollins.

International Organization for Migration (2022), *World Migration Report 2022*. https://worldmigrationreport.iom.int/wmr-2022-interactive/ (accessed February 13, 2023).

Jackson, M. (2017), "Poetry, Uncertainty, and Opacity," in A. Pandian and S. McLean (eds.), *Crumpled Paper Boat*, 91–3, Durham: Duke University Press.

Jones, A. (2015), "Material Traces: Performativity, Artistic 'Work,' and New Concepts of Agency," *The Drama Review* 59(4): 18–35.

Kaufman, M. (1998), *Gross Indecency: The Three Trials of Oscar Wilde*, New York: Vintage Books.

Kaufman, M. and the Members of Tectonic Theater Project (2014), *The Laramie Project and The Laramie Project: 10 Years Later*, New York: Vintage Books.

Kaufman, M. and B. Pitts et al. (2018), *Moment Work: Tectonic Theater Project's Process of Devising Theater*, New York: Vintage Books.

Kazubowski-Houston, M. (2010), *Staging Strife. Lessons from Performing Ethnography with Polish Roma Women*, Montreal: McGill-Queen's University Press.

Kazubowski-Houston, M. and M. Auslander (eds.) (2021), *In Search of Lost. Futures Anthropological Explorations in Multimodality, Deep Interdisciplinarity, and Autoethnography*, Cham, Switzerland: Palgrave Macmillan.

Kirmayer, L. J. (1993), "Healing and the Invention of Metaphor. The Effectiveness of Symbols Revisited," *Culture, Medicine and Psychiatry* 17: 161–95.

Kondo, D. (2018), *World-making. Race, Performance, and the Work of Creativity*, Durham: Duke University Press.

Koselleck, R. (2002), *The Practice of Conceptual History: Timing History, Spacing Concepts*, Stanford University Press.

Latour, B. (2005), *Reassembling the Social: An Introduction to Actor-Network-Theory*, Oxford: Oxford University Press.

Lehman, H.-T. (2004), *Postdramatic Theater*, London and New York: Routledge.

Lerman, L. and J. Borstel (2003), *Critical Response Process: A Method for Getting Useful Feedback on Anything You Make, from Dance to Dessert*, Liz Lerman Dance Exchange.

Lessing, G. E. (2019), *The Hamburg Dramaturgy: A New and Complete Annotated English Translation*, ed. W. Aarons, Natalya Baldyga, and S. Figal, trans. Natalya Baldyga, Abingdon, Oxon: Routledge.

Lio, P. (2019), "Milano Corso Como, così rinasce la passerella dello shopping: panche, fiori, luci colorate," *Corriere della Sera* [Milano], June 20.

Madison, D. S. (2005), *Critical Ethnography. Method, Ethics, and Performance*, Thousand Oaks: Sage Publications Inc.

Madison, D. S. (2018), *PerformED Ethnography & Communication. Improvisation and Embodied Experience*, London and New York: Routledge.

Manning, E. (2013), *Always More Than One. Individuation's Dance*, Durham: Duke University Press.

Manning, E. (2016), *The Minor Gesture*, Durham: Duke University Press.

Marcus, G. E. (2008), "The End(s) of Ethnography: Social/Cultural Anthropology's Signature Form of Producing Knowledge in Transition," *Cultural Anthropology* 23(1): 1–14.

Marcus, G. E. (2010), "Contemporary Fieldwork Aesthetics in Art and Anthropology: Experiments in Collaboration and Intervention," *Visual Anthropology* 23(4): 263–77.

Marsilli-Vargas, X. (2014), "Listening Genres: The Emergence of Relevance Structures through the Reception of Sound," *Journal of Pragmatics* 69: 42–51.

Martin, C. (2013), *Theatre of the Real*, New York: Palgrave Macmillan.

McCormack, D. P. (2013), *Refrains for Moving Bodies. Experience and Experiment in Affective Spaces*, Durham and London: Duke University Press.

McGranahan, C. (2015), *Anthropology as Theoretical Storytelling*. https://savageminds .org/2015/10/19/anthropology-as-theoretical-storytelling/.

McGranahan, C. (2016), "Refusal and the Gift of Citizenship," *Cultural Anthropology* 31: 334–41.

McLean, S. (2017), *Fictionalizing Anthropology. Encounters and Fabulations at the Edges of the Human*, Minneapolis: University of Minnesota Press.

Multiple Mobilities Research Cluster, Ticktin, M., R. Subramaniam, V.Hattam, L.Y. Liu, and R. Youatt (2017), "Images Unwalled," *Anthropology Now* 9(3): 24–37.

Myers, N. and J. Dumit (2011), "Haptic Creativity and the Mid-Embodiments of Experimental Life," in F. E. Marscia-Lees (ed.), *A Companion to the Anthropology of Bodies/Embodiment*, 239–61, Hoboken: Wiley-Blackwell.

Napolitano, V. (2015), "Anthropology and Traces," *Anthropological Theory* 15(1): 47–67.

Navaro-Yashin, Y. (2012), *The Make-Believe Space: Affective Geography in a Postwar Polity*, Durham: Duke University Press.

Ossman, S. (2021), *Shifting Worlds, Shaping Fieldwork. A Memoire of Anthropology and Art*, London and New York: Routledge.

Overlie, M. (2006), "The Six Viewpoints," in A. Bartow (ed.), *Training of the American Actor*, 187–222, New York: Theater Communications Group.

Overlie, M. (2016), *Standing in Space: The Six Viewpoints Theory and Practice*, Billings: Fallon Press.

Pandian, A. and S. McLean (eds.) (2017), *Crumpled Paper Boat*, Durham: Duke University Press.

Pandolfi, M. (2008), "Laboratory of Intervention: The Humanitarian Governance of the Postcommunist Balkan Territories," in M. J. Del Vecchio Good, S. T. Hyde, S. Pinto, B. J. Good (eds.), *Postcolonial Disorders*, 157–86, Berkeley: University of California Press.

Pandolfo, S. (2018), *Knot of the Soul. Madness, Psychoanalysis, Isalm*, Chicago and London: University of Chicago Press.

Peano, I. (2017), "Migrants' Struggles? Rethinking Citizenship, Anti-Racism and Labour Precarity through Migration Politics in Italy," in L. Lazar (ed.), *Where are the Unions? Workers and Social Movements in Latin America, the Middle East and Europe*, 87–106, London: Zed Books.

Pietila, A. (2010), *Not in My Neighborhood: How Bigotry Shaped a Great American City*, Chicago: Ivan R. Dee.

Pinelli, B. and L. Ciabarri (eds.) (2015), *Dopo l'approdo. Un racconto per immagini e parole sui richiedenti asilo in Italia*, Firenze: Editpress.

Pontalis, J. B. (1993), *Love of Beginnings*, London: Free Association Books.

Povinelli, E. (2011), *Economies of Abandonment: Social Belonging and Endurance in Late Liberalism*, Durham: Duke University Press.

Praspaliauskiene, R. (2022), *Enveloped Lives: Caring and Relating in Lithuanian Health Care*, Ithaca: Cornell University Press.

Radosavljević, D. (2013), *The Contemporary Ensemble: Interviews with Theatre-Makers*, Abingdon and New York: Routledge.

Recalcati, M. (2016), *Il mistero delle cose. Nove ritratti di artisti*, Milano: Feltrinelli.

Redfield, P. (2006), "A Less Modest Witness: Collective Advocacy and Motivated Truth in a Medical Humanitarian Movement," *American Ethnologist* 33(1): 3–26.

Riley, S. R. and L. Hunter (eds.) (2009), *Mapping Landscapes for Performance as Research: Scholarly Acts and Creative Cartographies*, New York: Palgrave Macmillan.

Roitman, J. (2014), *Anti-crisis*, Durham: Duke University Press.

Rosaldo, R. (1989), *Culture & Truth: The Remaking of Social Analysis*, Boston: Beacon Press.

Sánchez Criado, T. and A. Estalella (eds.) (2023), *An Ethnographic Inventory. Field Devices for Anthropological Inquiries*, New York: Routledge.

Sanyal, D. (2017), "Calais's 'Jungle': Refugees, Biopolitics, and the Arts of Resistance," *Representations* 139: 1–33.

Schechner, R. (1985), *Between Theater and Anthropology*, Philadelphia: University of Pennsylvania Press.

Schneider, R. (2015), "New Materialisms and Performance Studies," *The Drama Review* 59(4): 7–17.

Schweitzer, M. and J. Zerdy (eds.) (2014), *Performing Objects and Theatrical Things*, London: Palgrave Macmillan.

Scott, J. C. (1999), *Seeing Like a State: How Certain Schemes to Improve the Human Condition Have Failed*, New Haven: Yale University Press.

Sharpe, C. (2016), *In the Wake, on Blackness and Being*, Durham and London: Duke University Press.

Simpson, A. (2014), *Mohawk Interruptus: Political Life across the Borders of Settler States*, Durham: Duke University Press.

Simpson, A. (2017), "The Ruse of Consent and the Anatomy of 'Refusal': Cases from Indigenous North America and Australia," *Postcolonial Studies* 20: 18–33.

Smith, A. D. (1994), *Twilight in LA, 1992*, New York: Anchor Books

Spolin, V. (1963), *Improvisation for the Theater: A Handbook of Teaching and Directing Techniques*, Evanston: Northwestern University Press.

Stevenson, L. (2014), *Life beside Itself. Imaging Care in the Canadian Arctic*, Berkeley: University of California Press.

Stewart, K. (1996), *A Space on the Side of the Road*, Princeton: Princeton University Press.

Stewart, K. (2007), *Ordinary Affects*, Durham: Duke University Press.

Stoetzer, B. (2018), "Ruderal Ecologies: Rethinking Nature, Migration, and the Urban Landscape in Berlin," *Cultural Anthropology* 33(2): 295–323.

Strathern, M. (2004), *Partial Connections*, Walnut Creek: Rowman and Littlefield Publishers.

Taussig, M. (2006), *Walter Benjamin's Grave*, Chicago: University of Chicago Press.

Taussig, M. (2009), "What Do Drawings Want?," *Culture, Theory and Critique* 50 (2–3): 263–74.

Taussig, M. (2011), *I Swear I Saw This: Drawings in Fieldwork Notebooks, Namely My Own*, Chicago: University of Chicago Press.

Thomas, D. (2011), *Exceptional Violence: Embodied Citizenship in Transnational Jamaica*, Durham: Duke University Press.

Thrift, N. (2007), *Non-Representational Theory: Space, Politics, Affect*, London and New York: Routledge.

Ticktin, M. (2011), *Casualties of Care: Immigration and the Politics of Humanitarianism in France*, Berkeley: University of California Press.

Ticktin, M. (2017), "The Innocent Bystander," in *Multiple Mobilities Research Cluster*, 2017.

Tsing, A. L. (2005), *Friction: An Ethnography of Global Connection*, Princeton: Princeton University Press.

Tsing, A. L. (2015), *The Mushroom at the End of the World. On the Possibility of Life in Capitalist Ruins*, Princeton: Princeton University Press.

Turner, V. (1967), *The Forest of Symbols. Aspects of Ndembu Ritual*, Ithaca: Cornell University Press.

Turner, V. (1982), *From Ritual to Theater. The Human Seriousness of Play*, New York: PAJ Publications.

UN General Assembly, Convention Relating to the Status of Refugees (1951), United Nations, Treaty Series, July 28, Vol. 189: 137. https://www.refworld.org/docid /3be01b964.html.

Vendler, H. (1995), *The Breaking of Style*, Cambridge, MA: Harvard University Press.

Vidali, D. (2020), "Ethnographic Theater Making: Multimodal Alchemy, Knowledge, and Invention," *American Anthropologist* 122(2): 394–409.

Welch, R. (2016), "Time Out of Joint: Larsen's *End of Dreams* and Italy's 'Colonial Unconscious," in Refugees and the Crisis of Europe, Hot Spots, Cultural Anthropology website, https://culanth.org/fieldsights/time-out-of-joint-larsens-end -of-dreams-and-italys-colonial-unconscious.

Wilderson III, F. B. (2014), *We Are Trying to Destroy the World: Anti-Blackness and Police Violence After Ferguson*, Ill Will Editions. https://illwilleditions.noblogs.org/ files/2015/09/Wilderson-We-Are-Trying-to-Destroy-the-World-PRINT.pdf.

Winnicott, D. W. (1971), *Playing and Reality*, London: Routledge.

Wittgenstein, L. (1958), *Philosophical Investigations*, New York: MacMillan Publishing.

Woolf, V. (1984), *The Essays of Virginia Woolf. Volume 4: 1925 to 1928*, ed. A. McNeille, London: The Hogarth Press.

Worley, L. (2001), *Coming from Nothing: The Sacred Art of Acting*, Boulder: Turquoise Dragon.

Yalouri, E. (2019), "'Difficult' Representations. Visual art Engaging with the Refugee Crisis," *Visual Studies* 34(3): 223–38.

Zizek, S. (2006), "Notes Towards of Politics of Bartleby: The Ignorance of Chicken," *Comparative American Studies: An International Journal* 4: 375–94.

Index

Note: Page numbers followed by 'n' indicate note number(s).